Self and Identity in Adolescent Foreign Language Learning

MIX
Paper from
responsible sources
FSC® C014540

HeeKyeong Lee

SECOND LANGUAGE ACQUISITION
Series Editor: Professor David Singleton, *Trinity College, Dublin, Ireland*

This series brings together titles dealing with a variety of aspects of language acquisition and processing in situations where a language or languages other than the native language is involved. Second language is thus interpreted in its broadest possible sense. The volumes included in the series all offer in their different ways, on the one hand, exposition and discussion of empirical findings and, on the other, some degree of theoretical reflection. In this latter connection, no particular theoretical stance is privileged in the series; nor is any relevant perspective – sociolinguistic, psycholinguistic, neurolinguistic etc. – deemed out of place. The intended readership of the series includes final-year undergraduates working on second language acquisition projects, postgraduate students involved in second language acquisition research, and researchers and teachers in general whose interests include a second language acquisition component.

Full details of all the books in this series and of all our other publications can be found on http://www.multilingual-matters.com, or by writing to Multilingual Matters, St Nicholas House, 31–34 High Street, Bristol BS1 2AW, UK.

Self and Identity in Adolescent Foreign Language Learning

Florentina Taylor

MULTILINGUAL MATTERS
Bristol • Buffalo • Toronto

To John, who makes
the world go round

Library of Congress Cataloging in Publication Data
Taylor, Florentina.
Self and Identity in Adolescent Foreign Language Learning/Florentina Taylor.
Second Language Acquisition: 70
Includes bibliographical references and index.
1. Teenagers—Language. 2. Language arts (Secondary)—Social aspects. 3. English language—Study and teaching (Secondary)—Foreign speakers. 4. Interdisciplinary approach in education. 5. Second language acquisition. 6. Identity (Psychology). 7. Language and education. I. Title.
P120.Y68T34 2013
428.0071'2–dc23 2013011924

British Library Cataloguing in Publication Data
A catalogue entry for this book is available from the British Library.

ISBN-13: 978-1-84769-999-2 (hbk)
ISBN-13: 978-1-84769-998-5 (pbk)

Multilingual Matters
UK: St Nicholas House, 31–34 High Street, Bristol BS1 2AW, UK.
USA: UTP, 2250 Military Road, Tonawanda, NY 14150, USA.
Canada: UTP, 5201 Dufferin Street, North York, Ontario M3H 5T8, Canada.

The policy of Multilingual Matters/Channel View Publications is to use papers that are natural, renewable and recyclable products, made from wood grown in sustainable forests. In the manufacturing process of our books, and to further support our policy, preference is given to printers that have FSC and PEFC Chain of Custody certification. The FSC and/or PEFC logos will appear on those books where full certification has been granted to the printer concerned.

Typeset by Techset Composition India (P) Ltd., Bangalore and Chennai, India.
Printed and bound in Great Britain by Short Run Press Ltd.

Contents

Tables and Figures   vii

1   Introduction   1
       Research Background   3
       Aims and Outline of the Book   6

2   Self and Identity in Adolescence: A Relational Perspective   9
       From Self to Identity: Terminological Inroads   9
       Main Relational Contexts Shaping Adolescents' Identity
          Development   12
       From Actual to Possible Selves   17

3   Self and Identity in Foreign Language Learning   26
       Language and Identity   26
       Self and Identity in Language Learning   27
       Research Needed   38

4   A Quadripolar Model of Identity in Adolescent Foreign
    Language Learning   41
       Self System Components   41
       Self System Relationships   50
       Self System Types   52
       Amotivational Self Configurations   58
       Limitations   59

5   Participants' Self Systems in Four Relational Contexts   62
       The Submissive Self System   64
       The Duplicitous Self System   67

The Rebellious Self System   73
The Harmonious Self System   77
Self-systems: Preliminary Conclusions   83

6   Self Perceptions and Identity Display in Learning English
    as a Foreign Language   85
    Self and Language Learning Perceptions   85
    Identity Display   93

7   Of Students and Teachers   105
    To Be or Not to be 'Yourself' in the English Class   105
    A Reward-centred Ethos   108
    From Interested Teachers to Interested Students   111
    Internalisation Potential   116

8   Drawing the Line: Evaluation and Implications   121
    Model Evaluation   121
    Implications for Future Research and Practice   125
    Conclusion   127

    Appendix A: The L2 Quadripolar Identity Questionnaire   131
    Appendix B: The L2 Quadripolar Identity Questionnaire
                with Item Numbers   138
    Appendix C: Questionnaire Scales with Item Numbers   145
    Appendix D: Interview guide – Themes Covered, with
                Examples of Questions and Prompts   147
    Appendix E: Self System Graphical Representations and Vignettes 151
    Appendix F: Interviewee Profiles   153

    Glossary   170
    References   172
    Subject Index   191
    Author Index   193
    Country Index   198

Tables and Figures

Tables

Table 4.1 A quadripolar model of identity   42

Table 6.1 Descriptive statistics for the continuous self variables   86

Table 6.2 Descriptive statistics for other continuous variables in the questionnaire   87

Table 6.3 Gender differences (ANOVA)   89

Table 6.4 Correlation matrix for the main self variables   94

Table A Self systems summary   151

Table B Self system types and interview summaries for all 32 interviewees   154

Figures

Figure 4.1 A quadripolar model of identity with four relational contexts   48

Figure 4.2 The submissive self system   53

Figure 4.3 The duplicitous self system   55

Figure 4.4 The rebellious self system   56

Figure 4.5 The harmonious self system   57

Figure 5.1 Self system percentages by gender and relational context   63

Figure 5.2 Key concepts associated with the submissive self system   65

Figure 5.3 Key concepts associated with the duplicitous self system   67

Figure 5.4 Key concepts associated with the rebellious self system   73

Figure 5.5 Key concepts associated with the harmonious self system   78

Figure 6.1 L2 public/private and public/imposed correlations by gender and relational context   96

Figure 6.2 L2 declared achievement by self system in four relational contexts   102

Figure 6.3 L2 perceptions in the teacher self system (MANOVA)   103

1 Introduction

The research described in this book is rooted in my decade-long interest in what it is that helps students participate genuinely in learning activities that they consider personally relevant, and how these factors could be turned into learning capital in the classroom. Many library shelves have been filled with books about how to motivate students to learn, but we sometimes forget a simple truth that Kohn (1993: 198–199) reminds us of:

> ... children do not need to be motivated. From the beginning they are hungry to make sense of their world. Given an environment in which they don't feel controlled and in which they are encouraged to think about what they are doing (rather than how well they are doing it), students of any age will generally exhibit an abundance of motivation and a healthy appetite for challenge.

A control-free environment that nurtures personal growth and an appetite for challenge is particularly needed in adolescence – a child's apprenticeship to responsible self-determined functioning in society. Given teenagers' increasing bids for independence and autonomy, contexts that do not support their explorations and personally relevant choices lead to frustration and conflict. The situation is further complicated by the different relational contexts in which a teenager functions: family, school, peer groups and so on. If interactions with adults are restrictive and unappreciative of one's individuality, there is often a peer group that is happy to accept a youngster on condition that a particular code of conduct is adopted. Depending on the nature of the adopting group, this can be either detrimental or beneficial. Superficially displayed attitudes can end up reshaping one's identity, but it is a totally different matter if the change is triggered by, for example, a questionable street gang or by a well-intended teacher.

The developmental stage when identity processes are at their most complex peak – adolescence – is also the period when most foreign language learning occurs, given that foreign languages are usually studied in secondary school. Identity complexities inherent in adolescence therefore overlap with the identity complexities that are inherent in language learning. It is sometimes said that learning a language means learning a new identity. Being an adolescent also means learning a new identity: the identity that one will manifest in one's community, at the hub of an intricate network of social relationships. Just as a new language is learnt by trial and error, by pronouncing a word wrong until one gets it right or by making a grammatical mistake until it does not feel 'right' anymore, in the same way teenagers learn 'who they are' by trying out and discarding alternative selves until one of them meets with social approval and gets adopted and sometimes internalised into their own identity.

Foreign language classes can be either a curse or a blessing for an adolescent's emerging sense of self. Expressing ourselves in a language different from our own might expose us to ridicule, projecting a vulnerable self in the eyes of peers who may have fun counting our mistakes. However, expressing ourselves in a foreign language can also be an excellent tool for identity exploration, and that is especially relevant during adolescence, when identity exploration is of paramount importance. Genuinely communicative language classes would appear, in this light, as the most suited to identity development of all academic subjects. As long as students have learnt to express themselves fluently, the teaching has been successful. But for this they need to be able to express *themselves*, to talk about what worries and what thrills them, as well as about what helps them engage more and learn better. When such communication occurs in the foreign language itself, the teacher gains crucial insights into the learners' own motivational processes, while the students gain socio-communicative competence that they will be able to use later, in real-life encounters, besides exploring and consolidating their identity through this very communication. One could almost say that successful foreign language classes are CLIL lessons where the subject matter is the student's own identity.

However, the overlapping complexities inherent in adolescence and foreign language learning are not the only double-edged challenge in class. The classroom is a space where two socio-relational contexts overlap. Whereas the teacher is just a teacher at all times (except, perhaps, when the class is being observed by a superior member of staff), students are always both students and classmates, having to juggle with often contradictory social expectations: will they be (or pretend to be) hardworking and please the teacher, or will they be (or pretend to be) sworn enemies of learning and please their work-avoidant peers? The ensuing identity negotiations necessary to avoid conflicts are also encountered in adolescents' personal lives, when being in the same place with one's parents and one's best friends would often require the diplomatic display of particular context-dependent identities. It is these spiralling 'complications' that make foreign language learners' identity such a rewarding research topic.

Starting from such considerations, and having completed a study with Romanian learners of English as a foreign language (Taylor, 2008), which revealed a vast array of manipulative-escapist behaviours that students displayed in class when they were not appreciated personally and their views were not taken into account (see also Taylor, 2013a), an investigation into what helps students feel appreciated in class was a natural continuation for my research interests.

Research Background

This book reports on a research project that aimed to facilitate a better understanding of the adolescent foreign language learner caught in a web of social relations that may not always be self-actualising, with particular emphasis on the factors that may help learners feel personally appreciated in class and the ways in which these factors could be used to enhance their engagement and achievement. My chosen research context was the Romanian secondary-school system, because it is a context with which I am familiar both as a student and as a teacher, because my interest in this research topic was kindled by my previous study in a very similar research site, and because it is a medium where teaching is still regarded by many as knowledge transmission by an authoritative teacher figure, thus promising rewarding insights into differential classroom identity display. In addition, the student's identity and its relationship to language learning are significantly under-researched areas in this educational context.

The combination of strong international influences and developments, on the one hand, and a controversial political atmosphere with changes of government triggering changes in educational policy every four years, on the other hand, has taken Romanian education through a never-ending cycle of reforms and structural changes in recent years (European Commission, 2008a; Mihai, 2003). As far as the teaching of English is concerned, the result may be seen as an example of *less-than-healthy glocalisation* (Friedman, 2000).

Admittedly, monochrome Stalinist textbooks have been replaced by glossy materials featuring age-relevant issues (Andrei, 2006; Popovici & Bolitho, 2003), students watch English language films in class and may be assessed on projects more than on their proficiency in literary translation, regulations stipulating that by the end of upper secondary school productive and receptive skills are emphasised in equal measure (European Commission, 2008b). However, it is debatable to what extent these recent developments are truly *glocalised* in Romanian English language teaching. As Andrei (2006: 774) puts it, 'there still is a nostalgia for the past certainties, for more stable and more predictable curricula'. Although syllabi are in theory based on a functional-communicative model of learning and teaching (National Curriculum Council, 2007a, 2007b), in practice, however, teaching is still heavily driven by grammar-translation methodology, and the structure of the final examination – which for most pupils still represents the main reason for studying – has long contradicted the theoretical principles stated in the official documents, as emphasised by Mihai (2003). Project work was still an alien concept not long ago (Medgyes, 1997), whereas English classes are often *taught in Romanian* with only illustrative patterns written in English on the blackboard, and while some teachers still perceive themselves as *the* source of knowledge in class, many students have adopted an attitude of tolerance towards their tutors and, expending just enough effort to leave the impression that they are involved in classroom tasks, they actually attend to their own – not always educational – agendas (Taylor, 2008, 2009).

Paradoxically perhaps, many Romanian adolescents are proficient speakers of English. Their intrinsically driven competence, however, is often unrelated to their school foreign language lessons. They learn the language from the films they watch, from the music they listen to, from the computer applications they use, from online socialising networks where they use English for authentic communication about personally relevant issues (Constantinescu *et al.*, 2002; Istrate & Velea, 2006). In one of the very few investigations that have documented the mechanics of motivation and classroom involvement for Romanian foreign language learners, Taylor (2008) found that since they had started studying English at school, adolescents' excitement and interest for their language lessons had decreased, although their perceived confidence and declared proficiency had actually increased. Her participants also declared that they skipped about one third of their English classes and, when present, were engaged for about two thirds of the time, admitting to a wide range of activities they resorted to in class while giving the impression they were on task. The qualitative component of the study identified as the main reason for such conduct perceived teacher distance (or alleged arrogance), as well as perceived lack of acknowledgement and appreciation for students as individuals with personal values and interests.

Responding to a scarcity of research linking identity and foreign language learning in general, and in Romania in particular, the project reported in this book aimed to: (a) gain new insights into the identity of Romanian adolescent learners of English as a foreign language and its relationships to classroom involvement and declared achievement; and (b) serve as the initial validation of a new theoretical framework, *A Quadripolar Model of Identity* (see Chapter 4). Having a dual inductive–deductive purpose, the project was governed by a pragmatic research paradigm that called for a parallel mixed-method approach (Creswell, 2008; Teddlie & Tashakkori, 2009). The data collection methods were self-reported structured questionnaires and semi-structured individual interviews, which were combined according to the research strategy of concurrent triangulation and the principle of complementary strengths and non-overlapping weaknesses (Brewer & Hunter, 1993; Johnson & Turner, 2003). Specifically, questionnaires were used in order to seek validation for the new model of identity and to collect cross-sectional trend data, whereas interviews had the purpose of complementing and enriching the questionnaire data with rich qualitative insights.

The data collection instruments were a purposefully designed questionnaire (see Appendices A, B and C; available to download from http://www.iris-database.org) and interview guide (Appendix D), which were piloted prior to data collection with 82 similar students in a different Romanian county. The concepts measured/explored in these instruments were derived indirectly from my understanding of the background literature and directly from the theoretical framework detailed in Chapter 4. Both data collection instruments used the Romanian language, as it was important that participants' understanding of the questions, as well as their answers, did not depend on their English language proficiency. The quantitative data were analysed with the IBM SPSS® 19 package and the qualitative data were submitted to thematic content analysis using the NVivo® 9 software. The qualitative analysis was conducted in the original language, with selected quotations translated into English and used for illustrative purposes in Chapters 5 and 7.

My participants were 1045 Romanian learners of English as a foreign language, aged 14–19 (mean 16.47), in five maintained schools of various specialisms. 339 participants were male and 645 female (61 did not report their gender). These completed paper questionnaires during regular class time after written permission was obtained from head teachers. The participating classes were selected so as to ensure a balanced spread of levels and according to the classroom teachers' availability and willingness to participate. The five schools were selected through geographical cluster sampling from a city in central Romania with an ethnically and economically heterogeneous population. Participation was completely anonymous and confidential, and the students had the option to refuse to participate (which some did). The teenagers had studied English as a foreign language for periods ranging from 1 to 15 years in mixed-ability grouping, with kindergarten and primary school the only periods when foreign languages were optional subjects. Depending on their specialism, the number of English classes per week was between 2 and 7. Of the 1045 students who completed the self-reported questionnaire, several dozen volunteered to be interviewed and 32 were selected for an in-depth one-to-one follow-up discussion on the school premises.

Aims and Outline of the Book

The aim of this book is to raise awareness of concepts and relationships that have not attracted much attention in foreign language learning research, although they may be regarded by many to make intuitive sense. Many adults know, for example, that adolescence is a turbulent period of identity exploration and also a period when many students lose their interest in school while becoming more interested in finding a place for themselves in society. Many adults know that teenagers sometimes pretend to be engaged and interested academically when interacting with adults, while pretending to be disengaged when interacting with peer groups that do not have strong academic values. What processes determine our children to juggle with these identities? What factors determine their desire to become one type of person or another? What factors determine whether or not their intrinsic curiosity and fascination with learning survives the classroom atmosphere and peer pressure? And, crucially, how can we help them learn better and be more fulfilled as fully functioning members of society?

This book seeks to answer some of these questions by (a) discussing the previous literature and research exploring the role of identity in adolescents' development in general, and in foreign language learning in particular, (b) reporting on a study that was inspired by the need for more research into the role of self and identity in adolescent foreign language learning and (c) discussing the findings of this project in relation to other similar studies, commenting on practical, conceptual and research implications. The book has the following structure:

The next chapter provides a literature background to the self, identity and related concepts in social and educational psychology, with an emphasis on developmental processes in adolescence. Four of the main influences on teenagers' identity development – parents, friends, teachers and classmates – are discussed briefly before a summary of the literature discussing differences between private/public and actual/possible identity perceptions. The chapter ends with an overview of Carl Rogers' conceptualisation of 'fully functioning persons', a notion which is considered to incorporate key elements from all the literature strands reviewed before, and which has influenced the new theoretical model proposed in this book to a great extent.

Chapter 3 reviews previous research that has explored foreign language learning from a self or identity perspective. The chapter begins by defining the focus of this book and the research presented in it: the learning of foreign languages in countries where the L2 is not the official language, through limited contact time at school. Whereas identity has been a prolific research topic in the second language acquisition literature documenting the adaptation and integration of immigrants into their host countries, it has only relatively recently come into focus in foreign language learning research. Key studies that have reported on the self and identity in foreign language contexts are discussed, as are various motivational, self-regulatory and relational perspectives that may not be regarded to have researched the core concepts of this book but which have, nevertheless, had an important influence on the design of the research project reported later. The chapter ends with five reasons why more research is needed into the role of self and identity in foreign language learning.

Chapter 4 proposes a new model of identity, which constituted the theoretical framework of the study reported later in the book. The model incorporates the social and educational psychology concepts reviewed in Chapter 2, while also drawing on concepts discussed in Chapter 4. The Quadripolar Model of Identity regards identity as an aggregate of internal and external selves, both actual and possible, associated with one individual. The chapter describes the components of the self system, the main relationships that these components are hypothesised to engage in, and the main self system configurations that these components may cluster around. The chapter ends by acknowledging some of the limitations of the proposed model.

Chapters 5, 6 and 7 discuss key findings of the research project that served as the initial validation of the new identity model for learning English as a foreign language. Chapter 5 draws on the qualitative data, reporting on the insights gained about the main self system configurations with extensive quotations from the interviews. Chapter 6 discusses highlights of the quantitative findings, supported by qualitative data, which confirm many of the hypotheses described in Chapter 4. It provides evidence that strategic identity display was rife in the selected research context (with some interesting gender differences), that adolescents responded in the predicted manner to the expectations of the social circles they interacted with and that identity display that is not rooted in the participants' actual identity has serious consequences for declared achievement in language learning. Chapter 7 discusses in further detail the role of the teacher in the classroom, at the centre of many crucial identity processes that adolescents experience. It shows the complex negotiations that students have to orchestrate when deciding whether or not to reveal what they believe about themselves as individuals in language learning, although most of the time what appears to matter is that they obtain a pass mark by whatever means necessary, without much personal investment. The chapter ends by discussing the participants' view according to which the main condition for students to be engaged is that teachers themselves are engaged, and discussing the reasons why an important internalisation potential appears to go unused in this particular research context.

Chapter 8 provides an evaluation of the theoretical framework, discussing some of the hypotheses that were confirmed by this empirical study, as well as several unexpected insights and remaining questions that my project could not answer. Implications for future research comment on the need to test the proposed model and other such approaches through alternative methods, as well as in countries where English is the official L1, and where recent years have seen a decline in Modern Foreign Language study. Implications for the classroom reiterate the need for students – and teachers – to be valued for what they are as individuals. The chapter ends with a brief conclusion summarising the focus of the main study reported in the book and the ways in which this study has contributed to the discussion about the role of identity in foreign language learning.

2 Self and Identity in Adolescence: A Relational Perspective

Although 'self' and 'identity' are now everyday vocabulary items, it is not easy to define them, in a domain characterised perhaps more than anything by terminological wilderness – a 'self-zoo', as it has been called (Tesser *et al.*, 2000) – especially that self and identity have tended to generate parallel strands of literature. In addition, discussing the identity of adolescents engenders further complications, as this too has generated many different research approaches. An extra layer of difficulty is added by the influence on adolescents' emergent identity of various relational contexts. (In this book, the phrase 'relational context' is used to represent a given social situation where the individual interacts with other persons in a particular social capacity, responding to particular social expectations.) Accordingly, this section will aim to clarify some of the associated terminology (self, identity, self-concept, self-esteem, self-worth) before discussing the main characteristics of adolescent identity development and the influence of four main relational contexts: parents, friends, teachers and classmates.

From Self to Identity: Terminological Inroads

It has been said that no topic is more interesting to people than… people, although what many of us may be supremely interested in is the self. Being human implies the reflective consciousness of having a self, and the nature of the self is the very essence of being human (Lewis, 1990). From the large array of explanations that can be found in the literature, Baumeister's (1997: 681–682) definition is perhaps one of the most helpful: *self* is a general term which represents 'the direct feeling each person has of privileged access to his or her own thoughts and feelings and sensations'. In this view, therefore, the self comprises cognitive, affective and physical aspects, being regarded as a collection of thoughts about what the individual can and cannot do – both with their mind and with their body, what is important and what is not, as well as what they like or dislike.

However, the literature tends to differentiate the self from people's knowledge or beliefs about themselves and their relations to other people – these being incorporated in the *self-concept* (Byrne, 1996; Hattie, 1992; Wylie, 1989). Some authors use the notion of *self-esteem* to define the evaluation and approval/disapproval of the self-knowledge and self-beliefs that constitute a person's self-concept (Zeigler-Hill, 2013). Self-esteem is clearly a very popular concept, which is evidenced by the enormous number of volumes available on the market that promise to cure anything from broken relationships to low achievement by increasing self-esteem. However, the notion has attracted serious criticism (Baumeister *et al.*, 2003; Kohn, 1994), particularly for a reason emphasised by the very president of the International Council for Self-Esteem: that 'efforts limited to making students "feel good" are apt to have little lasting effect because they fail to strengthen the internal sources of self-esteem related to integrity, responsibility, and achievement' (Reasoner, 1992: 24). Consequently, attempts to boost self-esteem have been considered a superficial approach to improving people's feelings about themselves with-out actually tackling the roots of those feelings. A preferable notion is that of *self-worth*, which defines people's sense of personal value as a function of perceived ability (Covington, 1992; Horberg & Chen, 2010). As one's self-worth is regarded to depend on ability, boosting self-worth means increasing ability through increased effort, which is considered a far more sustainable approach (Dweck, 1999). Some authors include self-worth in the definition of self-concept, which they regards as 'a self-description judgement that includes an evaluation of competence and the feelings of self-worth associated with the judgement in question' (Pajares & Schunk, 2002: 16).

Developing from early adolescence, self-concept is the product of social relationships and interactions, reflecting the mores, norms and values of a particular social context (Côté, 2009). Given that people function in many different environments, it follows that multiple self-concept categories develop that correspond to distinct roles, relationships, and social contexts. Authors have considered these multiple categories to be organised as a system of schemata (Markus, 1977), as an associative network (Bower & Gilligan, 1979), as a hierarchy (Marsh & Yeung, 1998), or not to be organised in any particular way (Harter, 2012), some authors believing that self-concept is not a helpful notion in the first place (Baumeister, 1999a). Where many authors converge, however, is on the belief that the self has many social facets modelled on the different relational contexts in which individuals engage, these facets being aggregated into the notion of identity (Baumeister, 1997; Harter, 2012). As Vignoles *et al.* (2011: 2) explain, '... identity comprises not only 'who you think you are' (individually or collectively), but also 'who you act as being' in interpersonal and intergroup interactions – and the social recognition or otherwise that these actions receive from other individuals or groups'. This is also the meaning of identity around which this book is constructed: an aggregate of internal and external identity perceptions (or selves, as detailed later).

Identity is, therefore, inextricably linked to the social context and inevitably shaped by it through the mediation of self perceptions. As Schlenker (1986: 24) explains,

> People's ideas about themselves are expressed and tested in social life through their actions. In turn, the outcomes of these 'tests' provide a basis for crystallizing, refining, or modifying identity based in part on how believable or defensible these identity images appear to be.

In other words, living in society, people develop perceptions of what is and what is not desired in a particular context and display self images accordingly. The subsequent social responses determine whether the self image being tested is discarded or internalised. One direct consequence is that, functioning in several different contexts, individuals may display several different identity images, which are not always convergent (Jones & Pittman, 1982; Leary, 1995; Schlenker, 2003). These identity images are composed of particular traits that are sometimes called *self-defining goals* and which represent the interface between identity and behaviour (Gollwitzer & Kirchhof, 1998). For example, somebody who wants to become a pop star knows that being a pop star involves singing or playing an instrument, wearing a particular type of clothes, associating oneself with people who appreciate pop music and so on. As such, the person who is not yet a pop star but wants to become one will start by pursuing the self-defining goals of learning to sing, buying particular clothes and seeking the company of particular people. Authors differentiate between such identity strivings performed for expressive reasons – when the person genuinely wants to acquire that particular identity (Wicklund & Gollwitzer, 1982), and those performed for strategic reasons – when the person is trying to manipulate an audience for a particular purpose (Leary, 1995). The distinction will be discussed in more detail later.

Two essential factors in the development of self and identity are choice and control, which play important parts in self-determination theory (Deci

& Ryan, 1985; La Guardia, 2009). This framework postulates the existence of three basic human needs – the need for autonomy, the need for competence and the need for relatedness – stating that the self images a person adopts in society are all in the service of these three basic needs (Ryan & Deci, 2003). Identity-relevant behaviours can be assimilated into the self along a continuum comprising *external regulation* (compliance with rules), *introjected regulation* (self-/other approval, guilt, shame), *identified regulation* (behaviours consistent with personally important goals), *integrated regulation* (the most autonomous form of intentional, externally regulated behaviour) and *intrinsic motivation* (e.g. fun, inherent enjoyment). Both intrinsic and extrinsic motivation to act are in contrast to *amotivation*, a state characterised by alienation and helplessness, resulting from lack of choice and control over one's actions.

Another framework which stresses the importance of control in mastering one's environment is self-efficacy theory (Bandura, 1997), although its links with the self and identity are somewhat obliterated by its main focus being placed on cognitive behaviour regulation. Self-efficacy beliefs – or 'beliefs in one's capability to organize and execute the courses of action required to manage prospective situations' (Bandura, 1997: 2) – are task-specific and context-dependent, being thus different from the perceived competence conceptualised in other frameworks (for a comprehensive review see, for example, Pajares, 1997). Whereas the definition of self-efficacy is not always clear in the literature, being sometimes confused with self-concept, theorists emphasise that self-efficacy represents individuals' judgements of how capable they are of performing specific activities, whereas self-concept is a description of one's perceived self in relation to a social context (Bong & Skaalvik, 2003; Pajares & Schunk, 2001).

As mentioned above, the differentiation of self-concepts and the formation of a socially conditioned identity begin in early adolescence, together with the superior cognitive and social development that the person is experiencing. It is in this context that different self images emerge in different relational contexts.

Main Relational Contexts Shaping Adolescents' Identity Development

Early to middle adolescence (12–15 years) brings with it the differentiation of selves to accommodate the diverse relational contexts in which the individual functions, whereas social comparison for the purpose of self-evaluation becomes more and more covert (Harter, 2012). Young adolescents begin to compare themselves to their significant others, which results in the self displayed to a group of peers being frequently different from the self displayed to one's best friends or one's family. This can be the source of great inner conflicts as teenagers strive to accommodate emerging alternative selves, as well as contradictory pressures from different social groups, at the same time having to cope with age-specific anxiety and fear of rejection (Brinthaupt & Lipka, 2002; Csikszentmihalyi & Larson, 1984).

Towards late adolescence, however, individuals learn to accept their limitations and contradictions, beginning to understand that, while within-context inconsistencies are to be avoided, they are perfectly normal between contexts. Showing signs of the approaching adulthood, the adolescent now knows that one can be a slightly different person in different contexts without having to worry about being inconsistent. Research conducted by Harter and colleagues (Harter et al., 1997; Harter & Monsour, 1992) revealed that self descriptions produced by early adolescents for different relational contexts overlapped in proportion of 30% while the percentage for late adolescents was 10%, showing a rising difference in self-perceptions between diverse social roles and an increased degree of acceptance of this apparent contradiction as a normal characteristic of an adaptable young adult. However, as Harter (2012) emphasises, conflicts between social selves do not disappear completely in adolescence: they are still likely to occur in socialising environments that do not support the integration of particular self attributes. Whereas superior cognitive development allows for increasingly abstract thinking, late adolescents consolidate their identity by comparing themselves to future selves of their choice, be they internalised or self generated (Higgins, 1987; Markus & Nurius, 1986). As a result, the relational contexts that do not allow for such self-actualising manifestations are conducive to intra- and inter-personal conflict.

It is both intuitive and supported by a substantive body of literature that the main relational contexts shaping adolescents' identity are their family, their friends, their classmates and their teachers (Taylor, 2013b forthcoming). These four categories exert specific influences on the development of the teenager's identity and will be discussed below.

Parents

As the formation of a social persona starts at home, the family is an essential factor in identity development. While the socio-economic and educational background of the family is a strong determinant of the adolescents' subsequent path (Bell *et al.*, 1996; Blau, 1999), the essential role in a teenager's self explorations is played by parenting styles. Research has linked supportive parenting to a smooth transition through the stages of teenage identity development (Soenens & Vansteenkiste, 2005). Authoritarian parents, on the other hand, have been shown to discourage mature identity explorations and engender dependence on their guidance (McClun & Merrell, 1998). For a healthy exploration of identity in adolescence, families who adopt a democratic parenting style, allowing for individuality and genuine communication, while expressing 'tough love' – a combination of warmth and consistency – were found to be most successful (Lexmond & Reeves, 2009).

In a developmental stage when adolescents' bids for autonomy and independence are ever greater, while the time spent with their peers is increasing to the detriment of the time spent with one's family (Csikszentmihalyi & Larson, 1984; Harter, 2012), the likelihood of parent–child tension is also on the rise. Thus, a family environment that does not support exploration and the enactment of self relevant goals will lead to frustration and conflict (Holmberg, 1996; Lempers & Clark-Lempers, 1992). However, it has been emphasised that, although teenagers strive to liberate themselves from the parents' influence, they will always maintain a strong psychological bond to their families (Collins, 1990; Feiring & Taska, 1996; Steinberg, 1990).

Friends

Whereas parents' influence is maintained, during adolescence friends become an increasingly important source of self-evaluation and social support (Brown, 1990; Selman & Schultz, 1990). Many adolescents feel that adults cannot understand them (Elkind, 1998), therefore friends of a similar age can provide the emotional support and the mutual understanding necessary in honing teenagers' socio-integrative skills. Indeed, research has found that the highest level of genuine self-expression is triggered by close friends, usually of the same gender (Harter *et al.*, 1997; Lempers & Clark-Lempers, 1992).

Friends can have a consistent influence on educational aspirations and outcomes (Berndt & Keefe, 1996; Phelan *et al.*, 1991), as well as on the adolescent's emerging social identity. Although best friends' appreciation and support are a source of well-being in adolescence, consequences are not always positive, as youth will sometimes pay undesirable prices in order to gain acceptance to particular groups (Connor, 1994). This includes the display of particular behaviours that identify a teenager as a member of a gang, for example, and which can end up being integrated into one's self-concept (Ryan & Deci, 2003; Spergel, 1995).

Teachers

Filling a large proportion of the adolescents' time, the classroom is a micro social setting that leaves its socio-ideological mark on students' identity through the mediation of teacher beliefs and practices. The teacher's role in the classroom is crucial in fostering an autonomous cooperative atmosphere in which students learn to develop in synergy, celebrating one another's successes and working together to consolidate one another's weaknesses (Ames, 1992; Boggiano & Katz, 1991; Murdock & Miller, 2003). In addition, given that students tend to perceive the teacher's responses as assessment of themselves as persons rather than of their performance, the feedback given in class is also crucial: not only should it be informative rather than controlling, but it should emphasise effort rather than ability or intelligence. Praise for easily achieved successes and unsolicited help, as well as low teacher expectations, can also have debilitating effects on motivation and perceived competence, as pupils regard them as low ability cues (Deci & Ryan, 1985; Dweck, 1999).

Many studies have indicated that adolescence is associated with a decline in academic motivation and school interest, as well as a reorientation from academic achievement to peer-related goals, from intrinsic to extrinsic motives and from learning to performance orientations (Fredricks et al., 2004; Skinner et al., 2008; Wigfield & Eccles, 2002). There is also evidence to suggest that teachers' attitude and behaviour can hinder – or facilitate – the internalisation of academic goals into students' self-relevant representations (Assor et al., 2005; Reeve et al., 1999). Some studies have also revealed that, from several relational contexts, adolescents repress their self most of all when interacting with their teachers for fear of a negative affective reaction, as well as lack of validation and respect for one's views (Harter, 1996; Lempers & Clark-Lempers, 1992).

Classmates

For the developing teenager, classmates serve as potential companions and friends, being important socialisation factors. However, in the absence of a harmonious cooperative environment, they can also represent the source of social comparison in the classroom, with important repercussions for the adolescent's sense of self (Kindermann et al., 1996). This may be one of the reasons why classmates have been identified as generating the relational context in which adolescents feel 'least real' (Harter, 1996).

In Western society, many schools are competitive environments in which *performance orientations* are encouraged, to the detriment of *learning orientations*. A learning orientation (or goal) is a focus on enhancing one's competence through increased effort, whereas a performance orientation is concerned with winning positive judgements of one's competence and avoiding negative ones: a performance-oriented student will strive to *look smart*, whereas a learning-oriented one will aim to *become smarter* (Greene & Miller, 1996; Meece *et al.*, 2006; Seifert, 1995; Seifert & O'Keefe, 2001). In a performance-oriented framework, one's peers become one's rivals, in a constant struggle to outperform the other in *displaying* ability or intelligence, so that the other's failure is celebrated as an opportunity to *appear* better yourself; in a learning-oriented environment, however, rather than being rivals, peers are facilitators of self-worth through cooperation and mutual enabling of progress (Butler, 1992; Dweck, 1999, 2007a). The link between goal orientations and student identity has also been acknowledged through recent calls for the conceptualisation of a third goal – an 'exploratory orientation' – that places the student's self in the focus (Kaplan & Flum, 2010).

Perhaps the most consequential influence that classmates can have on a teenager's academic identity under the circumstances is the so-called 'norm of low achievement' or 'law of generalised mediocrity', which results in peers being penalised by the group for their achievement strivings (Ames, 1992; Covington, 1992; Juvonen & Murdock, 1995; Juvonen, 2000; Seifert & O'Keefe, 2001). Dweck (1999: 131) offers an expressive description of this prevalent type of peer pressure:

> [Competitiveness] creates *a system of winners and losers*, where there are a few winners at the top and a large number of losers under them. Many groups of adolescents have, understandably, rebelled against this by creating their own rule system in which working hard and getting good grades meets with strong disapproval. This is how students have conspired to undermine a system that designates winners and losers. *Through peer pressure they seek to eliminate the winners*. Then, those who would have been the losers no longer stand apart from the others. The norm of low effort also means that students' feelings about their intelligence are further protected . . . *If they don't try, a poor grade doesn't mean they're not intelligent*. (emphasis added)

Such pressure is quite inevitable in a society where self-worth is a factor of marks and test results (Covington, 1992), leading to self-serving shifts in one's attributions of effort and ability. That is, low marks are often explained through lack of effort, rather than lack of ability, which also leads to effort withdrawal, so that in case of failure lack of effort can be offered as an explanation by individuals looking to protect their self-worth by maintaining at least what may look like ability. According to Covington, this is very much the case in Western society (as it is in the research context that generated the empirical content of this book). For a learning-oriented student, effort represents one's chance to become better and better all the time, whereas for a performance-oriented one effort is a sign of low ability, or, as Seifert (2004: 141) puts it, 'Smart people do not have to try hard and people who try hard are not smart'. In consequence, classmates' silent bid for mediocre conformity can be much stronger than students' desire to succeed, leaving important marks on their and their peers' academic and social identity. However, research findings have indicated that resistance to peer pressure increases in middle to late adolescence, when youth become more interested in their own ideals and desired selves than in a group-imposed identity (Harter, 2012; Steinberg & Monahan, 2007).

From Actual to Possible Selves

Psychological literature distinguishes between one's real (or perceived) self and the self images that one displays in any given context, the two being engaged in a dynamic relationship described below. There is also a distinction, on a hypothetical level, between one's desired selves and other socially conditioned possible selves, which are also bound in a mutually influential relationship. These will be discussed below, beginning with the difference between one's private and public selves, and the process through which the latter can become integrated into the former, then reviewing the literature on possible selves that is most relevant for adolescent identity and finishing with an overview of Carl Rogers' notion of 'fully functioning persons', which is considered to incorporate key elements of all the literature strands discussed in this chapter.

Private versus public

Although the degree of dissimilarity will vary in space and time, there are important differences between what we believe we are and what we show other people about ourselves, just as there are differences between what we show (or think we show) other people about ourselves and what they perceive, in turn (Andersen et al., 1998; Hogan & Briggs, 1986). The two facets of identity have been called the *private self* and the *public self*, Baumeister's (1986: v) definition being, once again, illuminating:

The public self is the self that is manifested in the presence of others, that is formed when other people attribute traits and qualities to the individual, and that is communicated to other people in the process of self-presentation. The private self is the way the person understands himself or herself and is the way the person really is. ...

Private self is an alternative designation for self-concept – one's knowledge and beliefs about oneself crystallised through social interaction and past experience – the former being preferred in contexts where a differentiation is necessary between one's personal sense of self and its socially displayed counterpart (Baumeister, 1999b; Schlenker, 2003).

Whereas the public self is delineated by one's private self, in the sense that one cannot display an image that is very evidently at odds with one's conception of oneself, the latter is also shaped by public manifestations, both in response to social conditioning and through the internalisation of some of the self images displayed in public.

Self-presentation and internalisation: When the public becomes private

Just as we cannot always say what we think (for fear of causing offence, for example), our innermost persona is seldom communicated socially in its entirety, and even William James, as early as 1890, noted that people have as many social selves as the audiences they encounter. In his colourful words, 'Many a youth who is demure enough before his parents and teachers swears and swaggers like a pirate among his tough young friends' (James, 1890: 169). People are constantly caught between the desire to look competent – or incompetent, if that better serves them – and the need for social approval (Covington, 1992; Leary, 1995). Consequently, 'our intended social identities', Hogan and Briggs (1986: 182) comment, 'reflect the best compromise we can negotiate' in our interactions. It is the same mechanism that drives people away from their undesired selves (Markus & Nurius, 1986), as we would normally avoid being seen as maladjusted, immoral, socially undesirable etc. (Leary, 1995). Far from being a sign of insecurity or vanity – Leary explains – a certain degree of concern with the impressions one makes is essential for successful social interaction.

Such disclosure tactics are called *self-presentation* and, although this can be used manipulatively, it is normal for a person to perform a set of predetermined behaviours in a particular social context in order to render a particular impression and thus achieve a desired goal (Arkin & Baumgardner, 1986; Jones & Pittman, 1982; Leary, 1995). As Schlenker (2003) emphasises, perfectly valid information about ourselves needs as much presentation skill as fabricated information in order to have the intended impact.

The self-presentation 'set' consists of an actor, an audience and a social situation, the last two components determining the salience of a particular public self. Given that desirable self-presentations reflect 'the integration of what people would like to be and think they can be in a given social context' (Schlenker, 2003: 499), a parallel with possible selves emerges (see below). Whereas realistic possible selves are future self-guides based on the affordances in one's proximal social environment, self-presentations can be said to be the present enactment of one's desired selves (Baumeister, 1982; Higgins, 1996). It has even been suggested that, for a public self to be activated by a particular audience, the audience does not necessarily have to be present: research has indicated that imagined audiences are just as effective in influencing people's self-presentations (Doherty et al., 1991).

The selves disclosed in public are determined by the private self (or self-concept), which ensures that one's social images are within one's realistic capacity. The key mediators here are perceived competence and constant self-monitoring: for example, if they believe they do not have the ability to perform complex mathematical operations, most people will not present themselves in public as mathematics experts. But the dynamic relationship between one's private and public selves is nowhere better demonstrated than in the evidence that our public selves can actually change our private self. 'Act the part and it becomes incorporated into the self-concept', Schlenker (2003: 502) quips. The process is called *internalisation* or the *carryover effect* (Rhodewalt, 1998). Internalisation is also an important component of self-determination theory (La Guardia, 2009; Ryan & Deci, 2003), which explains how particular external orientations can be assimilated into one's self-concept to a lesser or greater extent.

The influence of public selves on one's private self is mediated by the emotional response the individual has to the audience's reaction. Being manifestly perceived in the intended way may motivate the individual to reduce discrepancies between the current private self and the desired public self (Leary & Kowalski, 1990). Thus, internalisation is a vehicle of change that plays a crucial role in private identity formation (Baumeister, 1982; Leary, 1995). Acquiring a desired identity (or self) requires the enactment of a particular set of self-relevant images pertaining to that identity (Gollwitzer & Kirchhof, 1998; Pin & Turndorf, 1990). For example, a new university lecturer projecting an image that is consistent with being a lecturer will help integrate this image into his/her self-concept, solidifying this new identity. Similarly, a rebellious teenager who wants to be seen as 'one of the gang' may display particular behaviours that will subsequently get integrated into the private self. Leary (1995) explains that, while enacting particular behaviours that are not yet part of their self-concept, people may learn new things about themselves; they may even come to understand that they actually *are* the way they presented themselves.

Intriguing studies conducted by Juvonen and colleagues (Juvonen & Murdock, 1993, 1995; Juvonen, 2000) have revealed that strategic self-presentation and manipulative attributional shifts are rife in competitive classroom settings. Not only do competitive contingencies encourage high-ability/low-effort attributions, but they also determine students to explain their poor performance by different causes depending on their audience. Thus, pupils tend to communicate low-effort attributions to peers and low-ability to teachers: in order to gain the group's acceptance, when talking to peers they display the image of smart teenagers who do not have to work hard, whereas when talking to teachers they strive to appear hard-working but not very able, as they believe that teachers appreciate effort and empathise with low ability. Although proving that students do act different social roles depending on the context, this is a case when internalisation of public selves can have devastating consequences for students' academic self, motivation and achievement.

Possible selves

Together with the differentiation of public selves for interacting with various relational contexts, adolescents begin to consider alternative future routes. When displaying particular public selves in particular social contexts, they try out possible selves that they may or may not internalise later (Dunkel, 2000; Oyserman et al., 2002). As such, these selves are always socially conditioned and contingent, the individual understanding from the social environment whether a particular self is acceptable or unacceptable (Oyserman & Fryberg, 2006; Wurf & Markus, 1991).

Desirable and undesirable self images have been shown to mediate long-term motivation by channelling the actions necessary for the achievement of a self-relevant goal. Dunkel et al. (2006) offer a four-step explanation for the pursuit and integration of a possible self into one's identity: (a) as individuals contemplate change, they generate possible selves; (b) as they decide to pursue change, they try to validate their chosen possible selves; (c) as they pursue some possible selves, they eliminate others; and (d) when possible selves are achieved, they are integrated into the current self-concept. The constant reiteration of the process takes the individual further along a desired path.

In order for possible selves to translate into reality, they must be based on the individual's own propensities. This has two immediate implications: effective possible selves are an expression of perceived personal control and agency (Erikson, 2007; Norman & Aron, 2003) and they must be placed within one's realistic potential (Dunkel et al., 2006). Accordingly, similar to self-presentations, possible selves have been considered to enter a mutually influential relationship to one's self-concept (Erikson, 2007; Strahan & Wilson, 2006; Wurf & Markus, 1991).

As Oyserman and Fryberg (2006) underline, in order for possible selves to be successful activators of behaviour, they need to fulfil two more conditions. First, they need to be 'balanced' (when a positive self-identifying goal is accompanied by an awareness of the personally relevant consequences of not meeting the goal), and second, the possible selves need to be doubled by a strategy for attaining the desired state. In the absence of an activating strategy, evoking the end goal means simply evoking a mere state, rather than the process of getting there, which may lack motivational power (Oyserman et al., 2004). Similarly, Oettingen and Mayer (2002) differentiate between possible selves and sheer fantasies or passive expectations. As they explain, merely fantasising about the future lacks the motivational force of possible selves, because a possible self is a future state one must strive to achieve (or avoid) by taking active steps, whereas a fantasy is already lived in the present (albeit a hypothetical one), therefore failing to generate action.

The role of significant others in generating possible selves is important, although people one has never met (such as celebrities, famous gangsters or fictional characters) can be equally powerful inspirations in selecting a desired self, especially for younger adolescents (Harter, 2012; Oyserman & Fryberg, 2006; Zentner & Renaud, 2007). Similar to triggering the display of divergent public selves, different relational contexts can inspire the adoption of contradictory possible selves. In other words, a particular self can be desired in one context and feared in another, like in the case of a diligent student who works hard in order to attain a particular desired self, only to be labelled a 'nerd' and excluded from peer groups for being 'too keen'. The link to the norm of low achievement and the decline in academic motivation is evident. The latter has been attributed to the fact that being academically successful loses its salience as a possible self as pupils advance through secondary school, when being 'a good student' is no longer an appealing goal for many of them (Anderman et al., 1999; Clemens & Seidman, 2002).

Nevertheless, the potential of possible selves to enhance school persistence and academic attainment has been revealed repeatedly (Anderman et al., 1999; Leondari et al., 1998; Oyserman et al., 2002). From this perspective, the teacher's role in the classroom is once again rendered crucial. Just as teachers can make the difference between a competitive or cooperative classroom environment, so too can they help generate and keep alive the motivational potential of the students' desired selves (Day et al., 1994; Hock et al., 2006).

Complementary to the possible selves model is self-discrepancy theory (Higgins, 1987; Higgins et al., 1994). Postulating the existence of three 'domains of the self' (the *actual self*, the *ideal self* and the *ought self*) and two 'standpoints on the self' (own versus significant other), Higgins and his associates maintain that discrepancies between one's self-concept (actual self) and the relevant self guides (ideal self and ought self) produce discomfort, which, in turn, activates the behaviour necessary to eliminate the associated negative emotions by resolving the discrepancy. Sometimes, a person will have several conflicting ought selves, Van Hook and Higgins (1988: 625) maintaining that such discrepancies can induce a 'chronic double approach-avoidance conflict (feeling muddled, indecisive, distractible, unsure of self or goals, rebellious, confused about identity)'. Being caught between two different expectations, the person will be in a no-win situation: approaching one ought self-guide entails avoiding the second, and approaching the second means avoiding the first – hence, a double approach-avoidance conflict (also, Higgins, 1996, 2006). Similarities with possible selves and self-presentation theories are easily seen, as they both emphasise that when a person has to accommodate contradictory social expectations (whether for the future or for the present), tension and conflict are very likely to emerge.

Fully functioning persons

Carl Rogers (1902–1987), one of the founders of the humanistic approach to psychology and initiator of person-centred counselling, appears to integrate (or anticipate) most of the theories reviewed so far in his writings about the 'fully functioning person'. Of utmost relevance for education is his book *Freedom to Learn*, revised, updated and published in its third edition by Jerome Freiberg (Rogers & Freiberg, 1994). In this book, Rogers conceptualises the 'fully functioning person' as somebody who has come very close to his/her *real self* – the optimal result of education that helps people learn how to learn, and of person-centred therapy. This is not a static achievement, but a process through which people become closer and closer to being a 'total organism'. The key characteristic of this process is moving away from conscious and unconscious façades towards an increasing awareness and acceptance of one's inward experiences. Describing fully functioning persons, Rogers explains (Rogers & Freiberg, 1994: 65):

> They find this development exceedingly complex and varied, ranging from wild and crazy feelings to solid, socially approved ones. They move toward accepting all of these experiences as their own; they discover that they are people with an enormous variety of reactions. The more they own and accept their inner reactions – and are unafraid of them – the

more they can sense the meanings those reactions have. The more all this inner richness belongs to them, the more they can appropriately *be* their own experiences ... These people are becoming involved in the wider range of their feelings, attitudes, and potential. They are building a good relationship with what is going on within themselves. They are beginning to appreciate and like, rather than hate and mistrust, all their experiences. Thus, they are coming closer to finding and being all of themselves in the moment.

The biggest obstacle in becoming a fully functioning person – Rogers maintains – is our social defence, which prevents us from trusting our experiential reactions, so that 'consciously we are moving in one direction while organismically we are moving in another' (p. 324). This social defence is mainly represented by the *values* that the individual introjects from society and which can determine the person to lose touch with his/her organismic reactions. We accept these values because we want to be loved or accepted, but more often than not these are 'either not related at all, or not clearly related, to our own process of experiencing' (p. 283). Rogers argues that this is the very root of the crisis that humanity is going through nowadays: not a loss of values, but a contradiction between one's socially conditioned values and one's personal organismic experience. Having relinquished the internal locus of evaluation for our own experience, having adopted the conceptions of others as our own, we have 'divorced ourselves from ourselves' (p. 284), bringing about the fundamental estrangement of the modern person from oneself, which results in insecurity and anxiety.

It is quite clear that the fully functioning person needs absolute freedom in order to enjoy this experiential living. Quite opposite to the external choice that we normally associate with the idea of freedom, this is an inner, subjective, existential liberty that allows the individual to realise: 'I can live myself, here and now, by my own choice' (p. 304). It is the courage to step into the uncertainty of choosing one's own self, the acceptance of responsibility for the self one chooses to be, the person's recognition that he or she is an emerging process, not a static end product. As Rogers shows, the fully functioning person is a self-organising system which, while being constantly interacting with the environment, is not causally determined by it. Thus, the fully functioning individual is both autonomous and dependent on the environment for this constant interaction (p. 310). Being open to experience, living existentially and trusting one's organismic reactions, this person is dependable but not specifically predictable. As the psychologist goes on to explain, 'it is the maladjusted person whose behaviour can be specifically predicted, and some

loss of predictability should be evident in every increase in openness to experience and existential living' (p. 325). As individuals approach this optimum of
complete functioning, although dependable and appropriate, their behaviour
becomes more difficult to predict and equally difficult to control.

According to Carl Rogers, such freedom characterises very young children,
whose locus of evaluation is established firmly within, and who learn about
the world through personal experience unmediated by any socially conditioned 'values'. Incidentally (or perhaps not), we know that this is also the
period of maximum natural inquisitiveness and intrinsic motivation to learn.
As the child grows and starts longing for acceptance in society, the locus of
evaluation for one's experience is externalised, and the individual undergoes
conflictual encounters between social values and personal organismic reactions. Reaching adulthood, the two tend to become reconciled again, although
quite differently from infancy. For the mature person, experience is no longer
limited to the here and now, as it is for the infant, but the meaning of experience goes beyond the immediate sensory impact. The adult has learnt the
rules of living in society and evaluates experience through this social lens. In
addition, psychologically mature adults use their organismic intuitions just
like infants, only they are able to do so knowingly: they are aware that sometimes they need to follow a particular route instinctively and only later understand why that was necessary. And, crucially, they have the liberty to do so.

If infants and adults can enjoy the freedom of organismic experience, for
teenagers the most vulnerable point is being themselves. For most students
– Rogers explains – appearing as a whole human being in the classroom would
mean showing indifference, boredom, resentment at perceived unfairness,
occasional excitement, envy towards classmates, suffering because of one's
family, disappointment or real joy about one's girlfriend/boyfriend, sharp
curiosity about sex or psychic phenomena and so on. Therefore, both students
and teachers accept the unwritten rule that 'it is much safer [for the student]
to button his [sic!] lip, preserve his cool, serve his term, cause no ripples, and
get his paper credentials. He is not willing to take the risk of being human in
class' (p. 43). Furthermore, teachers themselves rarely take the risk of being
human in class, of being 'unafraid' of their organismic reactions.

Traditional schooling is thus seen as a masquerade in which both teachers and students hide behind masks that are meant to conceal their true
human feelings – the teacher, in order to preserve the image of formal authority, and the student in order to create a well-calculated impression of interest.
In Rogers' saddening words (p. 42, my emphasis):

> If he wishes to be well thought of as a student, he attends class regularly,
> looks only at the instructor, or writes diligently in his notebook. Never

mind that *while looking so intently at the instructor, he is thinking of his weekend date*... He sometimes truly wants to learn what the instructor is offering, but even so *his attention is contaminated* by two questions: 'What are this teacher's learnings and biases in this subject so that I can take the same view in my papers?' and 'What is she saying that will likely appear on the exam?' ... *It makes no difference what he thinks* of the course, his instructor, or his fellow students. He shuts such attitudes carefully within himself because he wants to pass the course, to acquire a good reputation with the faculty, and thus move one step further toward the coveted degree, the union card that will open so many doors for him once he has it. *Then he can forget all this and enter real life*.

In this light, school appears rather like a prison term that students have to serve before they can finally afford the liberty of being themselves. It is easy to see that this is the exact opposite of the fully functioning person, who has the courage – and is allowed to – take responsibility for his or her true feelings.

Carl Rogers divides schoolchildren into two categories: *tourists* (described in the quote above) and *citizens*. Quite opposed to the former category, 'citizens' are allowed to be themselves in a classroom where they are 'stakeholders', are valued and appreciated for what they feel, are encouraged to make responsible choices preparing for their future place as fully functioning adults in society. Working with citizen-students, the teacher becomes a facilitator of change and learning. When the facilitator is truly himself or herself, prizes the students for what they are and shows empathic understanding for them as whole human beings, then 'feelings – positive, negative, confused – become part of the classroom experience. Learning becomes life and a very vital life at that. Students are on the way, sometimes excitedly, sometimes reluctantly, to becoming learning, changing people' (p. 161). Such an environment that nurtures opportunities to learn from one's experiences (and one's mistakes) is crucial for the self-discipline, commitment and social responsibility that we, as educators, have a duty to facilitate in our students.

Rogers' conceptualisation of 'fully functioning persons' incorporates key elements of all the literature areas reviewed so far and has influenced to a great extent the new identity model proposed in Chapter 4 and the empirical study that validated it – reported in Chapters 5–7. Before that, however, the next chapter discusses the application of concepts like self and identity to language learning research, identifying several areas where more research is needed.

3 Self and Identity in Foreign Language Learning

Having discussed a number of educational and social psychology theories that helped inform the empirical investigation reported later, the discussion will now turn to the application of self and identity to foreign language learning literature. As explained below, the discussion will not include research into second language acquisition and will only focus on key research perspectives that can help illuminate the learning of foreign languages in adolescence.

Language and Identity

The inextricable link between language and identity has long been acknowledged by psychologists, sociologists, anthropologists and philosophers alike. From language as the substance of the mind and the very core of the social self (Mead, 1934), to the dialogic appropriation of pre-existing linguistic codes for self-expression (Bakhtin, 1981), to language as cultural capital and personal power (Bourdieu, 1991), as the only means of expressing the me/other divide (Melucci, 1996) or as a symbolic elaboration of the self (Elliott, 2001), to verbal communication as a key to making sense of the world and allowing others to make sense of us (Durkin, 2004; Harter, 1999; Woodward, 2002), the link between linguistic expression and the self has been recognised consistently.

As the multiple roles that the self plays in society are mainly manifested through language, there is little wonder that over the last two decades studies in language acquisition have shown an increasing interest in the learners' identity. Goldstein (1995, 1997), Heller (1987), McKay and Wong (1996), McNamara (1987), Miller (2003), Norton (1997, 2000), Pavlenko and Blackledge (2004), Pavlenko and Lantolf (2000), Ricento (2005), Rubenfeld et al.(2006) and Toohey (2000) are only some of the authors who have researched and conceptualised the relationship between language acquisition and identity, regarding the language learner in interaction with the language-learning context. Whether researching young learners (Heller, 1987; McKay & Wong, 1996; Miller, 2003; Toohey, 2000) or adult learners (Goldstein, 1997; Norton, 2000; Pavlenko & Lantolf, 2000), what these authors have in common is their focus on second language acquisition, that is, the acquisition of an additional language (L2) after one's mother tongue, in a context where the L2 is spoken officially. This is the case of immigrants learning the language of their host community while striving to become functional members of that particular community (Bussmann et al., 1998). Most of the above authors' research has been conducted in the United States, Canada and Australia, with immigrants of various nationalities.

Learning a new language has been equated with learning a new identity (Kellman, 2003; Lightbown & Spada, 1999; Pavlenko & Lantolf, 2000), and the ensuing psychological conflicts have been well documented by the above-mentioned and many other second language acquisition researchers. Immigrants may struggle to negotiate a new identity while acquiring the new linguistic code, but they do usually benefit from rich cultural and linguistic input in their host communities, which helps smooth the process. However, the situation is very different in foreign language learning: in countries where the L2 is not an official language but is generally studied at school, through limited contact time and poor opportunities for real-life practice – for example, learning French in England, Spanish in Germany, or English in Romania (Bussmann et al., 1998; Gebhard, 2006). While foreign language learners can be reasonably expected to experience similar identity processes to learners of a second language in their host country, research linking identity or the self and foreign language learning is much scarcer.

This chapter will discuss previous studies that have either taken a self/identity approach in the study of foreign language learning or can be seen as relevant to the focus of this book through their tangential approach. The discussion will begin with previous work on self concept, self-efficacy, self-determination and self-esteem. Motivational and self-regulatory perspectives will then be discussed, before ending with an overview of relational approaches to the study of foreign language learning.

Self and Identity in Language Learning

Still a relatively new topic in foreign language learning research, the self and identity have generated rather sporadic empirical work. Not all the literature that uses 'self' terminology is related to the self or identity, as some perspectives use the term to emphasise autonomy or independence (e.g. self-access), rather than an individual perspective of the social world. This brief overview discusses key contributions that are relevant to the focus of this book and its empirical content, and concentrates mainly on adolescent learners. Adult language learning studies are mentioned where they are otherwise directly relevant to the focus of this book.

Self-concept

Distilling self-perceptions formed through interactions and evaluations within one's social context, where communication with one's social group is mainly carried out via language, self-concept appears particularly useful in foreign language learning. Marsh and colleagues (Marsh *et al.*, 2005; e.g. Marsh, 1990a, 1992) include it in their multidimensional and hierarchical model, according to which the overall self-concept is divided into academic and non-academic components, with the academic component being split further into a math academic self-concept and a verbal academic-self concept. Along with other subject-specific components, the latter also includes a foreign-language academic self-concept. The causal relation between these sub-components and achievement in the respective academic areas is believed to be reciprocal (i.e. high perceived competence leads to higher achievement and higher achievement increases perceived competence). Specific academic self-concepts have been found to correlate substantially with academic achievement, but not with non-academic components nor with a general overarching self-concept, which has cast doubts over the usefulness of a general measure – be it called overall self-concept or self-esteem (e.g. Marsh, 1990a; Marsh *et al.*, 1988; Marsh & O'Mara, 2008). However, it must be noted that other authors (e.g. Baumeister, 1997; Coopersmith, 1967) consider self-esteem the evaluative dimension of the self-concept, rather than an overarching aggregate of self-concepts.

An important contribution to understanding self-concept in foreign language learning is that of Mercer (2012), who borrowed the terminology used by Marsh and colleagues in large trans-national cohort studies and applied it to a qualitative exploration of foreign language learners at an Austrian university. Drawing on longitudinal case studies, language learner histories, self-descriptive narratives and in-depth interviews, she made the case for a fluid and ever-changing nature of language learner's self-concept. As this is presented as being influenced by myriad inter-related factors, language learners should be regarded as 'holistic individuals living complex situated lives', the author believes (Mercer, 2011: 10). This approach is very welcome in that it places the language learner in the social context, Mercer's findings showing that her participants resort to social comparison in order to better understand who they are. This is perhaps surprising, given that her respondents are university students and, by that age, their self-image should be crystallised, self-centred and independent (Harter, 2012), but the finding emphasises the crucial lifelong role that social relational contexts have on our identity development (see also Mercer, 2012).

The so-called Marsh/Shalveson hierarchical model of self-concept was also applied to language learning by Lau *et al.* (1999), although their participants were learners of English as a second – not foreign – language in Hong Kong. Taking the hierarchical organisation even further than Marsh and colleagues, they split the English self-concept into four skill-specific parts: listening, speaking, reading and writing self-concepts. Although they did find four different factors, particular research design ambiguities have raised questions regarding the validity of such a focused approach for academic self-concept research. Specifically, as Bong and Skaalvik (2003) explain, Lau *et al.*'s (1999) task-oriented approach to perceived confidence would be more suitable for self-efficacy than self-concept research (see Bong & Skaalvik, 2003, for an extensive discussion of differences between academic self-efficacy and academic self-concept). Essentially, self-efficacy is concerned with beliefs of competence with regards to performing a particular task, whereas self-concept is 'a self-description judgement that includes an evaluation of competence and the feelings of self-worth associated with the judgement in question' (Pajares & Schunk, 2002: 16). That is, self-efficacy is much more focused and task-specific than self-concept.

Self-efficacy

Although self-efficacy is related more to regulation and perceived competence than identity, it is nevertheless a useful tool when exploring the self, given that one's competency beliefs influence one's approach or avoidance of goals and tasks (Bandura, 1997), which indirectly shapes the type of person the individual will ultimately become. Working within this framework, Mills *et al.* (2007) found that higher-education American students enrolled in French courses were more likely to experience success in their French learning if they perceived themselves as effective metacognitive strategy users and had generally strong self-efficacy beliefs. Graham (2007) also found that, after a strategy-training project involving English learners of French, students' self-efficacy did improve, especially after detailed feedback, although much less than expected. Bong (2001) revealed that the self-efficacy perceptions of 424 Korean middle- and high-school students were moderately correlated across core academic subjects including English, and Bong (2005) concluded that the goal orientation and self-efficacy of Korean high-school girls in core academic subjects fluctuated significantly across the academic year, culminating in high performance orientation and low self-efficacy around examinations. Finally, studying American adults' motivation to learn foreign languages, Ehrman (1996) showed that self-efficacy was negatively correlated with language learning anxiety and positively with assessed language performance.

Self-determination

Another theory that is indirectly related to identity and has been applied to foreign language learning is self-determination theory (Deci & Ryan, 1985, 2002), introduced briefly in Chapter 2. Within the framework, Comănaru and Noels (2009) surveyed 145 university students of Chinese in Canada, the sample including Chinese native speakers, English native speakers of Chinese origin and English native speakers of non-Chinese origin. Assessing the respondents' motivational orientations, psychological needs (autonomy, competence and relatedness), learning engagement, community engagement and reasons for learning Chinese, the authors found that heritage learners (i.e. those whose families comprised native speakers of Chinese) considered the language a more important part of who they were than non-heritage learners, at the same time feeling more pressure to learn Chinese than the non-heritage group. Similarly, Noels (2005) questioned 99 university students enrolled in German courses at a Canadian university, some of whom studied German as a heritage language and some as a non-heritage language. Both types of learners endorsed all motivational orientations to a comparable degree, but heritage learners of German were more motivated by reasons related to their self-concept, indicating that heritage language learners were more integratively oriented (more motivated to interact with the German speaking community) than non-heritage language learners.

In her mixed-method investigation of 376 adolescents studying English as a foreign language in three Romanian secondary schools, Taylor (2008) also found that self-determination was positively correlated with involvement in class and learning orientations, the teacher's attitude and expectations playing a crucial role in determining the students' involvement or avoidance. Other studies found strong relationships between self-determined forms of behaviour and language learning motivation and performance (e.g. Goldberg & Noels, 2006; Noels et al., 2000, 2006).

Self-esteem

Another identity-related concept that has been applied to foreign language learning in an attempt to explicate learner identity is self-esteem, which – as seen in Chapter 2 – is concerned in some frameworks with the evaluative aspect of the self-concept. Rubio (2007) dedicates an entire volume to self-esteem in foreign language learning – a focus which, the editor declares, originates in the potential benefits of self-esteem in the classroom and the total lack of publications covering the theory, research and classroom applications of self-esteem. While this may be accurate, of the 11 chapters included in the volume, only one reports on primary research: de Andrés (2007). The chapter refers to an intervention programme which the author piloted in 1996 following small-scale action research undertaken in 1993. Her participants were 31 children aged 6–8 studying English as a foreign language at a private school in Argentina. Their responses to a closed-item questionnaire were corroborated with work samples, classroom observations and projective tests, as well as with teachers' and parents' opinions. The objectives of the intervention programme were: (1) to develop children's understanding of themselves; (2) to develop understanding of others; and (3) to communicate more effectively. One of the three sub-sections of the third objective was 'to improve English language skills'. This is the only reference to foreign language learning in the entire project, which consisted of games, story-telling, singing and arts & crafts activities understood to have been conducted in English. Based on answers to questions such as 'Did you like the project?' or 'Did the project respond to your child's needs and interest?', it was concluded that 'self-esteem work can be a vehicle for improving language acquisition' (p. 52) – a conclusion that might be considered rather arbitrary in the light of the evidence reported. In addition, although de Andrés started her chapter by reviewing the socio-psychological literature on the self (with reference to William James, Charles Cooley, Carl Rogers, Abraham Maslow and many others), there is little indication of how the theories reviewed informed the reported project.

The remaining ten chapters of Rubio's (2007) edited volume follow a similar pattern: a review of the general literature on self-esteem and associated constructs, complemented by the authors' assumptions or inferences about the applicability of the concept in the foreign language class. Self-esteem seems to be generally used in free variation with concepts such as identity, self-concept, self-confidence, self-worth, self-efficacy – all scarcely referenced and loosely (if at all) defined. Leaving such details aside, and ignoring the controversy that surrounds the concept itself in the literature (e.g. Baumeister *et al.*, 2003; Kohn, 1994; Marsh & O'Mara, 2008), there seems to be little empirical evidence regarding the usefulness of the concept in language learning and teaching.

Motivational self systems

A contribution that has generated considerable discussion and numerous follow-up studies is Dörnyei's (2005, 2009) *L2 Motivational Self System*, which is built around the ideal/ought self dichotomy (Higgins, 2006) reviewed briefly in Chapter 2. The model has three components: the *ideal L2 self*, the *ought-to L2 self* and the *L2 learning experience*. The strongest component of the model is the ideal L2 self, which the author characterises as 'a powerful motivator to learn the L2 because of the desire to reduce the discrepancy between our actual and ideal selves' (Dörnyei, 2009: 29). However, the model does not include an actual self and it is not clear how the ideal self can be a powerful motivator to reduce the discrepancy between one's actual and ideal selves when no attention is given to the actual self.

The model also dismisses much of the influence of the ought-to self on the individual's motivation and self development. In Dörnyei's view (2009: 32), 'because the source of the second component of the system, the Ought-to L2 Self, is external to the learner (...), this future self-guide does not lend itself to obvious motivational practices'. This is contrary both to a considerable body of literature showing that socially induced possible selves can enhance school persistence and academic achievement (see Chapter 2), and to the experience of all of us who have ever done anything because we felt we should, rather than because we really wanted to.

As such, the core value of the *L2 Motivational Self System* stands in reinforcing the motivational potential of the ideal self confirmed repeatedly in the literature, without, however, shedding any light on the language learner's identity or self. The contribution is also important in that it is one of the first and few comprehensive models of the self system in foreign language learning, although the instruments used to validate it were not designed specifically for this purpose. As Dörnyei explains (Dörnyei *et al.*, 2006: 91–94; e.g. 2009: 26–27), the *L2 Motivational Self System* is a recent reinterpretation of his Hungarian survey data collected in 1993, 1999 and 2004 with a questionnaire heavily influenced by Gardner's (1985) Attitude/Motivation Test Battery (built around the concept of integrativeness in second language acquisition contexts). The instrument used for collecting these data contained variables addressing the L2 learners' attitudes towards their host community, which made sense in Gardner's Canadian context, from whom many scales were borrowed, but not so much in the Hungarian foreign-language context. Scales such as integrativeness, instrumentality, attitudes towards the L2-speaking community, attitudes towards the L2, parental encouragement, L2 class anxiety and motivational intensity (including motivated learning behaviours and learning effort) have travelled on, in various combinations, from Gardner (1985) to Dörnyei *et al.* (2006), to Kormos and Csizér (2008), Csizér and Kormos (2009), Ryan (2009), Taguchi *et al.* (2009), Henry (2009), Busse and Williams (2010) and so on. Although the benefits of using (entirely or partially) already validated and established data-collection instruments are unquestionable, it is high time foreign language learning research moved beyond an instrument designed more than 25 years ago for a very different population, with different contextual effects and a different set of aims and research questions. (For a more detailed critical review of the *L2 Motivational Self System* and several empirical studies that have used this framework, see Taylor, 2010.)

The main limitation of the *L2 Motivational Self System* – ignoring the L2 learner's present or actual self – was addressed by Xu (2009) in his doctoral thesis, *English Learning Motivational Self System*, which he calls 'a revised version of the L2 Motivational Self System proposed by Dörnyei'. Although itself borrowing items from a Gardner-inspired instrument designed to validate Dörnyei's system (Taguchi *et al.*, 2009) and drawing on the same possible selves and self-discrepancy theories, Xu's data collection instrument was mainly based on 360 compositions that students wrote for him, describing their potential for learning English (Xu, personal communication). Working with 674 Chinese undergraduates studying English as a foreign language, he proposed and validated a model consisting of three components: the *possible English self*, the *present English self* and the *past English self*. Through exploratory and confirmatory factor analyses, Xu found that the present English self mediated between the past and the future English selves, 33% of the variance in the future self being explained by the present and past ones. With its strong emphasis on the impact that the present English self can have on a student's future identity and motivation, Xu's (2009) proposed system addresses an important need in the literature, in what appears to be a solitary multidimensional project in identity-focused research on foreign language learning to date. In doing so, however, he largely overlooks the social influences shaping the students' present identity and the contextual interactions in which they engage.

Other motivational and self-regulatory perspectives

In other relevant literature areas, Busse and Williams (2010) report on the first phase of a longitudinal mixed-method investigation into the motivational trajectories of 94 first-year undergraduate students enrolled on German courses at two British universities. Borrowing items from Gardner *et al.* (1997), Ryan (2008) and Taguchi *et al.* (2009), their instrument measured: *wish for language proficiency, intrinsic reasons, ideal self, instrumental reasons, integrative reasons* and *ought-to self*. For the qualitative component, they used a semi-structured interview schedule based on Ushioda's (1996a) doctoral exploration. Apart from their findings related to motivation – the main focus of their investigation – the authors also found some support for the ideal self, but not the ought-to self, in determining the students' motivational itineraries, the survey being corroborated by the qualitative content analysis of the interviews. Reminiscent of the literature generated by the *L2 Motivational Self System*, Busse and William (2010) did not elaborate much on the learners' present identity, being mainly concerned with the motivational potential of the ideal self.

Investigating students' motivation to learn a foreign language, Williams *et al.* (2002) conducted a mixed-method study with a total sample of 228 pupils learning French and German in England with the aim to elucidate key motivators and various differential effects. In their study, motivational factors were divided into four broad areas: attitude, identity, agency and external factors. The identity component consisted of perceived success and perceived ability, and rendered fairly positive values, although smaller for boys than for girls, smaller for Year 9 than for Year 7, smaller for low-proficiency learners than for highly proficient ones, and smaller for learning French than for learning German. Again, the self in foreign language learning was not the focus of Williams *et al.*'s (2002) research, which concentrated mainly on motivation.

In turn, Ushioda (1996b, 1998) reports on a two-phase qualitative study with 20 undergraduate learners of French as a foreign language in Ireland. Her aim was to explore motivational thinking in foreign language learning and its relationship with academic achievement. She found that internal attributions for success and external attributions for failure were related to students' academic achievement through the mediation of a positive self-concept. However, Ushioda's specific focus was not the participants' identity, and, in line with the purpose of her studies, 'self-concept' was used in a loosely defined manner.

More recently, Ushioda (e.g. 2009) has called for a 'person-in-context view of motivation', which would regard the language learner as a real person, rather than a 'theoretical abstraction'. Such a perspective would entail:

a focus on the interaction between this self-reflective intentional agent, and the fluid and complex system of social relations, activities, experiences and multiple micro- and macro-contexts in which the person is embedded, moves, and is inherently part of. (p. 220)

The author's words encapsulate an important need in research on foreign language learning identity: a view of the language learner as an active self-reflective agent in interaction with the social context. Ushioda's 'person-in-context view of motivation' is still in need of more solid conceptualisation and little published empirical research seems so far to have explored this line of thought.

A similar standpoint has been represented in discourse analysis by Riley (2006). He points out that, although much has been written over the years about learners' motivations and needs, very little attention has been paid to the learners themselves. He explains (p. 296):

> Although it is true that applied linguistics literature abounds with references to 'the learner', almost without exception this expression will be found to refer to a model or personification of the learning process, and not to real-life, flesh-and-blood individuals with their own subjective and social worlds.

Borrowing his approach from Vygotsky (1978) and Mead (1934), he regards personal identity as the result of an interplay between individual awareness and social identity, which is constructed in and through discourse. Riley (2006) analysed a corpus of service-encounter recordings with the aim of elucidating the high rate of dissatisfaction amongst foreigners engaged in such encounters in France, as well as the difficulty of Nancy tertiary institutions in communicating with an increasing intake of foreign students. His results suggested an interactive nature of identity production in pragmatic discourse, whereby self-expression entails confrontation, negotiation and reconfiguration of identities in social encounters. Although Riley emphasised the 'immediate implications [of his findings] for the foreign language classroom' (p. 316), his research was rooted in second-language-acquisition and language-immersion contexts.

A small qualitative investigation conducted by Syed (2001) also examined the identity of foreign language learners in their struggle to find their voice and place in society. Along the course of a semester, Syed interviewed repeatedly 5 female students aged 21-34 learning Hindi at a large American university. Two of these were learning Hindi as a foreign language, and three as a heritage language. He also conducted classroom observations and some interviews with the participants' language teacher. Noteworthy among his findings was the insight that these students' sense of self was being shaped by the expectations of their families and social circles, which had played an important part in their decision to study Hindi. In addition, a significant component of their learning motivation was their desire to forge a particular identity: as individuals moving between several cultural worlds, learning the language helped them define who they were.

Finally, Cotterall and Murray (2009) provided metacognitive strategy training to 400 Japanese undergraduate learners of English within a mixed-method longitudinal study. In the quantitative component of their research, 100 of the participants completed a beliefs questionnaire consisting of ten stand-alone items. Principal component analysis performed on the results revealed two factors, which the authors labelled 'identity' and 'metacognition'. Perhaps surprisingly, 'identity' included items like: 'I know what I need to do to learn English', 'I can identify my strengths and weaknesses as a student' and 'I know which aspects of my English I want to improve'. The authors equate the 'identity' factor with a future possible self and discuss it in the light of Markus and Nurius's (1986) theory, although only one of the five items making up the identity factor refers to the possibility of using English in the future. Whereas the contribution of the study to understanding identity is rather limited, the language learning histories, portfolios, course evaluation, interviews and focus groups used and reported on offer very interesting insights into metacognitive awareness.

Relational perspectives

Several authors have investigated the influence of relational contexts on students' attitudes to foreign language learning, in particular the influence of teachers, peers and parents – a relational focus (Taylor, 2013b, forthcoming) that is of particular relevance to the study reported later in this book.

Williams and Burden (1999) found that the teacher had a significant role in determining the students' cognitive attributional pattern, many teenagers judging their success by external factors such as teacher approval or marks. The two authors' qualitative study consisted in interviews with 36 English pupils aged 10–15 learning French as a foreign language, also including some ability ratings by teachers. Williams et al. (2002), mentioned briefly above, reported on a mixed-method investigation of English students' motivation to learn French and German, consisting of 228 questionnaires and 24 interviews with pupils aged between 11 and 14 (years 7–9). The teacher was again identified as an important determinant of students' motivation, followed by parents and the peer group. Although no significant gender differences were found in the perceived influence of significant others, girls were more motivated to learn foreign languages than boys, particularly in relation to French. Interestingly, French was considered 'the language of love and stuff', while German was equated to 'the war, Hitler, and all that' in the interviews, which led to boys preferring German and being teased by their peers if they showed an interest in French.

By contrast, Bartram (2006a) identified an anti-German learning culture in his 295 learners of French and German (aged 15–16) at comprehensive schools in England, Germany and the Netherlands. His longitudinal qualitative investigation of language-learning peer culture found that teenagers sometimes laughed at their classmates who tried to imitate the foreign accent in language classes, which had a detrimental effect on participation levels. As for gender effects, French was again perceived as 'girly'. In a separate publication, Bartram (2006b) reported a different component of his tri-national PhD study of attitudes to foreign language learning, this time emphasising parental influences. 411 learners of French, German and English (aged 15–16) in England, Germany and the Netherlands took part in his multi-method qualitative study, revealing that parents influenced their children's attitudes to foreign language learning in a number of ways, including positive and negative personal examples, the communication of educational regrets and perceived values, as well as through their own level of foreign language knowledge.

In turn, Kyriacou and Zhu (2008) explored the motivation of Chinese students to learn English as a foreign language and its relationship to the perceived influence of parents, teachers and peers. The responses they received to 610 questionnaires and 64 semi-structured interviews from 17- and 18-year-olds in seven Shanghai secondary schools indicated that English was not considered as important as other academic subjects, while significant others did not consider it particularly important that students did well in English. Of the three relational contexts analysed, the teacher was perceived to be slightly more important than parents and peers.

Block (2000, 2007) reports partial results of his doctoral study (Block, 1995) in which he interviewed repeatedly six Spanish students in their thirties learning English in a large language school in Barcelona, his main aim being to elucidate their perceptions of learning processes, lessons and teachers. Sustained tension was identified both in relation to the English teacher and with the peer group, which called for skilful negotiation by the students in order to maintain the balance of power, to avoid conflict and to ensure that learning took place. But one of the most striking examples of the influence that teachers can have on students' identity and attitudes to foreign language learning is depicted in Lantolf and Genung's (2003) case study of Patricia Genung's failed attempt to learn Chinese during her doctoral programme at a major North-American university. The account shows how she challenged (unsuccessfully) the perceived abusive power of the instructors manifested through explicit drilling, grammar translation and little communicative practice, which finally transformed her from a successful language learner into a 'successful' student who managed to obtain the necessary pass marks with little learning progress. While these situations represent adult experiences of foreign language learning, they do serve as important examples of the influence that relational contexts can have on the individual language learner.

Although this sub-section does not concern itself with identity specifically, it does reveal an important interface between language learning and identity in the main relational contexts discussed earlier. For students who gauge their learning success by the teacher's appreciation or assessment, language learning cannot be part of their true selves, and perhaps the same can be said of Kyriacou and Zhu's (2008) Chinese students, for whom learning English was mainly instrumental and less important than learning other subjects. The conflicting choice between self-relevant goals and socially imposed goals also calls into question the students' appreciation as individuals in the respective relational contexts and sheds light on the ensuing identity display that may have little relation to their real selves (for example, Patricia Genung's public self as a successful student – clearly at odds with her perceived failure to learn the language – or Williams *et al.*'s (2002) boys who might have liked learning French but had to opt for German in order to avoid peer victimisation).

Research Needed

This and the previous chapter have offered an overview of several theories and research strands that have facilitated a better understanding of the self and identity in adolescence and foreign language learning, and that have shaped the theoretical framework detailed in the next chapter. We have seen how notions such as self and identity are conceptualised in the literature and what specific factors are considered to influence identity processes in adolescence. The effects of four main relational contexts (parents, friends, teachers and classmates) were detailed. In order to clarify context-dependent identity display, concepts like the private and the public selves were reviewed, along with self-relevant and socially conditioned desired selves and internalisation processes through which external behaviours or goals are integrated into one's self-concept. Carl Rogers' notion of fully functioning person was also described, which was thought to incorporate elements of most theories presented previously.

When reviewing the research on identity in foreign language learning, several research studies were discussed that have taken a self- or identity-related perspective, such as the application of academic self-concept, self-determination and self-esteem to foreign language learning, as well as the inclusion of identity in motivational and self-regulatory models.

Comparing the two research areas – identity in adolescence and identity in foreign language learning – several areas become apparent where research on the adolescent self in foreign language learning is needed:

- *Private self.* The main under-represented area is clearly a conceptualisation of the language learner's present self. Mercer's (2011) empirical work has provided a wealth of qualitative data on adult university students' language learning self-concepts. Such an approach is yet to be taken with younger learners, the period of peak identity exploration – adolescence – being still largely overlooked by similar research perspectives. Every teacher entering a classroom encounters 20 or so different universes, each of them – just like the teacher – feeling that all the others revolve around itself. What do we know about these universes? How can we help our adolescent students understand that the subject we teach is 'good for them' if we know nothing about 'them' as complete individuals, at the core of a complex social network?
- *Public selves.* The intriguing insights provided by Juvonen and her colleagues (e.g. Juvonen & Murdock, 1993) into the strategic self-presentation that students resort to in the classroom have yet to resonate in foreign language research. Given the added identity complexities that learning a foreign language entails, especially in the context of adolescence – which has its own identity complexities – it is surprising that the public selves that language learners may display in class have not yet been investigated. Differences between the identities they display to their classmates and to their language teacher or parents would also be potentially revealing, as would the degree to which one's private L2 self influences the L2 identity display. Another promising research path that is still unexplored would be investigating to what extent the teacher can inspire the display of a language-learning self, which might later be internalised into the learners' self concepts, making the language and language learning 'their own'.
- *Socially imposed selves.* As we have seen, the ought-to self (representing duties and obligations imposed by parents, teachers and so on) has been investigated in a limited number of publications, but it was not considered to have any motivational potential, being external to the learner. However, it is very clear that adolescents do many things because they feel they have to although they would not if they had a choice, foreign language learning being in many cases one of them. It is also intuitive that many pupils start studying a language because they have to, and end up liking it and adopting it into their own identity (although the reverse is certainly true as well, in which case it would be worth investigating why an alternative imposed self was stronger than the language learning one). The mechanism of internalising a socially imposed self could also lend itself to insightful research, whether the internalisation is produced through the adoption of particular public selves, or through the integration of an imposed self with one's own ideal self.

- *Comprehensive models.* For the exploration of such elusive concepts and their pluridirectional relationships, a comprehensive model of identity would be needed. Any one such concept, however fascinating, could only describe a splinter of the learner's sense of self. It is clear that we could never describe or explain somebody's identity completely, but a multidimensional research framework would at least triangulate results and provide deeper levels of interpretation. Only seeking a comprehensive picture of the learners' identity at the hub of an entire social web can we hope to facilitate their progress towards becoming fully functioning members of society.
- *New instruments.* Finally, as these topics have not been researched in a systematic manner yet, new purposefully designed data collection instruments are necessary. Acknowledging the difficulties involved in designing and validating new research instruments, there is little point continuing to investigate these complex phenomena with instruments built decades ago for very different purposes, in very different settings.

The literature reviewed in these two chapters and this fivefold rationale have shaped the research design of the empirical study reported later, as well as the theoretical framework detailed in the next chapter.

4 A Quadripolar Model of Identity in Adolescent Foreign Language Learning

The previous chapter identified several under-researched areas of the literature on identity in foreign language learning. This chapter, in turn, represents the extended hypothesis and theoretical framework that guided the design of the present research project, which sought validation, confirmation and unanticipated insights for the postulates delineated below. The chapter, which regards identity as an aggregate of the internal and external selves associated with one individual, is structured in three main sections: a presentation of the four components of the proposed model of identity; a brief description of the multidirectional relationships in which the four self components are thought to engage; and a discussion of the main self system types that the self components were hypothesised to form. The chapter ends by acknowledging some limitations of this theoretical framework.

Self System Components

Stipulating the existence of two self dimensions – possible/actual and internal/external – the proposed model aims to incorporate both the future and the present aspects of the perceived self, as well as its inner and outer facets. Given that present identity is influenced by the emotional crystallisation of past experiences, the model may thus offer a tentatively comprehensive framework for understanding the synchronic and diachronic dynamics of identity (Taylor, 2013b; Taylor *et al.*, 2013) and their motivational implications.

The two self dimensions – possible//actual and internal//external – result in four components of the self system: the ideal (internal, possible), the private

Table 4.1 A quadripolar model of identity

Self dimension	INTERNAL	EXTERNAL
POSSIBLE	Ideal	Imposed
ACTUAL	Private	Public

(internal, actual), the imposed (external, possible) and the public (external, actual) selves, as shown in Table 4.1.

There are two important differences between the internal and the external dimension: the locus or origin of the respective selves, and their degree of integration. Thus, the ideal and the private self are personal to the individual, whereas the imposed and the public selves are not, but the latter two may be later internalised. The ideal and the private self are the results of internalisation of social values and beliefs combined with personal values and preferences (which, it could be argued, are in turn socially conditioned).

We have seen in the previous chapters that individuals sometimes display different public selves in different relational contexts. Accordingly, the external dimension of this identity model is expected to fluctuate depending on the context with which the individual interacts. There will be, therefore, as many imposed and public selves as the relational contexts in which the person functions.

These components of the Quadripolar Model of Identity will be described below, with an emphasis on their relevance for understanding identity in adolescent foreign language learning.

Possible selves

As already mentioned, this model hypothesises the existence of one ideal self and multiple imposed selves representing desired future states that originate in the individual and outside the individual, respectively. Being internal, the ideal self would tend towards unification, but the imposed selves would be plural because they originate in different contexts and audiences, which exercise different social pressures and have different – often contradictory – social expectations of the individual.

Ideal self

In the Quadripolar Model of Identity, the ideal self is understood to mean *a personal representation of what an individual would like to become in the future, irrespective of other people's desires and expectations about the individual.* Rather than suggesting a restrictive and inaccessible end state, the term 'ideal' is taken to represent the best possible combination of attributes that a person would like to have in the future, from a strictly subjective point of view. As some of these attributes are achieved and incorporated into the private self, new desired characteristics will replace them in one's ideal representation of oneself in the future, ensuring a motivational continuum. In this respect, the ideal self is a dynamic representation of one's desired future rather than a static perfectionist goal.

Although some of the possible selves literature speaks about multiple desired selves, in this framework one's ideal self is taken to represent the unitary combination of the most desirable attributes constituting the person's desired future identity. An adolescent could not be expected to say 'The dream of my life is to become a successful actor' and also 'The dream of my life is to become an excellent football player', but their ideal attributes would coalesce into one unitary desired identity. In accordance with the background literature discussed earlier, it is expected that differentiation of desired selves or contradictory self attributes would be greater in early adolescence, while teenagers experiment with various self attributes, a unitary ideal self emerging towards late adolescence. Nevertheless, the 'dream of one's life' does not have to be monochromatic. A teenager may want to become, for instance, a very successful actor who plays excellent football as a hobby, speaks five foreign languages fluently, travels to a different country every year, has friends all over the world and collects model motorbikes. But these would not all be different ideal selves – they would be facets or attributes of the same coherent ideal self that the individual would be striving to achieve. As some of these attributes would be more important than others, they would take priority and result in more effort being invested in achieving these self-relevant goals.

It is hypothesised that the more details one adds to one's ideal future self, the more motivational this would be in activating future behaviour, as a livelier, more concrete representation of oneself in the future would be more likely to be accompanied by a plan for achieving this desired state. As the research reviewed earlier has shown, the ideal self would be differentiated from sheer fantasy by the existence and implementation of a strategy for the attainment of the respective desired self. This helps explain why some people would love to speak a foreign language, for example, but are disappointed by their own performance. If wanting to achieve a goal is not accompanied by a clear strategy for achieving this goal, and if concrete steps are not taken with a view to reducing the gap between the current and the ideal state, then one's desired future state is little more than fantasy or day-dreaming.

The motivational force of the ideal self represents a mechanism similar to internalisation, only this time it occurs on the vertical or diachronic axis: activating one's ideal self in one's mind may act as a vicarious experience whereby the individual rehearses a future role in his//her imagination which will later be enacted in reality. A strong ideal self would also be accompanied by an awareness of the personally relevant consequences of not meeting the desired self goal. Such 'feared selves' may be part of the ideal self through their positive counterparts: if one's strong fear is failing examinations, for example, then being successful in examinations will be part of one's ideal self; similarly, teenagers who are afraid that they might be rejected by their peers would have peer acceptance as an important facet of their ideal self.

For the language learner, the ideal self would incorporate elements of linguistic proficiency that the student does not yet possess, but would like to and will internalise in the presence of the right strategy and concrete action. The role of the language teacher would thus be not only to help students create and maintain compelling self-relevant language speaking attributes, but also to help students integrate these into their ideal self through day-to-day activities. The difference between teaching the foreign language as yet another academic subject and teaching it as a personally relevant communication tool is very important here. As we have seen in the previous chapters, the ideal self cannot be imposed – it has to be personal, so the teacher needs to help students see the foreign language as a component of their own future self if it is to be taken seriously, rather than rejected as an external imposition. From this point of view, in countries where the communicative value of a foreign language is overtaken by it facilitating access to academic qualifications, to the job market or to particular social strata, the role of the teacher would be the same, although the ideal self of the students would differ slightly. Instead of having the ideal self of, for example, 'a successful consultant having international clients with whom they communicate in English', students' ideal self from this category may be more like 'a successful consultant who speaks English so well that finding a job in the country is not at all a problem'.

In language learning, like in any other life domain, the ideal self would have to be placed realistically within the limits of one's perceived ability, as well as be socially acceptable. In other words, people need to believe that they are able to achieve the desired goal, and that this goal will be acceptable in their relational contexts. Believing in one's ideal self may also be conditioned by an incremental theory of intelligence, by learning (rather than performance) orientation, and by internal, unstable and controllable attributions of success and failure. That is, such language learners would believe in expanding ability through increased effort, would work hard in order to reach the level of their ideal L2-speaking self, would enjoy challenges, would see mistakes as opportunities to learn more and would believe that success and failure depend entirely on how hard one tries. The importance of the language teacher in facilitating such an atmosphere in the classroom is, again, crucial, as the belief that achievement depends on effort rather than ability, and that mistakes are positive learning opportunities, will filter down into everyday decisions about teaching methods, assessment, teacher and student roles.

Imposed selves

In this identity framework, imposed selves are defined as *representations of other people's hopes, desires and expectations of what an individual should achieve, the number of such representations depending on the number of social relational contexts in which the individual functions.* As the name indicates, imposed selves originate outside the individual's volition and have only an indirect connection to one's personal desires. The degree of 'imposition' will vary from mild metaphorical (i.e. 'normal' social conditioning that results in all of us adopting beliefs that are promoted in our social context) to strong literal (for example, in the case of some teenagers who are forced to pursue a particular career against their will).

The various circles in which a person functions as a social being create different expectations about that person's identity – that is, different imposed selves. The foreign language class would be one such circle. Depending on the teacher's attitude, the classmates' behaviour, the general classroom atmosphere and many other factors, a student will form an understanding of what is expected of him//her in that circumstance and will decide whether or not to meet the given expectations, which will determine his//her future behaviour. In traditional competitive environments, for example, a controlling teacher would likely generate a strong imposed self for the learners, who would feel strongly expected to accept the teacher's authority without questioning it and will repress their own intentions that may be different from the teacher's. In many cases, this will result in students working hard in order to achieve good results and the pressure to do well may be subsequently internalised into their own desired future goals. It is also possible that students with particularly high metacognitive strategies, who know what they need to do in order to learn better, may not accept an inflexible approach in the classroom and they may either reject it openly or develop strategies to give the impression they are observing the teacher's guidance, while covertly pursuing their own goals (both cases are discussed later).

It is very possible for a person to have several conflicting imposed selves. The language learners in the above example may belong to a group of peers who maintain the norm of low achievement. These students would have to reconcile the expectation to be submissive and hard-working (coming from the teacher) with the expectation to avoid involvement, to procrastinate, to withdraw effort and to feel proud of it (an imposed self originating in the work-avoidant peer group). For many teenagers in competitive educational environments, this is actually the norm, which can only exacerbate their age-specific uncertainty, confusion and rebellion, as they are expected to be two very different things at the same time, while the stakes are very high in both contexts (high marks and teacher appreciation versus peer and social group acceptance).

Being the external counterpart of the ideal self, the L2 imposed selves may be associated with a fixed theory of ability, with performance orientations and with external, stable and uncontrollable attributions for success and failure. For example, a language learner with a very strong L2 imposed self would not have the freedom to develop in his//her own chosen way, being perhaps inclined to perform the expected role superficially, without genuine involvement, to put in as little effort as possible, to see failure as a threat to self-worth as it would imply low ability, and to attribute outcomes to forces outside one's control. For this reason, teachers who help their students recognise the personal relevance of an academic subject in the future will be more successful in creating sustainable motivation for learning than teachers who expect learners to accept and pursue an externally imposed goal, and who may thus only encourage work avoidance and superficial identity display. This would appear to be particularly relevant in countries such as the UK, where the global status of the L1 is sometimes seen as evidence that studying Modern Foreign Languages is obsolete and unnecessary. The role of the classroom teacher is so important in such contexts, that, even when the everyday relevance of languages is emphasised persuasively by visiting speakers, students are still unlikely to continue language study beyond the compulsory stage if they perceive classroom practices as personally irrelevant and unfulfilling (Taylor, 2012).

Actual selves

While possible selves define one's future self-guides, actual selves cover the dynamics of one's present-day identity. Reflecting the internal/external dimension of this identity model, and in accordance with the literature discussed earlier, one's actual selves are hypothesised to consist of one private self and as many public selves as the social relational contexts in which the individual functions.

Private self

In this framework, the private self is understood to mean *a person's intimate representation of his/her present attributes, which may or may not be disclosed in social interaction.* Just like the ideal self, the private self is likely to be unitary, although comprising several different facets – academic, social, familial etc. – which contribute to one's individual character. Thus, the language-specific component – the L2 private self – will be one facet of the academic private self or academic self-concept.

Being an appraisal of one's present attributes, the private self is a cognitive, emotional and relational crystallisation of past experience translated into perceived competence or ability and affective perceptions. What I believe I am as an individual at the moment is the result of what I believe I can do, what I like and do not like doing, what I tried to do – and succeeded or not – in the past, as well as how I believe I compare to my peers and to my own ideal representations of myself. In this way, the past influences the future via the private self, given that a strong future guide will have to be formed on the realistic basis of one's actual self appraisal: if a student believes, for instance, that she cannot pronounce English correctly because there is something wrong with her phonatory apparatus, it is quite unlikely that impeccable English pronunciation will be part of her L2 ideal self. Nevertheless, a language teacher who emphasises effort over ability and regards mistakes as learning opportunities will find ways to encourage such a student to be the best she can be and to work around perceived and real obstacles in order to achieve realistic personally relevant goals. In younger adolescents, social comparison will also be an important source of information for the private self, the way they compare to other people – as well as to themselves across life domains – determining their perceived competence, emotional responses and behavioural choices. A classroom atmosphere that encourages cooperation and learning from one another will, therefore, help build a strong private self and healthy peer interactions, leading to less contradictory social expectations and less likelihood that a generalised norm of low achievement will prevent students from striving to do well in order to gain peer acceptance.

An environment that allows individuals the freedom to be themselves, that values them for what they really are, that encourages the expression of true feelings and experiences would be an environment in which one's private self would move naturally towards one's ideal self. In the classroom, such students would be responsible 'citizens' rather than passing 'tourists', whose strong self-worth would be encouraged by teachers who trust them to be essentially competent human beings and who approach them with empathic understanding and an expectation that they can all make a meaningful and valuable contribution to the lesson. Thus, a language learner with a healthy L2 private self may think: 'I cannot really express myself fluently in this foreign language yet, but I am on the right track; I am encouraged and valued for the progress I have made so far, I know that making mistakes is a normal part of learning, I know what I need to do in order to make fewer mistakes in the future and one day I will get to my ideal stage of speaking this language with fluency and confidence in such and such situations'. Of course, few students will have such beliefs and confidence in the absence of a differentiated, learner-centred, teaching approach and without a tutor who would patiently help them overcome low confidence, perceived or real difficulty, apparent irrelevance and contradictory social pressures. Although this would be of help in any educational environment, working on building healthier L2 private selves in our students may, again, be a solution to the decreasing interest in foreign languages in English speaking countries, where negative peer pressure, perceived difficulties, perceived irrelevance of classroom activities and assessment practices are often given as reasons for disengagement with foreign languages (Carr & Pauwels, 2009; Graham, 2004; Mitchell, 2009; Rhodes & Pufahl, 2010).

Public selves

In the Quadripolar Model of Identity, public selves are the *various social presentations that a person may display depending on the relational context and audience*.

Owing to the inherently human need to belong and be accepted socially, a person's public selves will be directly related to one's imposed selves. Thus, every imposed self is hypothesised to have a corresponding public self (which can be either conforming or rebellious): a pupil's classroom imposed self will influence her classroom public self (either to conform or to rebel), her family imposed self will influence her family public self and so on (see Figure 4.1).

Given that imposed selves can be conflicting, one's public selves will also be conflicting at times, which requires skilful and strategic self-presentation. For example, when spending some time with her family, a teenager who

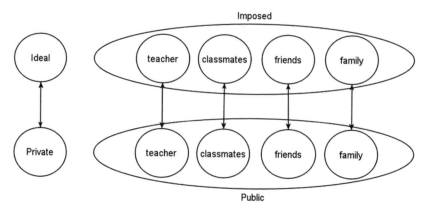

Figure 4.1 A quadripolar model of identity with four relational contexts

knows that her parents expect her to be a dutiful daughter may choose to play that part submissively, but later complain to her group of friends and blame her parents for being old-fashioned – an attitude that she knows may be appreciated by her peers. What the teenager in this example does is juggle with two different public selves, displaying an image that she feels is expected of her in the circle she finds herself in at a given moment (i.e. dutiful daughter versus independent teenager).

Of course, not everybody will conform to expectations. Some people may choose to defy a particular imposed self (or more than just one), seek a different affiliation, respond to a different imposed self and display a different public self. Conflict between one's imposed selves would thus trigger conflict between one's public selves. A familiar example would be a teenager who, caught in the presence of both parents and peers, may feel confused as to which public self she/he ought to display, exemplifying the 'double approach-avoidance conflict' conceptualised in the literature discussed earlier.

Especially in periods of identity conflicts such as adolescence, people may consciously adopt certain public selves in order to gain acceptance to particular groups (and they may internalise these public selves later, becoming genuine members of the respective groups). In school, particular stereotypes can generate public selves with important academic consequences – for example, boys not studying foreign languages because they are perceived as 'girly', or the generalised norm of mediocrity which would require everybody to withdraw effort and adopt manipulative and escapist strategies.

In situations when people do not feel comfortable disclosing their 'real' private self, conscious display of expected public selves is likely to occur. Students, for instance, who do not feel they can reveal their language learning anxiety or their low perceived ability in the classroom, may be inclined to adopt a disruptive public self, or an indifferent or even aggressive self – thus gaining acceptance, if not from the teacher, at least from similarly inclined peers. The opposite of responsible 'citizens', these will be 'tourists' in the language classroom, who will invest all the necessary effort not in improving ability, but in proving that they have ability by withdrawing effort, so that, if failure occurs, they can blame it on lack of effort rather than lack of ability. They will pretend to be involved in class while actually attending to their own agendas and will only be themselves when back with whatever group allows them to be truly themselves.

However, public selves can play a very positive role in the classroom as an internalisation instrument. For example, language teachers can help students create L2 ideal images, with their associated set of behaviours (related, for example, to the four main skills), and then help them adopt these behaviours into their L2 public selves. Provided all the conditions are fulfilled (personal choice, discrepancy from one's private self, social acceptance and so on), these may subsequently become part of the students' self-concept, thus helping them bridge the gap between their actual and their L2 ideal self.

Starting from the premise that a typical adolescent will usually interact with four main relational contexts, as discussed in the Chapter 2, a schematic representation of the quadripolar model of identity taking into account the self components described above might look like Figure 4.1.

Although this is a crude simplification of identity dynamics in social interaction, it does serve to illustrate the multiplicity of often contradictory social expectations and their influence on corresponding public selves disclosed in social interaction. The relationships that self components can engage in are, however, much more complex, each relational context being sometimes the origin of a configuration that is totally different from the others. A brief description of the main relationships that these self components can engage in is presented below, being followed by four key configurations of the self system that may be encountered in each of these relational systems. Before moving on, I should note that the fact that several of the notions discussed in this model of identity come in sets of four started as mere coincidence, but, given the evidence that our working memory can hold up to four conscious objects at any one time (e.g. Bor, 2012), the number was considered appropriate for the theoretical framework and data collection focus (for example, when asking participants to refer to their perceptions in interactions with each of the main four relational contexts).

Self System Relationships

The four self components described above are hypothesised to enter multidimensional identity processes which may include the following relationships and characteristics, in each separate relational context

- *Ideal self ↔ imposed selves.* The most unlikely influence is probably that of the ideal self on the imposed selves, as what an individual personally wishes to become may rarely change what other people want him/her to be. An exception could be the situation when public selves mediate this influence: the people around me may form expectations about my future depending on my public image, on my public behaviour, on my claims, on my apparent abilities and inclinations etc., and I may subsequently decide to adopt these expectations as my own desired self. However, the imposed selves will have a strong bearing on the ideal self: people's expectations and subsequent encouragement may persuade me to adopt a desired future for myself, as it happens with many children who do what their parents ask them to and are very happy to do so. Alternatively, people may decide to reject an imposed self, nurturing its very opposite as their ideal (as in the case of so many teenagers who rebel against various constraints at school, at home or in their peer groups).

• *Private self ↔ public selves.* It is rather obvious that my self-concept will have a direct influence on the image(s) I want to display in public. I may behave in a particular way in order to *prove* that I have – or do not have – a particular identity as a conscious manipulation of other people's impression, or, most likely, what I believe I am influences the way I present myself in my social circles without me even being aware of this influence. In turn, the public selves influence the private self through internalisation (the carryover effect). As the literature discussed above has shown, adopting a set of behaviours that pertain to an image we would like to display may influence the way we think about ourselves (sometimes facilitating unexpected insights into our own personalities) and they can even become part of our private self.

• *Ideal self ↔ private self.* In order to be realistic – and realisable – people's dreams must be within the limits of their potential. I cannot realistically wish to be a chess world champion if I hate board games, for example, and have no idea how they are played, nor any intention to find out. My ideal self will have to be strongly rooted in my perceived abilities and my interpretations of past experiences. Sheer boasting or empty daydreaming do exist, but without the necessary reality checks, these are not ideal selves proper. At the same time, an ideal self will influence the way people feel about themselves, especially if it is accompanied by strong self-relevant symbolism and the right promotional strategy: if I want to be a very good teacher and imagine myself interacting with my students successfully while taking the necessary steps to get there, I have every chance to become a very good teacher indeed. The ideal self may also affect the private self through the mediation of public selves: I may choose to display an image pertaining to a self that I would like to have, which I may subsequently internalise.

• *Imposed selves ↔ public selves.* As explained earlier, the way people behave in public is directly influenced by the audience and the context in which they find themselves at that particular moment. Thus, my L2 teacher imposed self will directly determine my L2 public self displayed in interaction with the teacher, whereas my family imposed self will trigger a particular family public self. This influence is not necessarily reciprocated, although it can be: what other people want me to become may influence the public image I display, but my social presentation would not influence other people's expectations in the same way. However, public selves can shape imposed selves by creating precedents (people may expect me to behave the way I have always done) or by generating estimations of my potential based on my publicly displayed identity.

- *Ideal self ↔ public selves.* Being cross-dimensional (see Table 4.1 at the beginning of the chapter), this relationship will be mediated by the private self, just like the next one is mediated by the public selves. What I would like to become may influence the way I behave in public, but it is my private self that decides my desired future and the public displays and behaviours that may take me to it. In turn, particular self-presentations may reveal surprising attributes of the private self, which may trigger the adoption of a different ideal self or the alteration of the existing one.
- *Imposed selves ↔ private self.* What I really feel I am is not always related to what other people would like me to become, but imposed selves do have a considerable impact on one's private self. A good example is the role of the teacher's expectations in defining the students' self-concepts: if the teacher constantly doubts and ridicules a student, it is very likely that the student will finally doubt herself, just as she will feel very positive and full of potential if the teacher believes in her and expresses genuine encouragement all the time. In turn, the influence of the private self on the imposed selves will occur through the public selves one displays, by creating precedents and expectations through behaviour.

Self System Types

In the transition from an actual towards a possible identity, both the ideal and the imposed selves can have motivational power. The ideal self may be a behaviour activator through the desire to resolve self-discrepancy, whereas imposed selves may motivate people to act either in the direction of somebody else's wishes for them or away from these wishes. Depending on these dynamic relationships, it is hypothesised that a person's identity may crystallise around the following main self system types:

- *submissive:* a strong imposed self generates responses against the ideal self;
- *duplicitous:* a different ideal and imposed self generate parallel responses;
- *rebellious:* a strong ideal self generates responses against the imposed self; and
- *harmonious:* equivalent ideal and imposed selves generate congruent responses.

These four possibilities are described briefly below, being accompanied by figures in which arrows represent motivated behaviour from present towards future, the = sign means equivalence or similarity and the ≠ sign means difference or opposition. For the sake of simplicity, the imposed selves and the public selves are treated as singular in these figures, but always bearing in mind that they are composite (as seen in Figure 4.1), one such self being salient at any given moment in one relational context. The labels given to these self systems are only intended as a convenient termonological shortcut and do not imply any value judgement.

The description of each system type will be followed by a vignette summarising the identity dynamics that a student may perceive in a given context. (For this reason, the vignettes use an informal style that a teenager might use when describing such identity processes.) Within the quantitative component of the study that validated this framework, participants were asked to choose one of these vignettes for each of the four relational contexts explored: the English teacher, classmates/peers, best friends and family. Within the qualitative component, all interviewees were also asked to comment on the suitability of these vignettes for describing their own identity processes in the four relational contexts, as well as to give concrete examples of how these dynamics might work in their own social interactions and contexts.

The submissive self system

In conditions of private/public self congruence and ideal/imposed self conflict, some people may relinquish their ideal self and adopt a certain imposed self as their future guide (see Figure 4.2). This may start as superficial compliance resulting in genuine internalisation at a later stage, which is not

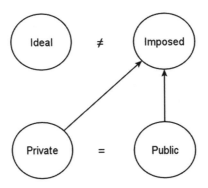

Figure 4.2 The submissive self system

necessarily a negative consequence, especially if the initial ideal self was less than socially desirable.

For instance, a student who is totally disinterested in school may decide to comply with the teacher's requests and end up realising that being academically successful may be quite fulfilling on a personal level. This could lead the submissive self system towards a harmonious one.

In language learning, students who were initially unmotivated to engage in class may also benefit from the process: if the environment is welcoming, they may try some learning activities, discover that they are good at them, feel appreciated and encouraged and adopt language learning into their ideal self (again, this would lead them towards the harmonious self system described below).

However, internalisation may not always follow submission to an imposed self. For some people, relinquishing their ideal self in favour of one or more imposed ones may lead to alienation, insecurity and frustration.

Vignette:

> *They know very well what sort of person I am. What they would like me to do in life is different from what I would like to do, so that's why I prefer to give up my intentions and do what they think is better for me. What they want me to do in life is more important than what I'd have liked, so I'll do what they say.*

The duplicitous self system

Presupposing the existence of major discrepancies between the ideal and imposed selves on the one hand, and the private and public selves on the other, the duplicitous self system results in two parallel types of behaviour (see Figure 4.3): on the internal dimension (left hand side), the person would work towards reducing the discrepancy between his/her private and ideal self in a covert manner, while on the external dimension (right-hand side) complying superficially with an imposed self – allegedly working towards reducing the discrepancy between a given public self and the respective imposed self. This state of the self system might not be long-lasting, as sooner or later the person would have to commit either to the ideal self (resulting in the rebellious type described below) or to an imposed self (as in the submissive type above). In either case, stating a particular position would also induce a certain degree of congruence between the private self and at least one of the person's public selves, given that by expressing this

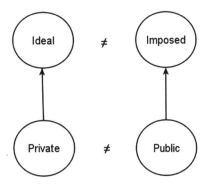

Figure 4.3 The duplicitous self system

preference the person will no longer have to pretend and hide his/her actual private self.

In the foreign language class, this may be the case of students for whom speaking the respective language is not part of their ideal self, but who choose to hide this from the teacher and comply superficially. Arguably, this may be the most challenging situation, given that the teacher has no direct means of assessing whether such students' activity in class expresses genuine learning involvement or strategic impression management. It is equally possible, however, that a self-directed student who does not approve of the teacher's approach may pursue his/her own learning goals covertly, while superficially complying with the teacher's requests out of obedience, consideration, fear and so on.

Vignette:

> *They don't really know what sort of person I really am, and it's not important for me that they do. They would like me to do something else in life than I would, and that's why I'll pursue my own dreams without letting them know. At the same time, I'll give them the impression that I do what they ask me to, even though I'm actually seeing about my own business. I know better.*

The rebellious self system

If a person's ideal self is very different from his/her imposed selves, but the private self is congruent with the public selves, as in the submissive system, another possibility is that the person may reject external impositions to the benefit of his/her ideal self (see Figure 4.4). The resulting behaviour

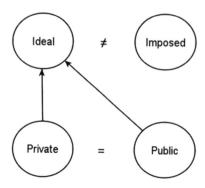

Figure 4.4 The rebellious self system

would be open defiance of imposed selves and relentless pursuit of one's ideal self both privately (self-concept) and publicly (social image).

In the classroom, this system is visible in the behaviour of students who refuse to observe the teacher's rules which are not personally relevant to them (i.e. are not part of their ideal self) or who resist peer pressure (peer imposed self) in order to pursue their own learning goals irrespectively. In this latter case, rebellion will be directed at the peer group, as from their point of view (as origins of the peer-group imposed self) the person is a rebel.

In highly controlling environments, students for whom learning a foreign language was initially part of their ideal self may reject this if it is perceived as being externally imposed (if the students feel that they *have to* learn the L2, some may resist even if they would themselves have liked to become successful L2 speakers). Owing to perceived lack of causality or control, their initial L2 ideal self would be regarded as an imposed self and, thus, rejected as a way of restoring personal causation. This ideal-imposed swap may occur in the case of numerous students who come to school genuinely interested and eager to learn, only to lose their initial enthusiasm in a few years when they start to disengage, play truant or even finally drop out.

Vignette:

> *What they would like me to do in life is different from what I would like to do, so that's why I'll pursue my own dreams even if I have to rebel against them. They know me well, I haven't got anything to hide, and if they want to force me into doing something, I am likely to refuse it openly. What they want me to do is less important than what I want.*

The harmonious self system

Providing what somebody would like to become is very similar to what other people would like this person to become, a harmonious self system is thought to emerge, as represented in Figure 4.5. This may be the perfect combination for the self system, which would result in galvanising motivated behaviour. As such, it is probably also the rarest form in many educational systems. Although it is theoretically possible to imagine a person with private/public selves incongruence in this system, these components are more likely to be convergent when the person does not feel hindered in his/her pursuit of the ideal self by any externally imposed future guides.

Students benefiting from a harmonious self system would work hard to bridge the gap between their actual and their desired states, while enjoying encouragement and useful informative feedback from the outside. They would feel valued and appreciated for what they are in the classroom, in their family, in their peer group or in their other social circles, their feelings would be acknowledged and cherished, their personal experiences would be regarded as intrinsically valuable. They would welcome mistakes as opportunities to learn more, they would seek challenges and would constantly expand their abilities. These people would make responsible choices about the persons they would like to be, having the freedom and the courage to be themselves in the present moment, without having to *prove* anything to anybody.

It is very important to note, however, that the harmonious self system would crystallise personal *and* social components of identity. The absolute

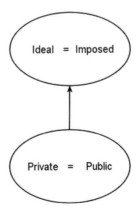

Figure 4.5 The harmonious self system

freedom of being oneself does not imply egocentric disregard for one's environment or other people's opinions. On the contrary, it implies high social responsibility and just the right amount of self-doubt necessary for allowing other people the absolute freedom of being themselves. Every individual is a complex system, but also a component of a larger complex system, which can only function if certain social rules are endorsed and observed.

Vignette:

> *They know me very well and appreciate me for what I am. My dreams for the future are very similar to what they'd like me to do in life. They don't want to impose anything on me, but give me the total liberty to choose, and they always appreciate my decisions about my future. They help me feel really fulfilled.*

Amotivational Self Configurations

The four types of self system delineated above are all motivational, in the sense that they generate behaviours necessary for making the transition from an actual to a future state. However, this may not happen in all cases. In the absence of an identity motivator – either an ideal or an imposed self – the system may behave in an erratic manner, may stagnate or may dwell on the past.

Intense momentary engagement with a particular activity – 'flow' (Csikszentmihalyi, 1990) – can be very strong in itself, but in the absence of a future self guide this engagement may not be sustainable. Indeed, as Csikszentmihalyi explains, for flow to occur, 'the important thing is to enjoy the activity for its own sake, and to know that what matters is not the result, but the control one is acquiring over one's attention' (1997: 129). If we take motivation to mean *moving* from one stage to the next (according to the Latin etymology), then we need to envisage the next stage we want to reach and know how to get there. Thus, it is questionable to what extent one can talk about truly motivated behaviour in the absence of possible selves (ideal or imposed), of a future-oriented vision and of a clear strategy for bridging the gap between one's actual and possible selves.

Learning can and does occur while we are engrossed in an activity that we find very interesting, but in order for our students' learning to be more than a fortunate by-product, we need to include it in a future-oriented strategy that is personally relevant to them. This can well begin with pure interest, which may lead to involvement, which in turn may lead to perceived competence and self-worth but at this stage that particular activity would have to be incorporated into one's ideal self in order to be truly motivational. Perhaps this is one of the differences between an infant (who can enjoy an activity for its own sake) and a social adult (who would also need a responsible long-term rationale besides pure enjoyment).

It could be argued that, in the foreign language class, performing an activity out of sheer enjoyment is a highly desirable goal, even in the absence of an ideal self. However, such enjoyment may not be durable and it may wane easily if the students do not find much personal relevance (other than pure enjoyment) in performing such activities. Personal relevance is exactly what makes an activity fit into one's future representation of oneself, and its presence would place such behaviours in one of the four motivational self systems discussed above.

Other amotivational self systems may include having an ideal self without visionary strength or procedural resolutions (i.e. fantasising or daydreaming), or generating gratifying public selves without the accompanying behavioural moves (i.e. sheer boasting or strategic impression management that is not rooted in reality). Helpless and self-handicapping dispositions may also be included here. If individuals dwell on past failures, which they attribute to external, uncontrollable and stable factors, they may lack the perceived competence and the desired selves necessary to activate motivated behaviour.

Limitations

Although it conceptualises four different self components and six reciprocal relationships leading to four possible main configurations, this model may appear to be a naïve oversimplification of human identity. Understanding a person's identity is clearly not a question of combining four elements into one of four configurations. The self systems will often occur simultaneously, in different relational contexts, each having a greater or lesser strength. This is easily understandable given that two of the components in this proposed model – the public and the imposed – are multifarious. Thus, for example, while in my peer group I may manifest a submissive self system (relinquishing my personal ideal for the sake of group acceptance and participation), at home I may benefit from a harmonious system, if my own goals are in agreement with my parents'. At the same time, if at school I have a language teacher who wants me to do grammar translation for hours on end and I know that is not my way of learning, I may be inclined towards a rebellious self system and pursue my own learning ideal irrespectively, or I may tend towards a duplicitous self system and pursue my goals in a covert manner. Nevertheless, even though several self systems are likely to act simultaneously in different relational contexts, one of them may tend to dominate, depending on the individual's priorities and inclinations, as well as on various external influences. This would happen both on the synchronic level (i.e. momentary dominance of a particular subsystem) and on the diachronic level (i.e. temporal transition from one dominant subsystem to another). An example of synchronic dominance would be Louise, who loves astronomy and feels harmonious in interaction with the astronomy teacher, while in her peer interactions she may feel duplicitous and pretend she is really interested in her friends' activities while really only wanting to get back to her telescope. In relation to teachers of other subjects, she may be submissive, accepting their externally imposed goals in order to meet the necessary pass standard, while at home she may be rebellious and explain clearly to her parents there is no chance she will ever become a language teacher, which they would like her to. But as everything Louise wants in life is to be an astronomer, the relational context that allows this dream to become achievable will be the most salient for her. On the diachronic level, Louise remembers her first astronomy class, when she thought this would be just one of those subjects in which she would have to submissively do what the teacher says and get her pass mark, while all she really wanted was to be with her friends. But this has now changed, her harmonious peer relations becoming duplicitous in the meantime, while dutiful submission to the astronomy teacher has now become rewarding harmony.

As each individual functions on numerous social levels and has numerous goals and intentions, some momentary, some durable, some conscious, some less so, it would be extremely difficult indeed to capture this whole wealth of identity dynamics in one theoretical model. The main limitations of this framework are, therefore, the very limitations that concern complex systems research in the social sciences. Although a complete concomitant representation of the self system would be very difficult to envisage, with the caveats above, the present framework can offer a useful if simplified snapshot of a person's identity and the findings discussed in Chapters 5–7 provide persuasive evidence that the model can help understand classroom engagement, motivation and achievement better.

One other limitation concerns the terminology used to identify the self components and self systems in this framework. These notions are used, for want of better labels, without any implication other than those explained in this chapter. By using this terminology, I am not implying that any individual can be characterised by any one word, concept, tendency, social relation or visible behaviour. The self components and self system labels, as well as the vocabulary used to describe them, are mere terminological tools that do not express any value judgement about the persons or processes identified, for the sake of simplicity, through these words.

5 Participants' Self Systems in Four Relational Contexts

This is the first of three chapters to present the findings of the research project that aimed to validate the theoretical framework presented in Chapter 4. The participants' self systems are discussed here, first from the point of view of their frequency in each relational context, which is then followed by a discussion of the qualitative interview data resulting from thematic analysis.

The self system vignettes that the participants chose from when completing the questionnaire can be seen in Appendix E, along with their conceptual labels and graphical representations, as well as in the questionnaire itself (Appendix A). Appendix F also provides a useful background to this chapter, as it includes the profiles of all 32 interviewees, with their chosen pseudonyms, gender, age, school, a summary of their interview and the self systems they chose for each relational context (English teacher, classmates, friends and family). The summaries were written by myself after the data analysis stage and consist of either direct citation or very close paraphrasing, concentrating on the salience of the students' reference to identity processes. By comparing the system types that the students chose for the four relational contexts with their interview summaries, it can be seen that my theoretical framework was supported by the interviews to a great extent: in most cases, the students' explanations match very closely my hypotheses about the system types and component relationships, besides demonstrating the complexity of experiencing different self system configurations in different relational contexts and the complex social negotiation needed to manage such differences.

The frequency of self systems declared by the participating students can be seen in Figure 5.1, which is split by gender. One striking difference between relational contexts is that the teacher and classmates are associated with the highest percentage of duplicitous self systems, whereas friends and families

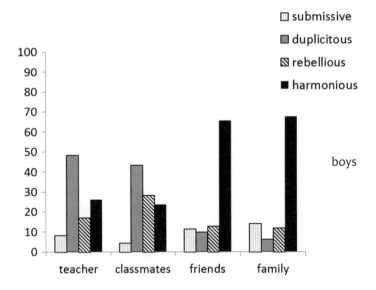

boys

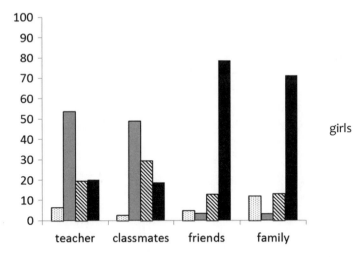

girls

Figure 5.1 Self system percentages by gender and relational context (Chi square significant only for friends, *p* < 0.001)

generate the most harmonious ones. This is the case for both genders, with only minor differences. Notably, more boys appear to feel harmonious in their interaction with the English teacher, although the difference is not statistically significant. Statistical significance (Chi square *p* < 0.001) was only obtained for the friends' relational context, showing that fewer girls than boys felt submissive or duplicitous with their friends, and more of them felt harmonious. Crucially, however, we see a clear difference between the academic domain (the teacher and classmates) and the personal life domain (friends and family), the former generating situations where participants feel the need to display an identity that has little to do with their personal self-beliefs, whereas in the latter domain most of them seem to feel appreciated and encouraged to develop along their chosen trajectory (and/or their chosen trajectory is aligned to that encouraged by their families and friends).

The qualitative data will help explain how the participants felt about these self systems, how they justified and illustrated their choices and, in some cases, why they felt some of the vignettes were not appropriate for their situation. (It must be noted, however, that they were not given the conceptual labels, either in the questionnaire administration phase, or during the interviews. As shown in Appendix A, there were simply asked to read the descriptions and choose between situations A, B, C and D, which were also used for probing in the interview.) For each of the four self systems, a diagram will be presented which crystallises the main themes that participants kept referring to in their interviews. These diagrams (Figures 5.2, 5.3, 5.4 and 5.5, see below) are the result of my interpretation of the data and their content represents key concepts identified through thematic content analysis.

When specific participants are mentioned, their own preferred pseudonym will be used to identify them, followed by their gender and age between brackets. Appendix F offers more background information for each participant, which will facilitate a better understanding of their responses and of this entire chapter.

The Submissive Self System

The submissive self system was governed by a need for authority and guidance from teachers and parents, accompanied by respect for their maturity and experience. These and other key concepts associated with it can be seen in Figure 5.2.

As opposed to friends and classmates, it was felt that teachers and parents had the right to have expectations and to guide one's path (*Maestru*, M, 18; *FC*, M, 15; *Sophie*, F, 15). They had been through similar experiences themselves and could advise one accordingly (*Pavel Jr*, M, 17), whereas peers were seen as immature, unreliable and believed that 'all that glitters is gold' (*Maestru*, M, 18).

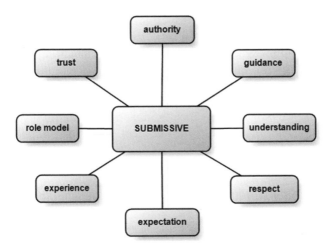

Figure 5.2 Key concepts associated with the submissive self system

Baubau (F, 14) gave a glowing account of her teacher:

Our English teacher has always been interested in our dreams, and she's always had a word of advice for us at the right moment. And she's been right most of the times. We've often been undecided and she advised us and in the end we saw it was good to do what she said. We've relied on her for so many times, that now we know what she says is right. (...) She's always known how to be both nice and useful. She's always known how to get involved where she needed to. Where she thought it unnecessary, she didn't, and it was very good what she did. (...) We're not the same with all the teachers, but when we see that she shows us this... enormous respect, then we like to do the same.

It is quite remarkable that she maintained this superlative opinion, despite believing that she was usually marked down in English. She explained that, although the teacher was 'a very, very kind person', she also knew when it was necessary to be strict, so the girl trusted her wisdom. If she were a teacher, she was happy to add, she would do exactly what her teacher did. *Foxy* (F, 16), who liked her teacher's approach very much and admired her for being so successful in helping them understand 'all English grammar and literature', also considered that strict and demanding teachers were the best, because they helped her pay much more attention in class than lenient ones.

Pavel Jr (M, 17) had very strong views about family. His mum and dad were the only people who knew him well and he believed that was the way it should always be. 'It's natural for children to do what parents say', he added, 'because they're a certain age, they've been through the same problems, they know what to do.' Conformity, he thought, was the key to a better world:

> Nowadays we need capable and responsible people, and my family is an example in this way. I follow their example and I think that's a reasonable way to live in society. I want to be like them, because the family is a model in society and if we all conformed, there would be a better society.

But society could also mean danger, *Pavel Jr* believed:

> In your family everything must be in the open, honest. Everything is based on honesty. But in society honesty can cause problems. Your honesty can be a weapon for other people to use against you. And society doesn't need all your information which is useful in the family. There must be a barrier between your personal and your social life.

Pavel also felt he needed the similarly high expectations that teachers and parents were entitled to have of him, in order for him 'to conform and get up there'. But for these expectations, he could never 'get his act together and get up there', he said.

Other interviewees also thought there was no questioning the teachers' or the parents' authority, whether for genuine or instrumental reasons:

> With my best friends I could negotiate things, but not with my family. That's something you've just got to do! (*Englezu*, M, 16)

> When a teacher asks you to do something, you can't say no! It's the teacher who gives you your marks! (*Maestru*, M, 18)

> I generally try to please the teacher, not the classmates, 'cause it's not them who give me marks, it's not them who teach me. (*Boomu*, M, 16)

Boomu too emphasised the link between the teacher's and the parents' expectations:

> I try to please my family. If I please my family, I necessarily please the teacher too – if I do my homework, work hard, get good marks and am active in class. [What makes you do that?] It's the fear of bad marks, there's nothing else I fear. Just the marks.

Sophie (F, 15) also thought one had to please one's family, although for different reasons. Recollecting her account conjures up the endearing image of a girl sighing pensively:

> Parents . . . Oh dear! You've always got to take care of them . . . Sometimes you've got to do what they say, otherwise they think you've betrayed them or say you haven't observed the family tradition. So you've got to do what they say.

Whatever their reasons, interviewees who were submissive to the English teacher or to their parents appeared to be happy and proud to be so, hardly any negative feelings being mentioned.

The Duplicitous Self System

The duplicitous self system stood under the sign of duty: a reluctance to 'play the game' doubled by a conscious decision to do so. Other key concepts that the participants associated with this system can be seen in Figure 5.3.

Many interviewees felt duplicitous to their English teacher for a variety of reasons, the most important appearing to be the teachers' lack of personal involvement and students' fear of reprisal.

A recurrent motif was that the English teacher was not interested in students as individual persons, and while many agreed the main reason was

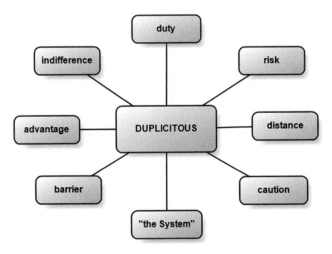

Figure 5.3 Key concepts associated with the duplicitous self system

lack of time, every teacher having to work with dozens or even hundreds of students in a school, they still thought that if the teacher knew a few things about each of them the information could be incorporated into the lessons, making these more relevant and enjoyable. *Freddy* (M, 18) said he had had a new English teacher every year, which made it impossible to bond and really care about each other. (*Anda*, F, 15, said the same but she chose the rebellious system.) *Sophie* (F, 15) and *Woolf* (M, 15) thought teachers were bored, their enthusiasm had run dry and they were only there for the money, simply waiting for retirement.

Several interviewees attributed the teachers' indifference to the generation gap and also a 'mentality gap'. It was rather interesting to see that these students (*Kiddo, 418353, Coca-Cola*), the oldest of whom had been born four years after the fall of Communism, believed they could not communicate with their teachers because the latter were Communist. *418353* (M, 18) thought this was the origin of the 'wall' that prevented genuine communication between teachers and students:

> There's a wall between the student and the teacher. You can't really reach the student. (…) Of course, the blame lies on both sides. Students can't open up for a certain reason – I don't know what that is. But they've both created this wall, both the teachers and the students, I think. [Why?] Because… I suppose every generation brings a change. Maybe an improvement to the previous generation, or just a change. And if you, as a teacher, can't understand this and try to manipulate the students – or maybe not to manipulate them, but to introduce them into the system that you're familiar with, of course you get this rift. And students don't agree with this and they get even further away. I suppose this may lead to defiance… Yes, you can get there. Or simply that 'can't be bothered' attitude…

Teachers' alleged boredom and failure to adapt to a new generation of learners also apparently translated into teaching routines that many of the duplicitous students found demotivating. Exercises on the board and question-and-answer sessions seemed to leave little time for fluency practice, especially as the teacher seemed to talk more than the students (often in Romanian, according to *Visator*):

> Some sit at their desk and dictate and we write stuff for 50 minutes without stopping. (…) Generally, we don't get a chance to speak in the English class – maybe we'll say a word or so in an hour. It's the teacher who talks, talks, talks, and we just sit there… I mean, if we could speak

too, if we could show that we know... Or even if we don't know, at least we learn, as long as we can speak... (*Kiddo*, F, 14)

I'd love something more interactive. I mean, not the teacher sitting at her desk, reading the question, and you answering from your desk. Right, [mark] 10 for an answer! Or for some ticks! That's how we'd develop our oral skills too, which we don't really [develop]... (*080081*, F, 17)

My idea of a perfect English lesson? I can't really describe it, because we've hardly ever had one. I guess one in which we speak freely, in which we express our views on things. Certainly not a class in which we write exercises on the board! (*Freddy*, M, 18)

Private tuition was sometimes thought to influence the teachers' attitude in class too. *Cercuri* (F, 18) had a teacher who only seemed to invest time and attention in the students who took private classes with her:

My English teacher has never been interested in me. (...) She's got her pet students – who aren't necessarily good at English! It's a question of private tuition. Nearly half the class takes private classes with her. The other half doesn't really matter much.

For *Sophie* (F, 15), a similar experience had a strong emotional impact in elementary school:

I really loved English and was trying to learn more, but she would say to me: 'Oh, you're bound to get it wrong, I won't have you answer this question!' And she always asked the best pupil, who was her private tutee, because it was clear he knew the answer. I used to feel like a real weirdo who didn't know anything and they knew everything. [Did you think you'd get it wrong when you put your hand up to answer?] I did, but I thought if I got it wrong then she'd correct me and I'd learn something new. But she didn't. [And you still put your hand up...] I did, and at some point she sent me to the board to write it up and when she saw I'd got it right she said I'd cheated. I felt like a right crook then. Really left out, I felt.

Another recurrent justification that interviewees gave for being duplicitous to the English teacher was their fear of reprisal. *Kiddo* (F, 14) and *Cercuri* (F, 18) thought it was typical of 'the System' for teachers to bear grudges and take revenge by giving bad marks if one got into trouble with them. It was safer to be on the teacher's side and to create the right impression from the very beginning (*Woolf*, M, 15), or certainly to do your 'duty' and avoid conflicts (*Freddy*, M, 18; *Visator*, M, 18). *Pinty* (M, 16) explained that being friends with the teacher was always a big advantage when he wanted to skip a class without being marked as an absentee.

Fear of retaliation sometimes prevented hard-working students from making the best of their English class. The 17-year-old girl who chose the nickname *080081* told of a situation when she got scolded really badly by her teacher for making a mistake in a lesson when they were practising a newly taught concept, and concluded: 'That's what makes people look up the answers at the back and fill them in before the lesson – and what have you done with that?' *Kiddo* (F, 14) also said that sometimes they were frightened to put their hands up and ask a question or confess they had not understood something.

Although *418353* (M, 18) blamed both the teachers and the students for this communication 'wall', there were indications that students regretted not being able to talk to teachers openly. Some had tried but did not meet with the desired response:

> I've noticed it's best to agree with the teacher, although sometimes I've got a different opinion. Because she often clings on to her view and I can't convince her that this is my opinion and my choice. Career options, for example. Maybe that's what I like, but she doesn't like it and is against it. It's a subjective thing. I've tried, but I've realised it's not worth it. (*080081*, F, 17)

> I'll normally tell you straight all I've got to say, and it's a compromise for me having to hide the truth and to take roundabout routes. I hate this. But I've got to do it to avoid conflicts, especially with the teachers but also with my parents. (*Coca-Cola*, M, 17)

Most of the participants who felt duplicitous to the English teacher appeared to be responsible and serious about their own learning. *Cercuri* (F, 18) and *Sophie* (F, 15), who were both unhappy in class, emphasised that they loved English and would like to learn as much of it as possible. However, there was also a risk that the negative perception of a teacher might lead to a negative perception of their subject. *Kiddo* (F, 14) explained:

> Well, you've noticed that the Romanian education system is very defective. (. . .) We don't learn the lesson from the classroom, which is very bad! (. . .) You go home to learn a lesson which maybe you're sick of, because

maybe you're sick of the teacher... That's what usually happens: when you don't like a teacher, you don't like the subject they teach either.

Some participants justified their duplicitous attitude through their desire to take English seriously, which appeared to be at odds with the teacher's and classmates' pursuits. A teacher stuck to unchallenging routines because the class was specialising in French so she thought they were not interested in English (*Cercuri*), another used most English classes for administration and form tutoring matters (*Kiddo*), while another one used the English grammar class to discuss superstitions – talking in Romanian (*Visator*). Similar frustrations were generated by classmates, who appeared unwilling to get involved and penalised the students who did: 'When I showed in class that I love English, they all went: "Oh, yeah! Teacher's pet! She takes private classes!"' [which she said she did not] (*Soare*, F, 17).

Of the participants who were duplicitous with their classmates and friends, most agreed that these were not interested in how well they did in school – friends because friendships should be based on honesty, not on how good one is at English, and classmates because they did not communicate enough to become interested in one another. The fact that classmates would only be with them for a few years and that friends may or may not be for life made most participants feel that friends and classmates were certainly not interested in their future. In the classroom context, competitiveness was also an important factor. *Soare* (F, 17) felt that her classmates wished her to fail because they could not stand her being good at many subjects; *Piaf* (F, 18) and *Aprilie* (F, 15) thought that students were afraid to speak in class for fear others might laugh at them and *Kiddo* (F, 14) explained this although her peers' alleged immaturity: 'They want you to make mistakes, so they can laugh. They're still children, and that's what children do.' Competitiveness was also illustrated by two participants who enjoyed appearing better than their peers:

I love it when I see that I know more than others and I can stand out. (...) I love reading out in class, because many of them can't pronounce some words and that makes me stand out. (*Prestige*, F, 16)

When people don't know the answer to a question, I really get out of my way to answer it, because for me it is easy and I think: 'Ah, come on, you don't know that?!' So then I'm always with my hand up. (*Airforce*, M, 17)

Whether because they spent too little time together and did not get the chance to know one another well (*Prestige, 418353, Englezu, Woolf*), because they were not encouraged to do projects or trips together (*080081*), because class-mates were immature and unreliable (*Maestru, Kiddo*), mean and envious (*Soare, Airforce*), or simply just indifferent (*Rares, Cercuri, 2244*), it was generally felt to be safer if classmates did not know one well. *Soare* (F, 17) summarised the precaution expressively: 'I've got this idea in my mind that if I show them who I am it can turn against me. So I'd rather show them the person I choose to show, and let them be shocked when they realise they were wrong and I wasn't!'

The interviewee who called himself *418353* (M, 18) justified his indiffer-ence to peers by a lack of desire to integrate with their group, suggesting – in my ulterior interpretation – that when one wants to be accepted into a circle one has to 'wear' a particular face:

> I'm not keen on being accepted to their group, so I don't feel the need to prove anything. If I wanted to be accepted into the classmates' group, I'd have to wear a face which isn't mine, and that's not worth it.

There were only two cases of duplicity in the family, both related to career choices. *Coca-Cola* (M, 18) felt nobody apart from himself really knew what sort of person he was and both his English teacher and his parents wanted him to choose a different career from what he wanted. Because his parents wanted him to be a vet, he let them think he was considering becom-ing a vet – 'so as not to let them down' – although he knew for sure he would not do that. Confronted with a similar problem, *Noiembrie* (F, 17) – who confessed she was preparing for a degree in Journalism – felt that only her friends knew her well and justified the communication break-down in the family through insufficient time spent together:

> Parents are busy with their jobs and with housework. They don't know you as you really are and can often be wrong about you. My mum and dad want different things to what I want – we've all got different opinions in my family. For example, my dad wants me to become a teacher because I loved playing teacher with the teddy bears and dolls when I was little. My mum wants me to do Medicine, but the problem is I hate blood and I'm not strong enough to do Medicine. (...) I give my mum the impression that I'm gathering stuff about Medicine, and my dad knows I'm considering getting into teaching, but it's hard to work with children – I can see it in my own group how hard it is for the teacher to keep everyone afloat.

Not everybody agreed with every aspect of vignette B (duplicitous). *Cercuri* (F, 18), for example, felt very strongly that the teacher and classmates would and should never be interested in her future. This would mean that they asked or expected something of her, which, in her view, was not the case – certainly not for the future. *Pinty* (M, 16), in turn, took issue with 'I know better' in the vignette, adding that he did not think he knew enough at his age. He also disagreed with the sentence 'it's not important for me that they know what sort of person I am', explaining that, in the teacher's case, this was very important for him although apparently not for the teacher. However, he still felt that vignette B was more suitable than the others.

The Rebellious Self System

Interviewees who chose the rebellious self system appeared in many ways similar to the duplicitous ones, but while they acknowledged other people's differences and expectations, they chose to go their own way. *Visator* (M, 18) expressed this view in unambiguous terms:

> If I'm told, 'Look, we want you to do this and that, and we expect great things from you', I will say, 'Fine, but I'll still do what I was going to do anyway, because it's for myself that I do it and I'll do what I feel is best'.

Some recurrent themes in these interviews are shown in Figure 5.4.
Career choices seemed to generate most problems, teachers and parents encouraging the teenagers to pursue their own professions. *Coca-Cola* (M, 18)

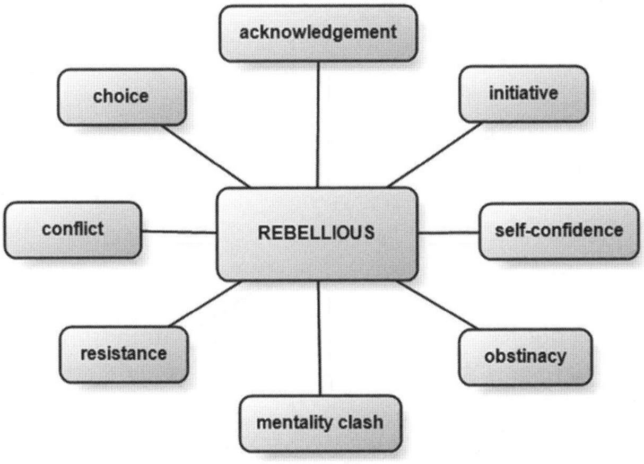

Figure 5.4 Key concepts associated with the rebellious self system

explained with saddening pragmatism why he was not going to follow his teacher's advice and become a teacher of English himself or a translator in Romania, where salaries were so meagre and it was so hard to make ends meet, in his opinion. *Noiembrie* (F, 17) had had an adverse reaction from her English teacher, when she told her she wanted to study Journalism and not Foreign Languages.

The student with the pseudonym *2244* also stressed that she would not do the degree her form teacher wanted her to do and *Titulescu* (M, 17) felt the same. A younger *FC* (M, 15) expressed his defiance by refusing to go to the English competitions his teacher wanted him to go to. *Englezu* (M, 16) and *Noiembrie* (F, 17) felt 'rebel' was too hard a word when it came to the English teacher. 'But you've got to follow your own dreams' – the girl said – 'because it's not the teacher who goes to university for you. You will go and you know yourself best of all'.

Visator (M, 18) spoke about the 'professional' relationship that he had with his parents, each doing his or her own 'job' in the family. He explained:

> They know, of course, what I intend to do, but I couldn't say they support me, because they don't. But I'll do what I think is best, because after all I'll spend 40 years of my life doing that job. They'd like me to do what they've done, but I don't want that, because I'm not attracted to it and we're different kinds of people. (...) There have been conflicts with my mum because of that. It's normal for a mum to want her child to succeed and if she's been successful to want the same thing for him, but she may not realise that he wants something else and he won't be happy going her way. (...) I have chosen a career that is right for my personality, my skills and my inclinations.

Rares (M, 16) had had difficulty convincing his parents to let him move to a different school when he realised school B was not right for him. Although he had given up in the end, he was determined to go to a university of his choice, justifying it: 'After all, it's me who's going to do that job – I've got to like it in order to feel motivated to be the best I can.' Although she did not feel too pressurised, *Piaf* (F, 18) also stated that her parents wanted her to get a degree in Medicine, whereas she was attracted to arts and puppeteering. She mentioned later that she did not feel she could open up in her family as she did with her friends and thought this might be strange. *Cerul* (F, 16) said she had a friend who kept pestering her about becoming a doctor, but she was not going to give in: 'Yes, I'll do what I want – I'll lead my own my life, nobody will lead it for me.'

Communism was again mentioned. *Coca-Cola* (M, 18) felt he could not express his honest point of view in class because the teacher was Communist.

Having been born in democracy, he maintained, he respected people's right to a free opinion, but she did not. Because he often preferred to state his view openly, he had had fights and conflicts with teachers ever since he started school, 12 years before. At the end of the interview, he expressed his hope that the results of this study would not be ignored by Romanian teachers, like so many others had been, and added: 'That's Romania for you! Many years must pass before something changes.'

Kiddo (F, 14) believed her mother was Communist and admitted she had the 'sick mentality' to always do the opposite of what her mum said. 'The more parents restrict you, the more obstinate you become', she explained. She also felt pressure from the family to be like her cousin, who had just been offered a place to study Medicine at the university. *Kiddo*, however, wanted to travel the world, do bungee jumping and save the whales, feeling that her own expectations of herself were far more important than her teachers' or parents' expectations.

Some students who chose the rebellious vignette for the teacher also expressed their disappointment with the English class. *2244* (F, 15) was sad because she had just been moved to an inferior set and claimed that the teacher sometimes shouted angrily and prevented her from concentrating. (Interestingly, her best friend – *Foxy* – a girl from the same class, thought the English teacher was wonderful.) *FC* (M, 15) said he only had good marks in English because every time they got a test they were informed beforehand, so they could prepare: 'This way, I can study, but I only study that chapter, or that lesson that I need, and that's why I get a high mark. If she were to assess me on the whole syllabus, it would be a disaster.' The girl with the nickname *Slot* (17) claimed that the English teacher mostly spoke Romanian in class, they did not get enough fluency practice and they were not pushed hard enough to become involved in the lesson. In turn, *Englezu* (M, 16) contrasted his present teacher to his previous one:

Our English teacher in elementary school took great interest in me. I was the second best in class and I really cared, and she talked to my parents and was interested. She gave me extra work to do and all that. Here, the teacher is not very demanding. (...) Other teachers get us to work hard even if their subjects are not important for our specialism, but English is like... well, let's just do a little thing or two... (...) I love discovering things, but we can't discover much in the English class, because the teacher is not too bothered. (...) There's a monotonous atmosphere: the teacher rambles on, we see to our own business...

Interestingly, he was surprised to be selected for the interview. He had written on the questionnaire that he was interested, but he then confessed that he had not expected the study to be conducted seriously. (One wonders whether he had got to a point where he thought no teaching staff was 'too bothered' with him at all.)

When it came to classmates or friends, most interviewees felt that rebelling against them was a non issue. *Freddy* (M, 18) explained: 'Let's say that a classmate tells me to go with him to I don't know what university, but maybe I want to go to a different one. (. . .) It's obvious I'll do what I want. It's my life, my future.' *Woolf* (M, 15) gave a similar answer: 'I can't let a friend tell me, for example, to go to the Economics high school with him 'cause it's nicer there, when I know I'm much better than that and I can get into a better high school than that!' (Incidentally, 'the Economics high school' he was talking about is school A in this project, which offers an interesting insight into inter-school perceptions.)

Pinty (M, 16) spoke about peer pressure pushing one not to do what the teacher said in class so as not to appear better compared to those who created conflicts. He also offered a noteworthy glimpse into the social aspect of peer pressure:

> At the end of the day, I'm only gonna be with these guys for four years and my future doesn't depend on them, so I'm not afraid to say 'no, I don't agree with this'. For example, most of them smoke and flaunt it, so when you spend a lot of time with them you feel the pressure to take up smoking too. It's not that they tell you to do it, but you know it would just feel right if you started smoking to be like them. But, no, I'm against it. I will never start smoking!! I hope.

FC (M, 15) did not feel he had been equally successful in his resistance:

> I've always wanted to be a model student, but it hasn't really worked so far. I mean, not to be a rascal, to get reasonable marks, that sort of thing . . . But I can't always behave the way I want! You see, if I sit next to a classmate, he cracks a joke, I crack another and. . . I just lose my ideas. I do everything the gang way, as it were. [And you think that's opposed to the model student you were talking about?] Yes, I think it is.

0590 (M, 19) had thought that in a Music school (C) everybody would be passionate about music and willing to work hard. However, he felt disappointed that he and his best friend (*418353*, M, 18) were considered strange because they wanted to become concert performers and were willing to practise for hours on end instead of going to clubs with their mates. They were always criticised that they worked too hard and never had fun, he said, but their dream to reach high performance levels was much stronger than their peers' attitude. *Noiembrie* (F, 17) thought that her classmates would be happy for her not to go to university, so that she stayed below their level. She explained this by being in a group in which they were all 'each for themselves', with no collegial feelings. This is why she said she never thought twice when it came to rebelling against them. 'I'll either have it my way or not at all', she added.

Nevertheless, many of the students who chose vignette C appeared quite happy in their respective relational contexts and said they would only rebel in the hypothetical case that they were forced to do something they felt was not right: *Aprilie* (F, 15), *Huggy* (M, 15), *Prestige* (F, 16), *Boomu* (M, 16). *Slot* (F, 17) chose the rebellious system for the English teacher for the same reason, but mentioned that in the past, when she expressed different views, the teacher had accepted them without any problem. Another example is *Anda* (F, 15), who admired her English teacher for asking them about their likes and dislikes from the very beginning, so that she would know how to approach the class. *Anda* thought this had an important effect on the students' motivation, who would otherwise think: 'If the teacher's not bothered about what I want, why would I care about what she wants?' She felt that when the teacher was interested, students too were interested.

The Harmonious Self System

Genuine communication seems to be the main thematic thread running through the interviews of the students who chose the harmonious self system, whether with their peers or with their teacher and families. Other recurrent themes are represented in Figure 5.5.

Perhaps considering it the default option, participants did not speak at great length about the harmonious system in their family, but many of them emphasised that they had their full support in everything they decided to do: *Soare* (F, 17), *Airforce* (M, 17), *080081* (F, 17), *Huggy* (M, 15). *Cerul* (F, 16) explained that her parents were determined to give her all the freedom of choice and all the support she needed because they had never had these when they were her age. On the contrary, their own parents had forced them to choose careers that they considered suitable, so *Cerul*'s mum and dad promised themselves never to do the same to their children. Similarly, *Huggy* (M, 15) benefitted from his family's generous support in learning English because he had shown a 'gift' for it since he was very young and his parents, who did

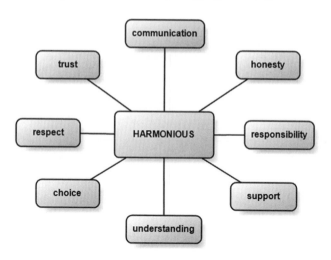

Figure 5.5 Key concepts associated with the harmonious self system

not speak any English, appreciated this and encouraged him. Expressing similar gratitude for his family's help, *Pinty* (M, 16) nevertheless spoke about a silent pressure that he perceived to come from his parents, which made him feel that, if he wanted their support, he had better do what they told him. Paradoxically, he felt it was his acceptance of their decisions for him that determined them to let him make his own. However, just like with teachers, he explained, it was always safer to be friends with your parents.

Kiddo (F, 14), *Piaf* (F, 18) and *Noiembrie* (F, 17) felt their best friends understood and knew them much better than their families did. Others (*Titulescu*, M, 17; *0590*, M, 19; *Pinty*, M, 16; *Freddy*, M, 18; *Sophie*, F, 15; also *Noiembrie*) considered that, in order to maintain harmonious relationships with both friends and family, when they were in the same situation with both, great care was necessary in displaying a certain type of behaviour usually expected by parents. *Freddy* and *Pinty* felt they owed their parents the respect to do that. *Titulescu*, who felt harmonious with his classmates, friends and family, but rebellious with the teacher, justified why he believed that in similar classroom situations friends should always understand if one chose to please the teacher rather than them:

> Any student tries to please the teacher, right? Because a satisfied teacher is a teacher who's on your side. [For...?] For marks, for better under-standing in class... (...) Classmates and friends can understand, it's normal for them not to have very high expectations, whereas teachers

and parents always want us to reach our maximum potential. Peers can understand more easily... not necessarily failure, but... not having such high expectations they are... more understanding? A friend should never ask too much of another friend.

An interesting connection emerges here between expectations and an understanding attitude, which seemed to be indirectly proportional. This was apparently supported by most harmonious students, for whom an understanding attitude appeared to obliterate the very notion of expectation. *Soare* (F, 17), *Anda* (F, 15) *Piaf* (F, 18) and *0590* (M, 19) emphasised that the only expectations they responded to were their own, which simply coincided with what other people wanted them to do. *Airforce* (M, 17) made sure the message was clear:

They're not really expectations. We simply think in the same way. So if my parents want something, I happen to want the same. Although I do listen to advice! [Are these expectations that you have negotiated together?] Not negotiated together! They are my personal expectations and ... theirs. The same as my parents' and teachers'.

In the absence of a developmental study, it is impossible to discern to what extent this is the result of internalisation and what the cause and effect are in the relationship between non-salient expectations and an understanding attitude. *418353* (M, 18), who did not feel harmonious either with the teacher or with his family, and for whom their expectations were quite prominent, suggested another intriguing perspective to internalisation: 'I'll mostly do what they expect me to do because, in a way, that helps me too. I mean... doing something for somebody else... trains me, in a way.'

Although friends were expected to be more understanding, their role was sometimes uncertain. (Classmates with whom the interviewees felt harmonious were also considered friends by them.) First, friends were not thought to care whether one was good at English or at school, in general: *Aprilie* (F, 15), *Pinty* (M, 16), *Airforce* (M, 17), *Sophie* (F, 15), *Rares* (M, 16), *Slot* (F, 17). (Perhaps this raises the question to what extent English is seen as an important part of these students' lives, or just another academic subject.) Second, friends were not always felt to care about one's future. As *Pinty* explained, the length of a friendship was often uncertain, which made him feel the vignette was not right to refer to the future too:

'My dreams for the future are very similar to what they'd like me to do in life' – this isn't really suitable for friends. Because I honestly don't know how interested they are in my future. I mean, we're friends at the moment, but you never know how long a friendship will last. You can have a really ugly fight with a guy and he stops being your best friend. [So it applies more in the present?] Yes, yes, that's it!

Nevertheless, *Kiddo* (F, 14) offered important insights into the influence that a peer group can have on a teenager. Emphasising that she thought this was something bad, she told me that all her friends played the guitar, which she had hated at first. However, 'in order to integrate better into this group', she was planning to buy a guitar and start practising. Asked whether now she liked the idea of playing the instrument better or she would do it just for the group, she answered that although at first she had hated it, she was now getting used to it and thought it was 'OK'. Talking about this group of friends, she also mentioned: 'They really understand me and I can be myself with them', which may suggest interesting differences between being 'an individual in a group' and being 'a group of individuals'. Like most interviewees who had chosen the harmonious self system for their peers, *Kiddo* stressed that if her friends – all much older than her – wanted to do something that she thought was wrong, she simply did not take part. She mentioned recreational drug use as an example. Considering the whole situation – and also remembering *Pinty*'s earlier account of pressure to start smoking which ended in a strong 'I will never start smoking!!' followed by a not-so-strong 'I hope' – we can see that being harmonious with one's peers poses important risks in certain situations, especially that internalisation is probably more likely to occur in a harmonious self system.

The most emotional accounts of harmonious systems were, however, inspired by the English teachers. All the seven interviewees who chose vignette D for the teacher emphasised the importance of being known as an individual in class, which they thought formed the basis for effective pedagogy. *Airforce* (M, 17) explained:

I've always tried to be very open and very honest in the English class. So my teacher knows all my good and bad sides. She knows what I'm up to, what sort of personality I've got... [How do you think this influences your motivation in class?] In the first place, she can be a better pedagogue through this. If she knows what motivates the pupil, she can use this as a weapon – in a good sense. So she can motivate that pupil by knowing his personality. And I think that's what every teacher should do: try to know the pupil's personality and then try to... manipulate that personality in a very good direction, or at least a good one. And I think this would motivate any pupil.

The condition, of course, is that teachers are interested in students as individuals and, in turn, students are genuine. In this way, teachers can offer them personalised advice when they are confronted with difficult decisions about their English and about their future, as *Rares* (M, 16) and *0590* (M, 19) said it had happened to them. (To *Soare*, F, 17, too, although only in school-related matters.) Other interviewees, who had chosen different systems for the teacher, also thought this was essential, although it did not really happen in their case: *Noiembrie* (F, 18), *Foxy* (F, 16), *2244* (F, 15), *Titulescu* (M, 17). For *Huggy* (M, 15) being genuine in class could not be more natural, being also accompanied by a positive attitude to doing what the teacher asked him to do:

> In the English class, I let my guard down, as it were. And I always feel good, I always try to feel good and... umm... respond well to what I'm asked to do. If, for example, the teacher asks me to describe my personality, I answer very honestly, usually in a jokey way, and everybody loves that. [So you feel you're appreciated for what you are...] Yes, I am!

He also made it clear that his genuine and open attitude in class was heavily dependent on the teacher:

> It depends on the teacher. If it's a good teacher, who knows how to approach the students, who also jokes with them and knows what to do... then I am really pleased to answer correctly, to work hard and all that. But if the teacher's not like that – mm, not really. [How would you define a good teacher?] One who has a sense of humour, who knows his or her subject well, who knows how to connect with the students, who understands them... That's about it!

Incidentally (or perhaps not), *Huggy* also confessed he had a real passion for English, which meant that every time he met somebody who spoke the language he started talking to them immediately, finding it very easy to 'connect'. He was certainly one student for which English played an important part in his life! *Airforce* (M, 17), who appeared similarly fortunate, explained that relevance for one's life was the whole point of education:

> [If I were a teacher], I'd give many life examples. I'm usually more motivated when I see the consequences in other people's lives. The fact that they didn't work hard, or that they didn't pay attention in class. (...) And we've got a teacher who doesn't only focus on teaching English, she teaches us how to live, she teaches us good manners, and all sorts of

things that are related to life. And then I feel much more motivated – I mean, look, that's really gonna help me, I can do something with that thing! (...) That's what school does to you: it teaches you how to live. It teaches you how to speak, how to be a person in society. And the whole thing boils down to society. Nobody would learn anything if they didn't live in social groups.

Anda (F, 15), who had chosen vignette C under the influence of her previous teacher, on the basis that she would refuse to do things she did not agree with if the teacher forced her to, also said that the way she would motivate her students if she were a teacher was to tell them exactly how everything she had done in school contributed to what she was now, considering that her real example would give the students a realistic motivation to work harder. She also mentioned that her favourite class ever had been the first English lesson in her new school, when the teacher asked the group to draw and write something about their personalities and, seeing that the students did not understand exactly what was expected of them, the teacher demonstrated on her own personality. (*Anda* was in the same group with *Huggy*, having the same English teacher.)

418353 (M, 18) considered that knowing the students as individuals would also help the teacher remove the 'communication wall': [If I were a teacher] 'I'd try to remove that wall I was talking about. I'd try to understand... to find their desire... to see where it comes from. And maybe to channel it in a certain way. If you've got the desire you can change a lot of things.' The teacher's trust and appreciation were also considered important factors in ensuring the student's wellbeing in class (*Piaf*, F, 19; *Rares*, M, 16). *Piaf* even suggested that the teacher's trustful attitude helped her know herself better: 'The trust that my teacher shows me influences me, yes. It helps me open up. But for myself, not for my classmates to see.'

The tutor's care for students as individuals, and perhaps for the relevance that English will have in the students' future, also translated into flexible teaching methodology, as *Rares* (M, 16) described:

I really do think that our teacher's style is a very good one. I don't know, maybe there is a better one, but I for one can't imagine that. And why? Because we don't stop at solving exercises from the book and writing... I don't know what English word equals I don't know what Romanian translation. And having vocabulary lists in your notebook and homework and that's it. No. We do a lot of essays, so there's room for artistic expression, for imagination, for developing your vocabulary – because we're always looking for new words and then using them in front of the class and speaking freely, and that's how they stick and we learn them.

Most of the interviewees who appeared rather disenchanted with the English class (and not harmonious with the teacher) confessed they would like to have challenging activities, free discussions, interactivity, projects. (*Soare* and *080081* also mentioned that some of their classmates had become their best friends because they had done projects together.) They would all have loved *Huggy*'s (M, 15) description of a perfect English class:

Desks in a circle, teacher in the middle... and fun! [What sort of fun?] Say we've had to do some reading in English – a book, a story, anything. And the teacher asks: What can you tell us about this? Everything would be relaxed, not tense or stressful. [As a teacher] I would joke very much. But I'd know where to draw the line, I wouldn't be crass, of course! And I'd do things differently, I mean I'd have diversity, to say so. Not just... every lesson: writing on the board, exercises, reading, full stop. I'd bring games and things, people would get involved, team work... stuff like that.

His description was actually not very far from what seemed to happen in his own English class. No wonder everybody knew him as 'the boy who laughs all the time'.

Self-systems: Preliminary Conclusions

It may be concluded that the 32 interviews provided support for most hypotheses related to the four self systems, although there were some unexpected insights too. For example, the indication that submissive students were proud to be so and showed respect for the source of their imposed self, as well as the suggestion that they thrived when relying on mature and authoritative guidance. The fact that for harmonious students the notion of expectation seemed to disappear altogether was again somewhat unanticipated, as were the indications that rebellious students felt confident, responsible and happy with the choices they had made. Very useful unanticipated insights were also offered by the students' comments on what they thought was not right for them in every vignette. All these findings will be essential in refining the theoretical framework and shaping the future projects that will emerge from this study.

An important role in shaping future investigations will also be played by several questions and uncertainties that emerged from the analysis of these interviews. Thus, it was clear that for some students (*Pinty, Airforce, 418353*) self systems had gone through a process of change recently. *Pinty's* (M, 16) account indicated that he used to be rebellious with the teachers, whereas now he chose the duplicitous system and there were suggestions he might be approaching a harmonious state; *Airforce* (M, 17) and *418353* (M, 18), in turn, explained that they used to care a lot more about what other people thought of them and displayed an identity consciously in order to be accepted to a particular group. The developmental side of these self systems would, there-fore, have to be addressed for a clearer understanding of the identity pro-cesses involved. This would also clarify the case of the younger participants, who had only just started their 9th year in a new school, and who were sometimes divided between strong impressions left by the previous teacher and new perceptions of the present one.

My investigation is also limited by only concentrating on the students' perspective – or rather my interpretation of the account they gave me of their perceptions, or of what they felt was right for them to say at that particular moment. It is impossible to know whether all of them where absolutely honest at all times or they were just recreating for me an image that they chose to display, for one reason or another. However, these qualitative con-tributions offer a useful perspective when read in conjunction with the quan-titative findings discussed in the next two chapters with links to the background literature.

6 Self Perceptions and Identity Display in Learning English as a Foreign Language

Both the qualitative and the quantitative findings provided strong support for the hypothesis that different relational contexts trigger the display of different public selves, which may or may not be related with what participants really believe about themselves as language learners (or, rather, what they were prepared to declare about their self beliefs when the data were collected).

These insights will be discussed in greater detail after some descriptive statistics will be presented to provide more details about the questionnaire scales.

Self and Language Learning Perceptions

The main descriptive statistics for the data collected through the L2 Quadripolar Identity Questionnaire are presented in Table 6.1 (self variables) and Table 6.2 (other variables). As can be seen in the two tables, skewness and kurtosis values indicate that the data are not perfectly normally distributed. However, it has been stated that a perfectly normal distribution, with skewness and kurtosis values of 0, is a 'rather uncommon occurrence in the social sciences' (Pallant, 2007: 56). Skewness is considered normal if its values lie within the range of −1 to +1 (Hair *et al.*, 2006). Other sources (e.g. Fabrigar *et al.*, 1999) recommend the cut-off values of 2.00 for skewness and 7.00 for kurtosis when assessing the normality of data.

Accordingly, only two of my self variables had relatively high values (although still well within the above-mentioned limit): imposed self teacher (present) and imposed self family (present). One of the findings of the study

Table 6.1 Descriptive statistics for the continuous self variables

Variable		Valid N	Range	M	SD	α (scale)	Distribution	
							Skewness	Kurtosis
L2 private self	Cognitive appraisals	1003	1–6	3.88	1.09	0.92	−0.26	−0.56
	Affective appraisals	1003	1–6	3.89	1.01	0.88	−0.30	−0.31
	Internal frame of ref.	1015	1–6	4.16	1.15	0.90	−0.41	−0.69
	External frame of ref.	1002	1–6	3.66	1.10	0.90	−0.06	−0.59
	Total (grand mean)	1042	1–6	3.90	0.99	0.92	−0.29	−0.64
L2 ideal self		1012	1–5	4.44	0.97	0.76	−0.66	0.25
L2 public self	Teacher	1007	1–6	4.74	1.11	0.90	−1.05	0.76
	Classmates	1001	1–6	3.05	1.22	0.91	0.01	−0.78
	Friends	994	1–6	3.49	1.19	0.89	−0.21	−0.45
	Family	991	1–6	4.73	1.10	0.88	−0.96	0.52
L2 imposed self	Teacher present	1015	1–6	5.26	0.75	0.83	−1.55	3.24
	Teacher future	1022	1–6	4.55	1.06	0.86	−0.93	0.71
	Teacher grand mean	1038	1–6	4.90	0.85	0.90	−1.21	1.70
	Classmates present	1004	1–6	2.96	1.15	0.89	0.00	−0.82
	Classmates future	1014	1–6	2.77	1.15	0.90	−0.01	−1.03
	Classmates grand mean	1032	1–6	2.87	1.10	0.94	−0.05	−0.93
	Friends present	1004	1–6	3.74	1.16	0.89	−0.36	−0.38
	Friends future	1018	1–6	3.56	1.13	0.87	−0.41	−0.36
	Friends grand mean	1034	1–6	3.64	1.08	0.93	−0.41	−0.30
	Family present	1003	1–6	5.22	0.84	0.84	−1.65	3.65
	Family future	1016	1–6	4.57	0.93	0.79	−1.01	1.34
	Family grand mean	1035	1–6	4.89	0.83	0.88	−1.35	2.53

M = mean, SD = standard deviation, α = Cronbach's internal consistency (reliability) coefficient

Table 6.2 Descriptive statistics for other continuous variables in the questionnaire

Variable	Valid N	Range	M	SD	A (scale)	Distribution	
						Skewness	Kurtosis
L2 learning orientation	1026	1–6	3.80	0.94	0.85	− 0.20	− 0.12
Perceptions of the English class							
Interest and relevance	1011	1–6	4.24	0.86	0.77	− 0.40	− 0.17
Appreciation as an individual	1022	1–6	3.18	0.97	0.82	0.22	− 0.47
Grand mean	1042	1–6	3.70	0.84	0.86	− 0.07	− 0.40
Attributions for success and failure							
Success – internal	1039	0–6	2.29	0.26	–	0.25	− 0.70
Success – external	1039	0–6	2.90	0.27	–	0.06	− 0.81
Failure – internal	1036	0–6	3.15	0.21	–	0.03	− 0.02
Failure – external	1036	0–6	2.13	0.22	–	0.39	− 0.24
Declared English mark							
Actual	1022	1–10	8.48	1.16	–	− 0.56	− 0.10
Deserved	1017	1–10	8.28	1.22	–	− 0.79	0.68

M = mean, SD = standard deviation, α = Cronbach's internal consistency (reliability) coefficient (calculated for cumulative/summative scales only)

is that most students rated their perceived imposed selves for the present very highly when referring to their English teacher and parents, as opposed to their classmates and friends. The means of the two variables are also considerably higher than others. Thus, negative skewness confirms the hypothesis and corroborates the finding that teachers and parents have very high expectations of my participants (i.e. high scores clustered towards the right-hand side of the distribution curve).

As far as kurtosis is concerned, positive values indicate that scores tend to cluster in the centre and negative values show that scores spread towards the tails of the distribution curve. As the instrument assessed complex attitudes with often contradictory responses depending on a multitude of unknown factors, a perfect bell curve would have been an unrealistic expectation. More importantly, my sample size places this study within very safe normality margins. It is known that, with reasonably large samples, skewness and kurtosis do not make a substantive difference in the analysis

(Tabachnick & Fidell, 2007). Pallant (2007: 56) interprets 'reasonably large samples' as more than 200 cases. In consequence, the small abnormalities in my data (already within the limits recommended in the field) were ironed out by the large sample size.

All the scales had high and very high internal reliability coefficients (α being measured on a scale of 0–1, the higher the coefficient the more reliable the scale). The main scales were tested with exploratory factor analysis (maximum likelihood with Promax rotation), which resulted in a reasonably clear factor structure with some cross-loadings. As the theoretically informed purpose of the analysis was to test the self scales, and not to reduce the variables, factors were not used in the analyses.

A brief look at Table 6.1 shows some interesting trends: students English private self (mean 3.90 on a scale of 1–6) is considerably lower than their English ideal self (mean 4.44 on a scale of 1–5), which shows they assess themselves lower than where they would like to be in relation to learning English. We can also see that they rate themselves in English better than in other subjects (internal frame of reference), but lower than their peers in learning English (external frame of reference). A pattern also emerges that groups teachers and families together and linking them to high imposed selves (expectations) and high public selves (expectation-linked identity display). The classmates' and friends' relational contexts also cluster together, being characterised by low imposed selves and generating low public selves. This is a clear indication that in these two relational contexts (and especially for classmates), students are not expected to do well in language learning, which, in turn, is reflected in the participants' low public selves, indicating that their response in relation to classmates and friends is directly proportional (i.e. low). Further analyses will explore this apparent strategic identity display in greater detail later on.

A few key statistics included in Table 6.2 show that L2 learning orientation is marginally higher than performance orientations on average (on a scale of 1–6, values closer to 6 show learning orientation and values closer to 1 show performance orientation). We can also see that students declare a relatively high level of interest and perceived relevance in the English class, but their perceptions of being appreciated as individuals by the teacher are lower, although they do appear to consider that the marks they receive in English are, on average, higher than they deserve. With regards to attributions for success and failure, we can see that the highest mean is represented by the internal attributions for failure ($M = 3.15$), followed by external attributions for success ($M = 2.90$). In other words, most of these teenagers explain their success through external, uncontrollable and often unstable factors, while explaining their failures through internal causes. When they

Table 6.3 Gender differences (ANOVA)

Self variable	Gender	N	M (mean)	SD	SE	F	Sig. (2-tailed)	Effect size (Cohen's d)
L2 private self	M	338	4.05	0.98	0.05	12.79	0.000	0.23
	F	644	3.82	1.01	0.04			
L2 ideal self	M	329	4.35	0.93	0.05	4.74	0.030	−0.15
	F	631	4.49	0.98	0.04			
L2 public self: teacher	M	329	4.55	1.15	0.06	20.87	0.000	−0.31
	F	624	4.89	1.03	0.04			
L2 public self: classmates	M	324	2.90	1.18	0.07	9.85	0.002	−0.22
	F	622	3.16	1.23	0.05			
L2 public self: friends	M	324	3.16	1.19	0.07	46.05	0.000	−0.46
	F	616	3.70	1.14	0.05			
L2 public self: family	M	323	4.56	1.14	0.06	16.30	0.000	−0.27
	F	614	4.85	1.04	0.04			
L2 imposed self: teacher	M	336	4.82	.91	0.05	5.91	0.015	−0.16
	F	643	4.96	.80	0.03			
L2 imposed self: friends	M	332	3.41	1.05	0.06	29.73	0.000	−0.37
	F	643	3.80	1.04	0.04			
L2 imposed self: family	M	323	4.43	.95	0.05	12.47	0.000	−0.25
	F	637	4.66	.89	0.04			
perceived T appreciation	M	329	3.27	.93	0.05	4.24	0.040	0.13
	F	634	3.14	1.00	0.04			
L2 internal attributions for failure	M	335	3.04	1.27	0.07	4.26	0.039	−0.14
	F	644	3.22	1.26	0.05			
L2 mark deserved	M	336	8.41	1.22	0.07	4.34	0.012	0.16
	F	635	8.21	1.22	0.05			

M = male, F = female, n = subsample, SD = standard deviation, SE = standard error of mean, df = degrees of freedom, Cohen's d effect size obtained using the online calculator available at http://www.uccs.edu/~lbecker/

do well in English, they may think they were lucky – when they do not do so well, they may think they are not very capable. Alternatively, internal attributions for failure may mean that they consider themselves capable but admit they have not invested enough effort in the respective activity, or indeed effort may have been withdrawn in response to the classroom norm of low achievement.

However, gender differences were also identified – regarding both attributions and other variables. Table 6.3 shows only the statistically significant differences, so it is worth mentioning that, although the mean values were different for boys and girls, no statistically significant difference was found for the following: the affective components of the L2 private self, the classmates imposed self, interest/perceived relevance in the English language class, learning orientation, attributions for success, external attributions for failure and declared mark. This shows that boys and girls liked English (and learning English) in equal measure, perceived a similar level of peer pressure and achieved similar declared results. However, Table 6.3 shows that boys have stronger L2 private selves (cognitive appraisals, internal and external frame of reference), believe they are appreciated by the English teacher more than girls do and believe they should be given a higher mark in English than girls do.

Overall, this indicates greater levels of language learning confidence for boys, in contrast to the female participants, who, although having stronger L2 ideal selves, have lower private selves, higher internal attributions for failure, higher public selves and higher imposed selves in all relational contexts except classmates (statistically non-significant difference). Female students would therefore appear to be less confident language learners, who blame themselves more when their results are less than pleasing, who feel the social pressure more acutely than boys and who respond more willingly to this pressure by displaying an identity that they feel is expected of them. Are boys in the five Romanian schools better language learners than the girls? This would go against decades of popular stereotypes, as well as the literature suggesting that girls may be better at languages than boys (Barton, 1997; Callaghan, 1998; Clark, 1995; Kobayashi, 2002; Little et al., 2002; Nyikos, 2008; Place, 1997) and that male students may avoid foreign languages – or at least some of them – because they are considered inappropriate for boys (Bartram, 2006a; Carr & Pauwels, 2009; Williams et al., 2002). Yet, there are also a handful of studies with similar findings to mine. For example, Bügel and Buunk (1996) show that Dutch girls obtain slightly but consistently lower scores than boys in national English language examinations, and Boyle (1987) found that male Chinese learners of English had better oral comprehension of vocabulary than girls. An in-depth contextual analysis would, however, be necessary in order to elucidate any causal relationships in such situations.

My research design did not include an objective measure of my respondents' actual performance and achievement in English – a measure which would be virtually impossible to obtain even in a carefully designed experimental study, given that actual performance and competence depend on past performance and the emotional processing of past outcomes (Hattie, 1992; Marsh, 1993). Neither did I seek access to registers or other 'objective' measures of students' proficiency because, as I have argued In the Introduction, evaluation and assessment are not always seen as reliable in the Romanian education system, and it was also important that I maintained the participants' anonymity at all times. I relied instead on students' self-perceptions, as well as their actual declared marks in English compared to the marks they believed they deserved. Under the circumstances, it is impossible to know for sure why boys and girls had different scores, but two possible explanations may be (a) that boys in my research context are better than girls at English, and (b) that they *think* they are better. Both possibilities are discussed in further detail below.

Some of the data collected, especially the interview data, suggested that the participants' competence in English may not originate in the English class, but in their free time, when they watch films, play video games and socialise in virtual environments – all of these using English, all of them using computers. One gender difference that has received consistent research support is that boys tend to be overall more interested, more confident and more experienced in computer use than girls (Busch, 1995; Shashaani, 1997; Siann et al., 1990), especially in high school (Whitley, 1997), and that female participants have less positive attitudes to interactive communication systems (Kay, 2009) and they keep a lower profile on online platforms than male participants (Pedersen & Macafee, 2007). In recent years, there have been indications that this gender gap is closing (Imhof et al., 2007), but even though the skills gap may be closing, girls may still have lower perceived competence, which affects their internet usage patterns (Hargittai & Shafer, 2006). Considering this evidence, it is possible that my male participants are inded better at English than my female participants, as they may use it more for real-life purposes, outside the classroom.

There is also evidence to suggest that boys tend to overestimate their abilities, whereas girls tend to be more self-effacing or to underestimate their competence (Cole et al., 1999; Dweck, 2007b; Miller et al., 1996). It is possible, then, that my male respondents genuinely thought they were better, while the female respondents genuinely thought they were weaker, although their different perceptions may not be mirrored by differences in proficiency.

Interestingly, there was no significant gender difference in the declared mark they usually got in English, which may support this second explanation as to why boys' L2 private selves were stronger. Some authors (Dweck, 1999; Furrer & Skinner, 2003; Hansen & O'Leary, 1985) maintain that girls tend to underestimate themselves especially in competitive environments, which do not welcome their alleged propensity for cooperation, communication and relatedness. As we have seen, my research site is an environment where students do not feel appreciated personally and/or prefer to hide their 'real' identity, concentrating instead on obtaining high marks and displaying whatever identity brings the most benefits in the classroom. Cooperation was not salient, especially that numerous interviewees claimed they hardly ever did any projects and worked in teams with their classmates. Instead, as many said, everybody followed their own interest, celebrating each other's mistakes and prospects of not going to university so they could appear better by comparison. It would be hard to comment on gender differences in the perceptions of my interviewees, but two of the girls (*Soare* and *080081*) believed that there was so much competition in their group precisely because they were never encouraged to work on projects collaboratively. They also mentioned that some of the classmates with whom they had been involved in projects in the past were now among their best friends.

Many authors have shown that gender differences in the classroom often originate in the teachers' differential responses to boys and girls, the consensus being that boys insist on and are given greater attention by the teacher (Sunderland, 2004; Swann, 1992), that teachers respond more to boys, both to praise and to reprimand them (Jones & Dindia, 2004; Merrett & Wheldall, 1992), that boys talk more in the classroom, both to teachers and in group work (Dart & Clarke, 1988; Swann & Graddol, 1994), boys are asked more questions, especially more challenging questions, and are given more instructions (Kelly, 1988), boys are reprimanded more because they tend to be more disruptive than girls (Delamont, 1990). The result is that, overall, boys receive more attention and more speaking time in the classroom. If this happened in English classes at my five Romanian schools, the boys' stronger L2 private selves could be explained through extra opportunities for practice and, therefore, better chances of improved proficiency. Nevertheless, we have seen that my participants felt they hardly ever got a chance to speak in the English class, that the teacher spoke most of the time, and sometimes only in Romanian. But even if my male participants had not improved their English skills through more speaking opportunities in class, they could still have improved their perceived competence by receiving extra attention from the teacher. This is sometimes called the 'Matthew effect' in the literature, from the Biblical parable which says that the rich will get richer and the poor will get poorer – an effect which has been shown to contribute to individual differences in the classroom (Lamb, 2011; Stanovich, 1986; Walberg & Tsai, 1983). My data support this interpretation, suggesting that more teacher appreciation is associated with higher perceived competence, whereas less teacher interest is associated with less love of English in the boys from two schools. Although there was no gender difference in the boys' and the girls' interest in the English class, overall boys felt more appreciated as individuals by the teacher), although the effect size was not great (see Table 6.3).

Identity Display

In Chapter 4 it was hypothesised that adolescents would tend to display particular public selves in response to perceived imposed selves, and that these would differ from one relational context to another. Based on the literature and on my experience as a teacher and student, four main relational contexts were expected to have an impact on language learners' identity: their language teacher, their classmates, their best friends and their families. Indeed, not only were my participants' public selves correlated highly and significantly with their imposed selves, but the correlations between their L2 public selves and their L2 private selves were minimal. The interviews confirmed the statistical results and offered valuable insights into the reasons and mechanism of this context-dependent self-presentation. In terms of similarity and difference between relational contexts, on the one hand, the teacher was very similar to the family in that they both generated very high public and imposed selves, whereas classmates and friends gave rise to similarly low public and imposed selves. On the other hand, the teacher was very similar to the classmates in inspiring most of my respondents to choose the duplicitous self system, while for the family and friends a large majority chose the harmonious self system.

Five important insights follow from these findings, supporting the inference that differential (strategic) identity display is frequent in the research context studied:

- There is little relationship between one's private and public selves.
- Public selves are directly proportional to their respective imposed selves.
- Significant others exert different, context-dependent, types of influence on the adolescents' identity.
- There seems to be a distinction between English-as-an-academic-subject (part of students' 'professional' lives at school) and English-as-a-communication-tool (part of their personal lives).

Table 6.4 Correlation matrix for the main self variables (boys below the dashed diagonal, girls above the dashed diagonal)

Pearson correlations (N = 1045, pairwise deletion)	1	2	3	4	5	6	7	8	9	10
1. L2 private self	–	0.59**	0.28**	0.14**	0.20**	0.19**	0.13**	ns	0.12**	0.13**
2. L2 ideal self	0.44**	–	0.32**	0.20**	0.30**	0.34**	0.21**	0.10*	0.27**	0.43**
3. L2 public self – teacher	0.20**	0.33**	–	0.39**	0.47**	0.72**	0.52**	0.23**	0.29**	0.43**
4. L2 public self – classmates	ns	0.25**	0.43**	–	0.65**	0.44**	0.29**	0.69**	0.44**	0.31**
5. L2 public self – friends	0.16**	0.35**	0.42**	0.77**	–	0.62**	0.32**	0.48**	0.73**	0.47**
6. L2 public self – family	0.14*	0.34**	0.65**	0.53**	0.58**	–	0.42**	0.29**	0.45**	0.66**
7. L2 imposed self – teacher	0.12*	0.30**	0.56**	0.26**	0.20**	0.33**	–	0.36**	0.39**	0.52**
8. L2 imposed self – classmates	ns	0.17**	0.31**	0.70**	0.55**	0.40**	0.40**	–	0.59**	0.34**
9. L2 imposed self – friends	ns	0.32**	0.37**	0.54**	0.66**	0.40**	0.43**	0.69**	–	0.52**
10. L2 imposed self – family	ns	0.46**	0.41**	0.39**	0.42**	0.63**	0.53**	0.42**	0.52**	–

**Correlation is significant at the 0.001 level (2-tailed). *Correlation is significant at the 0.05 level (2-tailed).
ns = non significant

• Identity perceptions have important implications for declared achievement.

These insights will be discussed in the next five sections, supported by evidence and linked to the background literature, where relevant.

Private versus public perceptions in language learning

Table 6.4 presents the correlations between the main self variables measure in the questionnaire. (For the imposed self, which measured perceptions about the present and about the future, the overall mean value is included in this analysis. Likewise, the private self is represented by the overall mean, incorporating all four sub-scales.) Although boys and girls had similar declared perceptions, these correlations are presented separately for each gender (boys below the dashed diagonal, girls above the diagonal), to illustrate some interesting, albeit minor, differences. For example, we can see there is no relationship between what girls believe about themselves as language learners (private self) and the type of person their classmates would like them to be with regards to language learning (imposed self – classmates). This is also the case for boys, although in their case we can also see that what they believe privately about themselves as language learners is also unrelated to what they show their classmates publicly and to what their friends and families would like them to be with respect to English language learning. It is possible that this gender difference may indicate a closer link between social expectations and self beliefs for girls, possibly reinforcing the stereotype that 'girls do languages'. However, such inferences cannot be based on correlational data.

Although other minor differences can be seen between the two genders (alternate cells greyed out for ease of comparison on the diagonal), it is clear that both girls and boys respond publicly to the identity imposed on them in the four relational contexts. That is, the correlations between the public self and the imposed self are high and very high, in social sciences terms (from $r = 0.52$ for girls in the teacher relational context, to $r = 0.73$ in the girls' friends relational context). These correlations, all significant, show clearly a strong relationship between what participants feel is expected of them and what they display publicly in their social interactions. This will be discussed in more detail in the section below.

One crucial insight that these correlations facilitate, however, is that there is little connection between the selves that these students show publicly in response of the selves imposed on them socially and what they actually believe about themselves as language learners. This crucial difference can be seen more clearly in Figure 6.1.

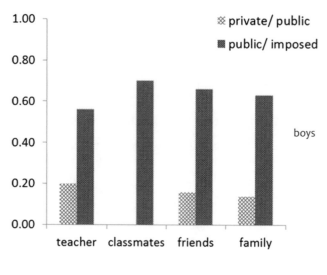

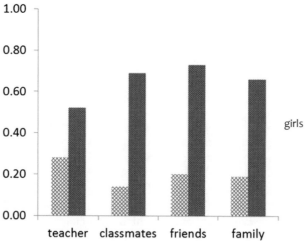

Figure 6.1 L2 public/private and public/imposed correlations by gender and relational context

Figure 6.1 is a graphical representation of two types of correlations: between the participants' private self and their public self (light bars), and the correlation between their public selves and imposed selves (dark bars) in each relational context, separately for the two genders. The small private/ public correlations (light bar) indicate a tendency for participants to hide their private beliefs in social interaction, or to give impressions that they personally think are not part of their private self. It is interesting to note that, for boys, there is no correlation whatsoever between what they believe about themselves and what they show their classmates about themselves as English language learners. In stark opposition, the relationship between the public selves that these students display and the perceived imposed self is very strong in all relational contexts (strongest of all for friends and class-mates), for both genders. This is an indication that students participating in this project resort to identity display that serves them best (e.g. showing their teachers and family that they are academically engaged and interested, while displaying the expected academic disaffection in their peer interac-tions, as seen in Table 6.1), all this being very different from what they believe about themselves as English language learners.

This difference may show that my participants feel the need for social approval, which determines them to display an identity that may not neces-sarily be their own in order to acquire a particular social status (Covington, 1992; Leary, 1995; Leary & Kowalski, 1990). Given that my research context can be considered a high-competition/low-achievement motivation environ-ment, performance orientations seem to have superseded learning orienta-tions (Elliott & Dweck, 1988; Meece et al., 2006; Miller et al., 1996). What matters, therefore, is that one appears to have particular characteristics, whether or not one truly has them being less important. There are indications that such discrepancies between a student's 'real' identity and a school-imposed identity act as barriers to academic engagement and well-being (Phelan et al., 1993; Wortham, 2006) and it has been suggested that such identity conflicts may be more to blame for poor achievement than lack of ability or skills (Klos, 2006).

Public selves directly related to imposed selves

We have seen in Table 6.1 that the teacher and the family had high L2 learning expectations of my participants, whereas the expectations of their classmates and friends were quite low. However, the correlation between the public self and the imposed self was very high (in social-science terms) for all four relational contexts, namely a high imposed self was related to a high public self, and a low imposed self to a low public self (Table 6.4, Figure 6.1). While it is not possible on the basis of the data available to know whether this correlation implies causation and, if it does, what its direction is, this relates well to the impression management literature, which shows how the audience determines the salience of a particular public self in a particular social context (Leary, 1995; Schlenker, 2003; Schlenker & Weigold, 1992).

This confirms the hypothesis that individuals tend to display a self that they feel is expected of them in a given relational context, even though this public self may be unrelated to their private self beliefs. This echoes Juvonen's results (Juvonen, 1996; Juvonen & Murdock, 1993), who found that school children presented themselves as eager but unable to the teacher, as they believed the teacher would be more sympathetic and supportive as a result, while presenting themselves as able but disengaged to their peers, thinking this would reinforce their image of 'cool' teenagers who do not need to work hard. In foreign language learning, similar strategic identity display in peer interactions was found, for example, by Williams et al. (2002) and Bartram (2006a). However, comparing the selves displayed in several relational contexts – between them, as well as to private self perceptions – and identifying clear differences between what individuals believe about themselves and what they display in response to social expectations does not seem to have been done before in language learning research. The same quantitative instrument and theoretical model described in this book were also recently used in a large European study with 4409 student and teacher participants from Bulgaria, Germany, the Netherlands and Spain (Taylor et al., 2013), with very similar results, which provided further validation for this model. The cross-sectional European study, which explored identity perceptions in the learning and teaching of English as a foreign language and Mathematics (a control subject), identified the same pattern in student identity dynamics: low correlations between what individuals thought of themselves as English/ Maths learners and the selves they displayed publicly; and high correlations between the selves that they displayed in social interaction and the selves that they perceived as imposed on them in the main relational contexts with which they interacted (teachers, peers, families).

Context-dependent influences on adolescents' identity

We have seen above that, depending on the analytical perspective take, the four relational contexts cluster in two different ways, indicating that the influence they may have on adolescents' identity is context-dependent. From the point of view of self systems, Figure 5.1 showed that teachers are similar to classmates, in that they are associated with the highest frequency of duplicitous self systems. This was in opposition to friends and families, who were associated with the highest incidence of harmonious self systems. The distinction showed that the participants tended to display an identity they thought was expected of them at school, while at home they felt free and encouraged to be 'themselves' (academic vs. personal identity domains).

However, when focusing on the expectations originating in the four relational contexts and the identity display these trigger, we have seen (Table 6.1) that the four interactions cluster in a different way: teachers and families are associated with high L2 imposed selves, which are mirrored by high L2 public selves in interaction with the two, whereas friends and classmates were associated with low L2 imposed selves and low public selves.

These context-dependent identity processes are also suggested by the interviewees' profiles (Appendix F), where the complexities of interacting on four different levels and juggling with different expectations and perceptions are evident. This is in accordance with the literature showing that different relational contexts influence adolescents in different ways (Harter, 1996; Harte *et al.*, 1998; Lempers & Clark-Lempers, 1992; Phelan *et al.*, 1993) and is, again, a perspectives that has hardly been taken in foreign language research before.

English-as-an-academic-subject versus English-as-a-communication-tool

A trend that is visible in Table 6.1 above is that the L2 imposed selves for the future are always lower than the imposed selves for the present (all statistically significant, $p < 0.001$, paired-sample t-tests, with very large effect sizes for teachers and parents). This can be taken as an indication that, although the teacher and the family wanted my participants to be good language learners in the present, they were less concerned with the role that English might play in their future. (Less concern with the future is also present in the friends and classmates' relational contexts, but the differences are smaller.) This may suggest that English was considered simply an academic subject that one had to study in order to graduate before moving on to more personally relevant pursuits. Friends' indifference to one's English learning at school may be another indication: many interviewees highlighted that their best friends knew them very well and appreciated them for 'what they really were', therefore one might surmise that, had the English class been part of 'what they really were', their friends would have been more involved. Several interviewees confirmed this bivalent view of the foreign language, stressing that they loved English but not the English class, while others declared that they did not feel the English class helped them develop communicative skills but they had learned the language through genuine communication in their own free time. Although in a totally different cultural context, this result echoes S. Ryan's (2009) analysis of English language teaching in Japanese secondary schools, which was found to be purely instrumental, with no sustainable communicative function. Similar findings are also reported by Taylor (2012), who found that many of her Year 9 learners of Modern Foreign Languages in English maintained schools loved learning languages for their communicative and personal development value but had reservations about the teaching methodology and assessment used in their language classes at school. Even when becoming much more enthusiastic about language learning as a result of listening to external speakers describe their everyday experiences of using – or desperately needing – foreign languages, many of these teenagers still refused to choose a language GCSE (General Certificate of Secondary Education) as they did not like the way these were taught in class, in their experience.

Implications for learning achievement

If students' public selves are in close relation with their imposed selves, it follows that identity conflicts will, at times, be inevitable. We have seen that such accounts surfaced in the interviews, when probing and follow-up opportunities revealed the stress that teenagers have to face at times when they are in the same situation with both their parents and friends, with their friends and classmates, or with their classmates and teachers. (No mention was made of such a situation involving one's parents and teacher, but as these two relational contexts generate similarly strong public and imposed academic selves, conflicts may be less likely to occur.) My participants did not imply that these situations were characterised by tension or strong negative feelings, but they did speak about the care needed to balance several public selves so as to ensure that the good will of all parties involved was maintained. Although it would be hard to generalise, such identity conflicts seemed to occur particularly in situations when the student could not reveal what they believed was their 'real' identity.

A serious complication of differential identity display and of the discrepancy between one's private and public selves appears in the context that is most relevant for this project: the classroom. *Pinty* (M, 16) explained in no ambiguous terms how doing 'your duty as a student' in class entailed conflicts with the classmates, who would turn against one for betraying them and their initial agreement that nobody would bother about the teacher. This is what Van Hook and Higgins (1988: 625) called the 'chronic double approach-avoidance conflict' appearing when somebody has several conflicting imposed selves (or rather *ought selves*, in their terminology), and which results in feelings of being 'muddled, indecisive, distractible, unsure of self or goals, rebellious, confused about identity'. The tension that sometimes arises when students straddle different relational contexts with divergent expectations has also been documented by Phelan and her colleagues (Phelan *et al.*, 1991, 1993, 1994), who showed that this could have debilitating effects on the academic engagement and socio-emotional functioning of their Californian high-school students. They found that excessive pressure to achieve academically (from teachers or parents) led to 'learning to play the game' rather than 'learning to learn', an emphasis on marks and competition affecting students' intrinsic motivation to participate in classroom activities. While teachers and parents often represented sources of tension through excessive emphasis on academic achievement, friends provided understanding support and release from pressure. However, friends could also be the source of a different type of pressure: that to engage in behaviours that adults would not condone, like truancy, drinking, or excessive partying. Nevertheless, when the different relational contexts that students were involved in were congruent and the transition from one to the other was smooth, they enjoyed a balanced, well-adjusted, academic and social life. Although in a very different cultural context and with a very different approach to the investigation, my results appear to confirm Phelan and her colleagues' findings to a considerable extent.

Questionnaire respondents were also asked for the average mark they normally achieve in English. Although the Romanian marking system ranges, theoretically, from 1 to 10, with a minimum pass mark of 5, no respondent declared a mark below 5. The responses were recoded into a three-category nominal variable, for which the following response percentages were found: satisfactory (marks 5–6) 5.5%, good (marks 7–8) 41.3% and excellent (marks 9–10) 53.2. Being a measure of declared rather than actual achievement, these marks must, of course, be treated cautiously. It is rare for a student to fail in foreign languages in Romania, but an overall average mark of 8.48 (SD 1.16) is probably a bit too high to be taken too seriously. Nevertheless, an interesting pattern emerges. As shown in Figure 6.2, a harmonious self system in the teacher relational context is associated with the highest percentage of excellent results and the lowest percentage of satisfactory marks, whereas the lowest percentage of excellent results appears in the submissive category (Chi square significant at the $p < 0.05$ level). This is an indication that the students who feel appreciated as individuals in their interaction with the teacher are more likely to have excellent results in English – or, indeed, that students who achieve excellent results are more likely to feel appreciated and encouraged to develop as individuals in the English class (see the self system descriptions in Appendix E). The fact that students who chose the duplicitous and rebellious self systems for the teacher were more likely to achieve excellent than good/ satisfactory results could indicate a tendency for these participants to study autonomously when they disapprove of the classroom teaching methodology, to improve their English outside the classroom or perhaps a tendency for the students who feel duplicitous or rebellious in class to claim higher results than

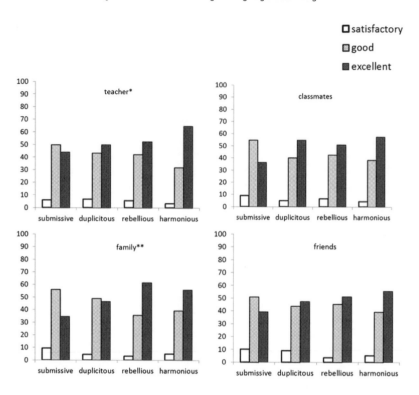

Figure 6.2 L2 declared achievement by self system in four relational contexts (teacher sig. $p < 0.05$; family sig. $p < 0.001$)

it may be the case in order to maintain their self-worth in what may be seen as a conflicting teacher-student relationship.

Figure 6.2 also shows that participants who chose the submissive self system for their family were more likely to have good, rather than excellent, results in English, the highest percentage of satisfactory marks also being recorded in this category (Chi square significant at the $p < 0.001$ level). Just like in the teacher self system, this may suggest that teenagers who comply with their families' (or teachers') guidance unquestioningly and follow their parents' advice although they would personally prefer a different course of action class (see the self system descriptions in Appendix E) do not do so well in English than the other categories of respondents. Interestingly, the participants who chose the rebellious self system for their family appear to have the best declared results, which may be linked with the apparent tendency discussed above, for parents (and teachers) to encourage English language study for the present but less so for the future. Many interviewees mentioned that their parents steered them in more lucrative professional directions (e.g. Law, Medicine) than a career to do with languages, so respondents who really love English and are good at it may have to disregard their parents' career guidance in order to follow their desired path.

The interaction of classmates' and friends' relational contexts with the participants' declared achievement in English was not statistically significant, but it is rather telling that the lowest percentage of excellent results were associated with the submissive self system in these two settings. In the context of friends and peers, where we have seen that academic expectations are much lower than in other relational contexts, a student who follows external guidance disregarding their own academic goals would perhaps be expected to do less well than a student who follows their own goals or who interacts with academically engaged peer groups.

These are important interactions, which show that the way students feel in class does have a bearing on their declared results. Significantly (both statistically, $p < 0.001$, and practically), the teacher self system also interacts with the main self perception variables: the L2 private self and L2 ideal self, as well as the respondents' perceptions of the English class (feelings of interest & personal relevance, and feelings of being appreciated as an individual) – see Figure 6.3.

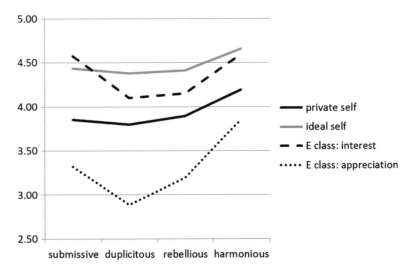

Figure 6.3 L2 perceptions in the teacher self system (MANOVA sig. $p < 0.001$; range 1–6, except for ideal self: 1–5)

As the teacher is regarded as the most decisive factor in the classroom (Birch & Ladd, 1996; Harter, 1996, 2012), the results presented in Figure 6.3 are critical, as they show that students who feel submissive or harmonious in their interactions with the teacher declare the highest L2 private self, L2 ideal self, interest in the English class and feelings of individual appreciation by the teacher – the harmonious self system being associated with the highest values. Combined with the results above, this is quite possibly the first empirical connection between identity perceptions and foreign language learning achievement. The validity of these inferences, and of the model itself, was strengthened by the fact that very similar evidence was found in the larger cross-sectional project that used participants from four European countries, referred to earlier (Taylor *et al.*, 2013).

More results emphasising the crucial role of the teacher in the classroom are discussed in the next chapter.

7 Of Students and Teachers

Although it is clear to everyone that the teacher has a tremendous influence in class, not much research has previously documented the complex identity negotiations that students have to engage in when interacting with the teacher and the potential that these negotiations have to help students adopt language learning, as a self-defining goal, into their identity. This chapter presents evidence to this effect, discussing the quandaries of being 'oneself' in the English class when the dominant ethos is assessment-oriented, as well as the potential of teacher engagement to inspire student engagement in class. The largely overlooked potential for internalisation of language learning into the student identity is also discussed.

To Be or Not to be 'Yourself' in the English Class

One of the most important findings of this project was that few of the participants declared they felt appreciated personally in the English class – with the corollary that they did not feel they could disclose their 'real' selves to their teacher or classmates. The extent to which they felt appreciated was much lower than their declared interest in the class, and several interviewees explained that they had initially tried to communicate with the teacher genuinely, only to realise that it was always safer to 'do their duty' and pretend they agreed even when they did not. Of the four self system types, most students chose the duplicitous one for their English teacher and classmates, while for their friends and families a large majority chose the harmonious self system. Both the quantitative and the qualitative data indicated the existence of a clear barrier between the classroom environment and the after-school environment that seemed to communicate the necessity of a 'professional' identity display in the former, whereas being 'yourself' and feeling appreciated for it was reserved for the latter. This entailed a distinction between the English class and the English language: while many participants had an affinity with the language and wished to be proficient speakers of it, few seemed to consider the English class part of their true self.

More importantly, the students' self systems had a significant interaction with their declared proficiency levels. Whereas students who chose the duplicitous self system for the teacher (52.5% of the 1045 respondents) had the lowest values for all components of the English private self, those who felt harmonious with the English teacher – implying, among other aspects, that their 'true' self was known and valued in class – had the highest scores on all components of the English private self, learning orientation, interest and appreciation in the English class, as well as the highest internal attributions for success. In addition, students who chose the harmonious self for the teacher also had stronger English ideal selves and higher declared marks. These two types of students are reminiscent of the categories described by Carl Rogers (Rogers & Freiberg, 1994): classroom citizens and classroom tourists. Rogers' theory – later supported with more recent research findings by Jerome Freiberg – indicates that students who can be themselves in the classroom and feel valued for what they are by a caring and interested teacher become responsible citizens (or 'stakeholders') who take an active and personal interest in their learning process and community. Research has shown that they learn more, are more creative and exhibit stronger problem-solving skills. By contrast, students who work with bored and indifferent teachers learn to be bored and indifferent themselves. These are like tourists who do not take an active responsible interest in classroom activities – 'never involved, never excited, never chosen … simply here [in the classroom]' (Rogers & Freiberg, 1994: 9).

My participants also declared that when they could not be themselves in class they did not get involved genuinely and only invested enough effort to give the impression they were on task. This confirms the results obtained by Rollett (1985, 1987) and Taylor (2008), who found that low levels of autonomy support in class were associated with high levels of avoidance motivation and misleading identity display, as well as truancy and a wide range of escapist behaviours that students resorted to in order to regain autonomy in the classroom. These findings also corroborate the evidence found by Harter (e.g. 1992) to indicate a strong link between intrinsic reasons for learning and increased perceived competence, through the mediation of positive affect. Preference for challenge was an associated factor in Harter's findings, and this resonates well with my interviewees' declarations: the disaffected ones felt that more challenge in the English class would determine them to engage more, while those who found challenge and appreciation in class declared high levels of engagement and perceived competence.

The link between intrinsic reasons for learning and increased perceived competence has also been documented extensively by the self-determination literature (Deci & Moller, 2005; Deci & Ryan, 1992; Noels *et al.*, 2000; Reeve & Jang, 2006). However, self-determination theory postulates that increased perceived competence results if the other two basic human needs – autonomy and social relatedness – are fulfilled. Given that most of my participants felt they could not afford to be themselves in the English class and they were not appreciated for what they were as individuals – either by the teacher or by their peers – it is evident that their need for relatedness was not fulfilled at school. The same seems to be the case with their need for autonomy, as few participants felt they had a say in the organisation of the lessons. As such, it is not surprising that the English class did not seem to have much impact on the perceived competence of the students who had intrinsic reasons for learning the language in their own time.

My participants' precarious level of self-determination is also suggested by their cognitive attributional patterns. As we have seen in the previous chapter, there was a tendency to internalise the causes of failure and exter- nalise the causes of success, which follows naturally from their perceived lack of autonomy and choice in a context where success means high marks (which do not always match the students' competence level). Thus, when these stu- dents do well in English, they explain their success through external uncon- trollable factors (i.e. 'luck', or the teacher's benevolence), whereas when they do not they explain it through lack of ability of effort, as reinforced over and over in the interviews. This is the attributional pattern associated in the lit- erature with learnt helplessness, a condition which has been proved to impair performance even in the case of high ability and high effort (Burhans & Dweck, 1995; Jarvis & Seifert, 2002; Peterson *et al.*, 1993; Seligman, 1992). As attribution theorists explain, helplessness leads to low achievement motiva- tion and self-handicapping, whereby effort is withdrawn in an attempt to restore ability perceptions (Covington, 1992; Rhodewalt & Hill, 1995; Weiner, 2005). Other authors have shown that lack of control over one's learning outcomes impairs academic performance (e.g. Stipek & Weisz, 1981) and that a high self-concept leads to internal attributions for success, which in turn strengthen one's self-concept, the same mutual reinforcement principle deter- mining a low self-concept to internalise causes of failure, especially in com- petitive environments (Ames, 1992; Ames & Archer, 1988).

Whereas in the absence of certain relevant measures it is not possible to infer that these explanations are unquestionably valid for the present project, they do help clarify the academic consequences of not being a fully function- ing autonomous agent in the classroom, as well as the crucial link between internal attributions for success and a strong L2 private self. Other research- ers investigating foreign language learning have indeed found that perceived control over the learning process and personal relevance led to more learning engagement and more positive results (Comănaru & Noels, 2009; Landry *et al.*, 2009; Noels *et al.*, 2006; Taylor, 2008, 2012). The attributional tendency resulting from my data – internal attributions for failure, external attributions for success – is in exact opposition to the attributional pattern that Ushioda (1996a, 1998) identified in her academically successful participants: she found that external attributions for failure and internal attributions for success were related to a positive self-concept, which, in turn, led to higher academic achievement. However, the external attributional cues that my participants used to gauge their success in the foreign language class corroborate Williams and Burden's (1999) findings, whose English adolescent participants learning French as a foreign language in the UK judged their success by the teacher's approval and the marks they received, without much awareness of communicative skills development.

We have seen that most of my participants felt duplicitous in their classroom interactions, and many interviewees talked about the 'duty' they had as students, or the 'role' they had to play, or the 'image' or 'face' they had to show, which they thought was expected of them. As some of them explained, this involved attending classes; doing homework (although sometimes by simply copying 'the answers' from a classmate or from the end of the book) or pretending to have done it; looking interested – but not too interested, as *Sophie* (F, 15) quickly added; agreeing with the teacher or pretending to; declaring they would pursue a certain university degree even when they knew for sure they would not; hiding their hobbies and declaring others that they thought the teacher would approve of; even sitting 'correctly' at their desks, in some cases. Many believed that this would guarantee the teacher's friendship and, with it, safe marks and a carefree school life (language proficiency and skill development appearing to be less important by comparison). Marks, it turns out, were the nub of the entire ethos in my research context, as many participants explained.

A Reward-centred Ethos

Almost all of the 32 interviewees mentioned marks without being prompted, and when *FC* (M, 15) said that marks were 'the only thing that matters' he expressed a view held by many. If students do not feel appreciated as individuals in the English class and lessons are often irrelevant for their future, caring about marks appears as a natural part of what many of them called 'my duty as a student'. The English class may not be part of what they really are or of what they would like to become, but it is a curriculum component that they need to pass in order to graduate. I did not ask explicitly for a definition of 'passing', but all evidence would indicate that in my chosen research context it means simply getting a certain mark, sometimes with little relevance for the student's actual competence in English. This interpretation is supported by the fact that the mean value of their declared mark in the questionnaire was 8.48 (out of 10 – the minimum pass mark being normally 5) and yet most of the interviewees emphasised that the English class did not provide opportunities for much skill development. Another interpretation may again be that their perceived competence originates outside the classroom, where language skills are honed through genuine communication on social networking sites and so on, or indeed that most of my participants had an intriguing tendency to exaggerate their formal achievement in English. (It is, of course, also possible that their marks were an accurate representation of their competence and that they learnt very much from their English lessons even if they declared they did not.)

As generalised a practice as it is on an international scale, it is known that marks, like any other form of contingent reward, undermine students' intrinsic motivation to learn through the so-called overjustification effect (Lepper & Henderlong, 2000): an activity that is intrinsically pleasing loses its appeal when we are rewarded for performing it, as the extrinsic incentive becomes more salient than the intrinsic one (Deci & Ryan, 1985). Although some authors have contested the detrimental effects of extrinsic incentives, there is overwhelming evidence to show that an emphasis on assessment and marks has negative consequences for students' intrinsic motivation and learning engagement (Deci et al., 1999; Kohn, 1993; Lepper & Greene, 1978; Lepper, 1983; Ryan & Deci, 2000; Vansteenkiste & Deci, 2003). While external incentives – whether good marks, gold stars, praise and so on – can motivate students to act in the short term, when the incentive is withdrawn, the motivated behaviour ceases. The more incentives are given, the more they are needed (Kohn, 1993), as they become the reason why the respective behaviour is maintained. Furthermore, it has been demonstrated that incentives impair conceptual learning and can only produce immediate rote memorisation – which is also lost to a greater extent if rooted in extrinsic incentives, compared to intrinsic motivators (Deci & Ryan, 1985).

One of the most serious problems associated with marks and other external incentives, however, is that these are instruments for controlling people's behaviour (Deci & Ryan, 1985; Kohn, 1993). It is behaviourism in its purest sense: do this and you will get that; work hard and you will get a high mark; behave nicely and I will let you pass. (Pretend to) agree with the teachers and they will be your friends – as some of my interviewees believed. In such a context, all the control is in the teacher's hands and it is the teacher and the teacher alone who decides what is acceptable and what is not in the classroom. From all the data that I have discussed so far, it is quite clear that my Romanian participants were quick to learn the game. If being themselves in class did not bring them the expected friendship and appreciation, as several of them declared, they learnt that if they pretended to agree, to be interested, to work 'hard, but not too hard', they were safe.

Smith (1986: 82–83) offers a rather unflattering explanation of incentives (i.e. marks, praise, bonuses) as compensation for poor teaching, which prevents learning from being intrinsically rewarding:

> The underlying implication of 'learning should be fun' is that learning *will be* a painful and tedious activity unless it is primped up as entertainment. Learning is never aversive – usually we are not aware of it at all. It is failure to learn that is frustrating and boring, and so is having to attend to nonsensical activities . . . . It is meaningless teaching, not learning, that demands irrelevant incentives. (emphasis in the original)

In his book *Punished by Rewards: The trouble with gold stars, incentive plans, A's, praise and other bribes*, Kohn (1993) explains that it is not the marks themselves that are the problem, but the way they are used and the messages that they give to pupils – whether they draw their attention to what they are doing or how they are doing it. Dweck (e.g. 1999, 2007a) and other authors describe this as learning orientation versus performance orientation: are students preoccupied to increase their ability or to show that they are more able than others? Marsh (Marsh *et al.*, 2004; Marsh, 1990b) describes it in terms of internal frame of reference versus external frame of reference: is the student better at English than other subjects, or is the student better at English than other students? Deci and Ryan (e.g. 1985) explain it in terms of informative versus controlling feedback (the former – constructive and empowering, the latter – restrictive and distrustful). Many of my interviewees mentioned bad marks being given for bad behaviour or as a form of revenge and punishment, while good marks were given as a prize, as an incentive to work harder, so as not to spoil the student's final average or as a biased token of recognition for the teacher's private tutees. Such feedback could hardly be considered informative, as it does not give the students any clue as to how they could improve their skills, or what their strengths and weaknesses are. As we have seen, their helpless attributional pattern indicates they do not feel much in control of their academic outcomes. When they do well, they explain it through uncontrollable external causes – when they do not do very well, they blame themselves for it, internalising the guilt and shame. Williams and Burden (1999) found a somewhat similar situation with their British learners of French, who did not seem aware of their skill development and gauged their academic success entirely by marks and the teacher's opinion. This led the two authors to conclude that French was taught like any other school subject, with little importance granted to understanding or effective communication in the foreign language. Several other researchers found that students used marks as the main indicator of progress and competence (Blumenfeld *et al.*, 1986; Butler, 1988, 1989; Sansone & Morgan, 1992).

In such a reward-centred environment, it is fairly clear that the teacher, who controls the marks, controls all these mechanisms in the classroom. Discussing the teacher's role in such processes, Kohn (1993: 221) reminds us:

> Every teacher who is told what material to cover, when to cover it, and how to evaluate children's performance is a teacher who knows that enthusiasm for one's work quickly evaporates in the face of control. Not every teacher, however, realizes that exactly the same is true of students: deprive children of self-determination and you deprive them of motivation. If learning is a matter of following orders, students simply will not take to it in the way they would if they had some say about what they were doing.

This quotation encapsulates two important facts: that teachers themselves are caught in a network of strong imposed selves and hidden private selves that may not be fully appreciated for what they really are (Taylor *et al.*, 2013), resulting in very possible identity display; and that, despite frequent institutional constraints, it still depends largely on the teacher to make learning personally meaningful for students (Taylor, 2010). As Ciani, Middleton, Summers and Sheldon (2010) found, an autonomy-supportive teacher who encourages a community spirit in the classroom can even attenuate the effects of performance orientations typical of a deeply rooted competitive ethos.

From Interested Teachers to Interested Students

Most of my interviewees thought the teacher had the power to motivate them more, in one way or another. Although this may mirror the helpless thought pattern of youth who feel that the teacher holds the key to their positive or negative academic outcomes, it also confirms a significant body of literature emphasising the crucial role that a teacher can have in students' classroom engagement and academic itinerary. In addition, not just helpless students thought this. Harmonious and balanced people who felt competent and happy in the English class thought they would feel more motivated to invest in the lessons if the teacher could make these more personally relevant to them. Measuring their engagement precisely was not among the objectives of this project, and it would clearly be hard to do it in a reliable way. But where the context facilitated it, students were asked in the interview how much they thought they invested in the class out of their total potential. While a few happy ones gave percentages as high as 90%, many giggled and admitted to utilising 40%, 10% or even 5% of their perceived potential.

It was one of the interviews' leitmotifs that, if teachers knew what motivated students personally, what passions and interests energised them, what made them feel 'themselves' in or out of school, then teachers could incorporate this information into lessons and make them more personally meaningful, relevant and engaging. We have seen *Airforce's* (M, 17) strong opinion of this, whose slightly jarring manipulation-focused discourse might reflect the mores of his speech community. *Airforce* – harmonious with the English teacher – explained:

> I've always tried to be very open and very honest in the English class. So my teacher knows all my good and bad sides. She knows what I'm up to, what sort of personality I've got ... In the first place, she can be a better pedagogue through this. If she knows what motivates the pupil, she can use this as a weapon – in a good sense. So she can motivate that pupil by knowing his personality. And I think that's what every teacher should do: try to know the pupil's personality and then try to ... manipulate that personality in a very good direction, or at least a good one. And I think this would motivate any pupil.

Another young man (*418353*, 19) thought this was the key to removing the 'communication wall' that he felt prevented students and teachers from genuine interaction:

> [If I were a teacher] I'd try to remove that wall I was talking about. I'd try to understand ... to find their desire ... to see where it comes from. And maybe to channel it in a certain way. If you've got the desire you can change a lot of things.

Unwittingly, this student almost quoted Kohn (1993: 226): 'We *can* get children hooked on learning – if that is really what we are determined to do.' (emphasis in the original)

Of course, the prerequisite is that both students and teachers are interested in genuine engagement, communication and mutual understanding.

However, we saw in the previous chapter that the situation may be quite different in my research context. A statistically significant effect showed that students felt they were considerably more interested in the English class, than teachers were in the students as real persons, the two correlating quite highly. This shows that students' interest and teacher's interest are directly proportional – a statistical result that found solid support in the interviews, most students declaring that if the teacher is interested and appreciates them as real persons, then they are more interested in the class themselves (7.2). *Kiddo* (F, 14), we have seen, presented the negative side of this correlation:

> We don't learn the lesson from the classroom, which is very bad! (...) You go home to learn a lesson which maybe you're sick of, because maybe you're sick of the teacher ... That's what usually happens: when you don't like a teacher, you don't like the subject they teach either.

The implication is dramatic: if, on the one hand, the teacher is genuinely interested in the students, this increases the students' interest and engagement too; on the other hand, if the teacher has not managed to bond with the students for one reason or another, this may diminish the students' interest and affective propensities for the subject they teach. The beginning of *Kiddo*'s quote is also essential, as she made a direct link between failure to learn in the classroom and not liking the teacher, therefore not liking the subject. The need for student autonomy could not be greater here. It is obvious that not every teacher will be liked by every student at all times, but if students are autonomous and understand that they are learning for themselves, not for the teacher, then the relationship between not liking the teacher and not liking the subject would be considerably weaker. This would also happen with less emphasis on marks (i.e. a product) and more emphasis on learning (i.e. a process). If students are genuinely interested in improving their skills, they would be more inclined to make the best of every learning situation – including, perhaps, a teacher they may dislike at first.

Whether students focus on products or processes depends, once again, on the teacher in no small measure. We have seen that the teachers' communicative style in the classroom and the type of feedback they normally give can make all the difference. Just like with marks, rewards, and any other event, it is important whether the message is informative or controlling. Even praise – criticised for its potential to orient children towards social comparison and performance rather than mastery (Dweck, 2007c; Mueller & Dweck, 1998) – can be informative or controlling. The difference between 'you've done well' and 'you've done well, as you should' is the crucial difference in locus of control: said to a student, 'you've done well' means I am appreciating you for your efforts and I am pleased to see you are making progress, whereas 'you've done well, as you should' means you are managing to raise to my expectations, which set the limits for how much you can develop (Deci & Ryan, 1985; Reeve & Jang, 2006).

We have seen that my Romanian participants tended to show helpless attributions for success and failure, and that the marks they get tell them little about their actual competence in English. We have also seen that they have little say in the organisation of the lessons and that they hardly ever feel they can be themselves in class. It is not hard to understand that the cues they receive in class may not be particularly informational. Moreover, for students to receive constructive informational feedback about how they could improve, the teacher must *know* the student well in order to decide what type of feedback would facilitate development, and genuine communication must be frequent in class. As we have seen, neither of these seems to happen much. Many interviewees maintained that it was mainly the teacher who talked in their English class – sometimes mostly in Romanian. Oral assessment too seemed to consist of little more than question-and-answer sessions and some of them ridiculed the reliability of an educational system in which the teacher, sitting at her desk, reads out a question and the student stands up to answer in order to get a mark. Hardman (2008: 133), who calls this pattern the 'recitation script', explains that this all too frequent practice 'requires students to report someone else's thinking rather than think for themselves, and to be evaluated on their compliance in doing so'. It would be hard to find a better definition of control in the classroom. As the author argues, genuine classroom talk, higher order questioning and informative feedback strategies help students develop their thinking skills and shape their engagement, learning and understanding. It is rather sad to see that this potential may be wasted in foreign language classes, which should thrive on communication rather than hanker after it.

Apart from finding out what the students' needs are in order to be able to address them – as teachers' opinions have been known to differ significantly from the students' (e.g. Spratt, 1999) – genuine communication in the foreign language class would allow students to develop communicative and social skills for life. Many of the students I interviewed were saddened that they could not see the real-life relevance of their English lessons. They would have liked to understand why they were expected to do particular things in class and how doing those things had helped the teacher and other adults become successful professionals. They wanted to discuss their view of things, to argue, to debate, to negotiate, to collaborate and to be allowed to make mistakes. With heart-warming insight, some of them explained to me that *even their mistakes* would help them learn – if only they could talk in class. There is a striking similarity between these Romanian teenagers and the British teenagers studying Modern Foreign Languages in maintained schools in England (Taylor, 2012), who show intuitive understanding of pedagogic principles and deserve a voice in the classroom (Taylor, 2013a). A teacher who cares about students, who respects them and treats them like real people rather than a passive audience for one's (passive) recitation, will find many ways to get them involved in the organisation of the lesson, negotiation of common responsibilities and decision making (Clarke, 1991; Kohn, 1999; Ushioda, 2008, 2009). It would be hard to think of a better way for these students to learn the discourse of mutual respect, responsibility and negotiation in a foreign language than putting it to real use in genuine classroom exchanges.

Nonetheless, the solution is not as simple as telling teachers to support their students' communicative competence and autonomous development – it is very unlikely that this would be a novel idea for any of them. Research has shown that controlling teacher behaviour is a consequence of perceived control and administrative pressures (Flink et al., 1990; Reeve et al., 2004). Just like students feel controlled by the teacher and have their autonomy stifled, so too teachers feel controlled by higher order factors. Furthermore, their autonomy and intrinsic joy of teaching can be stifled both 'from above', through curriculum constraints, performance standards, challenging colleagues, and 'from below', through disruptive and amotivated students (Pelletier et al., 2002). Often excluded from curriculum and syllabus design, deprived of opportunities for peer interaction and professional development, burdened with too much accountability, teachers can feel 'deskilled' and disempowered (Crookes, 1997). Many of them experience high levels of stress, job insecurity and dissatisfaction, low salaries and sleep deprivation deriving from excessive administrative duties and lesson preparation (Burke et al., 1996; Gilbert, 2005; LeCompte & Dworkin, 1991; Vandenberghe & Huberman, 1999). Apart from all these problems, Romanian teachers have also had to endure a degrading social status in recent years and bear the brunt of the very frequent educational reforms brought about by every change in government (Popa & Acedo, 2006).

Elsewhere (Taylor, 2009, 2010) I have argued that, while change is absolutely necessary in the Romanian education system, it is unlikely that this will be a top-down process in the near future. Rather than bemoan the miserable status quo and move towards burnout in sure large strides, teachers could start their own bottom-up educational reform each in their own classrooms before it is too late. In a previous research project (Taylor, 2008), I found that Romanian students from three different schools in a different county, deprived of self-determination in their interactions with the teacher, regained their autonomy by resorting to various escapist-manipulative behaviours that allowed them to feel in control of their actions. In the present project, it seems that my participants may try to restore their self-determination in the peer relational context, through the norm of low achievement. Two important insights follow from this: that Romanian teenagers can be self-determined and have great potential for self-regulation; and that this potential is largely overlooked in the English class. In both my previous and current project, it emerged that many students utilised this potential outside the classroom, learning English through real-life encounters and pursuits, showing academically fruitful intrinsic motivation. But when the English class appears not only to do little to help them acquire the necessary language skills, but also to potentially threaten their intrinsic interest in the language, it becomes very clear that immediate change is imperative.

Internalisation Potential

In Chapter 5 we saw that, in order to integrate better into her friends' group, *Kiddo* (F, 14) had bought herself a guitar and learnt how to play it. She confessed that at first she had hated the very thought of it, but later came to realise that, after all, it was not such a bad thing. All *Kiddo*'s friends played the guitar. They also consumed recreational drugs. In a similar vein, *Pinty* (M, 16) spoke about the silent pressure that his peer group exerted on him to start smoking. 'It's not that they tell you to do it' – he explained – 'but you know it would just feel right if you started smoking to be like them.' *FC* (M, 15) took the peers' influence into the academic context, confessing that, although he had always wanted to be a 'model student' he had so far been unsuccessful, as he found himself doing everything 'the gang way' despite his resolution 'not to be a rascal [and] get reasonable marks'. Several other interviewees also mentioned that students were sometimes reluctant to speak in the English class for fear others might laugh at them if they made mistakes (a fear probably exacerbated by question-and-answer practices that were reportedly prevalent in all the five participating schools). This echoes Bartram's (2006a) findings, which show that teenagers sometimes laugh at their peers who try to produce a correct accent in the foreign language they are learning. I do not have any objective evidence for this assertion, but my personal feeling as a language learner in a Romanian classroom was always that of a constant battle between 'I'll show them what a cool accent I can produce' and 'who does (s)he think (s)he is, talking like that?!' We have also seen that some of my interviewees felt particularly motivated to answer in class when other students did not know 'the answer' or – in *Prestige*'s (F, 16) case – when they could not read out a text as nicely as she felt she did.

Figure 6.2 showed that students who were submissive to their friends and classmates had the lowest levels of declared achievement and we saw in Table 6.1 that peers had the lowest expectations of academic engagement, mirrored by the lowest drive to show academic engagement. This may indicate the internalisation of the so-called law of generalised mediocrity or norm of low achievement (Covington, 1992; Dweck, 1999; Juvonen & Wentzel, 1996; Seifert & O'Keefe, 2001). As Dweck (1999: 131) explains, this unwritten law is the adolescents' way of rebelling against a 'system of winners of losers' which, by focusing on competition and assessment, allows for a few winners at the top and a majority of losers at the bottom. The author further explains that teenagers seek to eliminate these winners through peer pressure, so that 'those who would have been the losers no longer stand apart from others', their perceived ability being also protected: if they have not even tried, a poor mark does not mean they are not able to succeed if only they wanted to.

In the absence of a longitudinal investigation, it is not possible to surmise whether or not my participants' public selves will ultimately get internalised into their private ones, or whether their present private selves are the result of past public selves adopted in search for social approval in the classroom. However, this is quite likely to be the case. Ryan and Deci (2003) maintain that the self images a person adopts in society are all in the service of the three basic human needs that self-determination is built on: the need for autonomy, the need for competence and the need for social relatedness. We recall that my data suggested a problematic level of self-determination in my participants, who appeared to be deprived of autonomy and relatedness in their interactions with the English teacher. But the classroom is an arena where two relational contexts meet, the teenager having to wear the hat of a student and that of a classmate at the same time. If the relational context centred around the teacher does not allow for much self-determination, it would appear that these students compensate by gaining self-determination in the peer relational context, where all three basic needs can be fulfilled through the norm of low achievement: autonomy – because they may feel it is up to them whether or not they do what their peers, being of the same age and social level dictate (and several interviews confirmed this); competence – because they may protect their perceived ability by withdrawing effort, as Dweck (1999), Covington (1992) and many others explain; and relatedness – because, if nobody works hard or cares too much about the teacher, then the peer group may feel like a nice big fraternity where everyone is accepted and appreciated as long as they accept the rules of the game. If these three human needs are fulfilled through the norm of low achievement in the classroom, then the risk of internalising these practices into one's self-concept is very serious.

However, internalisation can also serve crucial educational purposes. Explaining what determined him to respond to adults' expectations, the student who chose the pseudonym *418353* (M, 19) said: 'I'll mostly do what they expect me to do because, in a way, that helps me too. I mean ... *doing something for somebody else ... trains me*, in a way' (emphasis added). This was one of the uncountable serendipitous insights that the questionnaire alone would never have uncovered, and which offered some compensation for the lack of a longitudinal investigation. This student understood that doing something you do not necessarily believe in can be very educational in itself, opening up developmental possibilities which a teenager of limited experience might never try otherwise. *Pinty* (M, 16), too, gave a revealing account of his turbulent process of adaptation to his new school ethos. He recalled how in his first year at the present school he used to 'fight with every teacher', feeling that everybody had something against him. Then his form teacher, who was also a psychologist, advised him to be more reserved in his outbursts with the teachers and he realised she was right. In time, he came to understand that *even the lessons were better* since he had changed. (Unless he had been really disruptive, it is quite unlikely that the quality of the lessons improved all of a sudden. However, his perceptions and wellbeing in class certainly did, as did his potential for acquiring new knowledge, once he became more focussed on the lesson content.)

These are only two edifying examples which show how internalisation can help a teenager experience a more fulfilling school life. The strong correlations between my participants' public selves and the imposed selves originating in all four relational contexts show a huge potential for internalisation – especially in the adult relational contexts, where very strong imposed selves triggered very strong public selves. For a variety of reasons, these adolescents are very eager to please the adults they interact with. However, it is quite clear that, in order for a particular public self to get internalised, teenagers need to trust and respect the source of its corresponding imposed self (as many interviewees explained) and, more importantly, to consider the associated set of behaviours personally relevant (Rhodewalt, 1998).

It is rather sad to see that, in all the four relational contexts, imposed selves related to the future were significantly lower than those relating to the present, with very large effect sizes for the teacher and parents. As I have commented earlier, this is an indication that neither the teacher nor the parents expected English to play an important part in the students' future. In other words, the two main adult agents in the teenagers' lives seem to be concerned more with the students' success in English-as-an-academic-subject (i.e. achieving good marks, passing examinations), rather than English-as-a-communication-tool (i.e. the acquisition and development of a skill for life). However, my interviewees could not emphasise enough how much they wished lessons would prepare them for real life, and how much they wished they could bring their real life into the lessons. This echoes the solid body of literature showing that learning needs to be personally relevant in order to be engaging and effective in the long run (Assor et al., 2002; Little et al., 2002; Reeve et al., 1999; Roeser et al., 2006; Ushioda, 1996c, 2009; Wigfield et al., 2006).

Investigating students' attitudes to learning mathematics, Miller et al. (1996) showed that desire to please the teacher and desire to please the family were distinct factors which correlated positively with each other but not with the adolescents' learning orientation. In addition, pleasing the teacher was related to cognitive engagement and achievement, but pleasing the family was not. Pleasing the teacher appeared not to be an end in itself, but a strategy used in the pursuit of other goals, while pleasing the family as a rationale for doing academic work emerged as detrimental to students' cognitive engagement and achievement. Thus, Miller et al.'s (1996) conclusions appear to be confirmed by my findings that students often do their 'duty' and observe what the teachers say in order to secure their friendship and a hassle-free time at school, but they may sometimes internalise these public selves and can benefit academically from what was initially just external compliance. As for Miller et al.'s finding that pleasing the family as an end in itself was detrimental to cognitive engagement and achievement, this reflects my own results which showed that, in the family relational context, the lowest L2 private self values came with submissive students (i.e. those who relinquished their own ideal in order to do what parents said), while the strongest L2 private self belonged to rebellious students (i.e. those who, feeling an affinity with the English language, chose to pursue it despite their parents' wish that they progress towards more lucrative vocations).

One surprising insight facilitated by the interviews was that students who felt harmonious in the two adult relational contexts seemed to have lost the notion of social expectations altogether. Many of them emphasised that it simply happened that they and their teachers or parents wanted the same thing for the future. Given that possible selves are usually rooted in one's immediate social context (Marshall et al., 2006; Oyserman & Fryberg, 2006; Wurf & Markus, 1991), it is quite probable that these students' ideal selves are former imposed selves which have either been internalised via the public self and then private self, or have simply been transferred from an external possible self (i.e. imposed) to an internal possible self (i.e. ideal).

Moreover, not only did the harmonious students feel that their wishes coincided with their teacher's and parents', but they also declared themselves eager to do what they were told in class, while paradoxically feeling totally free and unrestrained. They also had the highest scores in all components of the L2 private self, the L2 ideal self, learning orientation, and internal attributions for success. These students are clearly on their way to becoming fully functioning persons, whom Carl Rogers (e.g. Rogers & Freiberg, 1994) described as self-organising systems which are constantly interacting with the environment but are not causally determined by it. Being trusted and learning to trust themselves, they become integrated, whole, unified individuals whose organismic reactions tell them what is the right thing to do.

This also confirms the autonomy and self-regulation literature (Little et al., 2002; Rigby et al., 1992; Ryan et al., 1992; Sansone & Smith, 2000; Ushioda, 1996c; van Lier, 1996), which distinguishes between internally regulated behaviours (intrinsically and extrinsically motivated) and externally regulated behaviours (extrinsically motivated). Althoughvintrinsically motivated learning rooted in fun and enjoyment is an ideal that every student and teacher would love to see in class, it is clear that not all aspects of language learning would appeal to all students personally at all times. The crucial solution here is internalisation: students' appropriation of learning goals that they come to see as personally relevant. In this way, even gaining high marks, passing exams or securing lucrative jobs can be highly motivational pursuits, with positive academic and self-actualising consequences. They do, however, need to be internally regulated for their motivational potential to persist. If marks and language certificates are ends in themselves (i.e. purely extrinsic motivators), rather than means to other ends (i.e. internalised, personally relevant, motivators), the students' academic conduct may not exceed the level of instrumental identity display with little connection to skill development, only to be abandoned as soon as the external stimulus is no longer present (Deci & Moller, 2005; Hidi, 2000; Sansone & Smith, 2000; Shah & Kruglanski, 2000).

Given the intimate connection between language and identity, language classes may be particularly fertile ground for internalisation if students have the freedom to be themselves and to bring their own world into the classroom. This may also be a solution for English speaking countries considered to be characterised by a foreign language crisis (e.g. Australia, USA, New Zealand, UK) and where top-down interventions and policy changes seem to be less influential than the students' day-to-day classroom experience (Martin, 2005; Rhodes & Pufahl, 2010; Shearn, 2003; Taylor, 2012).

8 Drawing the Line: Evaluation and Implications

Having discussed the findings of my empirical study, which used a new theoretical model, it is now the time to evaluate my proposed Quadripolar Model of Identity, which has guided my research design and the creation of the data collection instruments, and has helped in the interpretation of the findings. The evaluation will be organised into three sub-sections: confirmed hypotheses, unexpected insights and remaining questions. The chapter will end with implications for future research and classroom practice.

Model Evaluation

It is clear that many of the results presented in the previous three chapters confirm the postulates outlined in Chapter 4, as well as the insights shaped in the literature review. There were, however, also unexpected findings, and many questions are yet to be answered by future research.

Confirmed hypotheses

Many hypotheses expressed in the theoretical framework (Chapter 4) have been confirmed, the Quadripolar Model of Identity receiving substantive support as a comprehensive representation of adolescents as real persons caught in a web of complex social relationships. The four different L2 selves – private, ideal, public and imposed – emerged as discrete concepts interacting largely in the predicted manner. The four self systems received very strong support as well, apart from developmental processes, which were not the focus of this cross-sectional study. However, many important insights were gained into self system evolution too.

Public selves have been shown to fluctuate in tandem with imposed selves – a strong imposed self being associated with a strong public self and a weak imposed self being associated with a weak public self. It was also shown quite clearly that the four main relational contexts generate different imposed selves and, through them, different public selves. The hypothesis that conflicting imposed/public selves would require skilful self-presentation and impression management was also confirmed in the interviews.

It was postulated and fully supported that, in the transition from the actual towards the possible, both the ideal and the imposed selves can have great motivational potential. This was shown to work mainly negatively in the peer relational context (through the norm of low achievement) and positively in the teacher relational context (mainly though the internationalisation of superior social values). Personal relevance and interest were confirmed to play crucial roles in the process of internalisation.

It was expected and confirmed that the Romanian teachers would exhibit controlling behaviours towards their students and that this would thwart the harmonious development of their language learning selves (although it was rather surprising that students should interpret this as 'Communism'). The fact that many Romanian adolescents learn English through self-directed real-life means in their own free time was another confirmed expectation.

My new data collection instruments were shown to work well, although subsequent fine-tuning of the questionnaire will facilitate the elimination of particular ambiguities and lacunae evident only in hindsight. Finally, an important confirmation is that the Quadripolar Model of Identity can integrate successfully several key psychological theories, with great traditions of research validation and confirmation: self-presentation, impression management, possible selves, self-discrepancy and self-determination. Future research addressing the questions still left unanswered about identity in foreign language learning can thus build upon the solid bases of these theories, as well as on the confirmed hypotheses of this new framework.

Unexpected insights

A surprising result were gender differences: boys having stronger private selves and feeling more appreciated as individuals by the teachers, whereas girls appeared helpless and performance-oriented in relation to English language learning, as they internalised the causes of failure, felt social pressure more strongly and responded with stronger identity display.

Doing 'one's duty as a student' emerged as a stronger trend than had been hypothesised, and the fact that a large majority of students were duplicitous to their English teacher and to their classmates contradicted my anticipation that most of them would be rebellious. Regarding the rebellious self system itself, the hypothesis that it would be associated with disruptive and perhaps aggressive behaviour was not supported. Instead, most students felt it was too much to say they would rebel against authority, as even those who chose the rebellious self system manifested rather duplicitous identity display. (It is also possible that no disruptive 'rebels' volunteered for the interview, denying me the chance to understand their perspective better.)

It had also been unexpected that submissive students would show so much respect and admiration for the sources of their imposed selves, just as it had not been anticipated that they would appear to thrive on authority and to need it for a fruitful academic and social development. The fact that for harmonious students the notion of social expectation seemed to have disappeared altogether was again somewhat unanticipated, although careful consideration indicated that this was very likely the result of complete internalisation of imposed selves.

Finally, it was surprising that some of the students were so indignant at the possibility that their friends and classmates would give as much as a thought to their English language learning – certainly not for the future. And, generally, peers and friends had been expected to generate stronger L2 imposed and public English selves than they appeared to do.

Remaining questions

Being a cross-sectional study with restricted access to developmental insights only allowed by the participants' limited accounts and reported perceptions, the study could not explore many of the mutual and multidirectional influences that the four self components had been hypothesised to exert. As most analyses were correlational, when a strong association was detected it was not possible to comment on its causes. Whether two correlated variables influence each other or are both influenced by a third, perhaps not yet identified or expected, is impossible to surmise in the absence of a longitudinal and/or experimental design.

For the same reason, the question still remains whether younger teenagers are pressurised into more identity display, which decreases as they learn to accept themselves and their private self becomes stronger. My present data did reveal various age differences, but they could not be integrated into a coherent conceptual explanation at this time.

On the basis of the literature, it was also hypothesised that, displaying particular public selves, people may learn new things about themselves and subsequently integrate these into their private selves. Not much support for this assertion emerged from my data, although one of the older participants did believe that doing what other people expect him to do 'trained' him in a way. The hypothesis that public selves would be influenced by the private self is also still unclear, my data indicating there may be no link between the two, but this is very likely to differ from one relational context to another and from one individual to another.

An important question that my project could not have answered in its actual form is whether the display of a public self in response to an imposed self is always conscious, always unconscious or both depending on circumstances, and under what circumstances (un)consciousness may influence decision. Also, internalisation processes have not been clarified entirely. Of utmost interest for this project was whether or not internalisation of imposed/public selves could be used to motivate students and help them achieve better results in foreign language learning. Unfortunately, as the students' language-related future did not appear to be important for the adults concerned, this question too is still without a definite answer, although internalisation was shown to work in social domains (both for the better and for the worse).

Starting from the literature reviewed, the ideal self was expected to be much stronger, to energise behaviour and to be accompanied by a strong future vision and clear strategy for reaching the desired state. Little support was found for these postulates, although the ideal self did contribute very important insights into identity and motivational processes. No interviewees mentioned strong future visions of themselves as proficient language learners and it is not clear whether such strong ideal selves can be found in Romanian teenagers. As for clear learning strategies resulting from classroom instruction, these are likely to be rare in my research site, where students' autonomy and self-regulation did not appear to receive much encouragement at school. It is also still unclear on the basis of my data whether the private self and the ideal self are unitary entities incorporating different contingent facets.

A final remaining question is to what extent these results can be generalised to other contexts. As we have seen, several similarities have been found between my Romanian participants and British, American, Chinese, Dutch, French, English and German students, although with different research designs and questions. A larger project with participants from Bulgaria, Germany, the Netherlands and Spain (Taylor *et al.*, 2013) did corroborate most of the findings of this study, thus confirming the validity of the theoretical model and data collection instruments. The crucial importance of students' perceptions in the foreign language classroom, and their relationship to achievement and desire to continue/discontinue studying the language have also been confirmed in the context of learning Modern Foreign

Languages in England (Taylor, 2012), although the Quadripolar Model of Identity has not yet been tested in this context.

Implications for Future Research and Practice

Most implications for future research and for classroom practice have already been outlined directly or indirectly, but I would like to emphasise here what I believe are the essential points.

Future studies

The questions left unanswered in my project, as well as the new ones generated by it, would have to be addressed in longitudinal and/or experimental investigations consolidated by in-depth ethnographic analyses of the larger community in which these teenagers function.

For a better understanding of the proposed framework, it is also necessary to test it with other foreign languages (also community and heritage languages), and with other academic subjects altogether. A science-oriented analysis would prove particularly revealing by facilitating insights into the extent to which identity processes are involved in the learning of a foreign language by comparison to a positivist academic subject. A preliminary follow-up study that compared the learning of English and the learning of Mathematics in Europe (Taylor *et al.*, 2013) suggested that identity display may be even more pronounced in Mathematics, but the findings clearly depended on myriad contextual factors and no in-depth qualitative data were collected on this occasion.

Different participants altogether – perhaps teachers and other professional categories – as well as representatives of different ethno-cultural groups would also help understand social identity processes better, as well as test the extent to which this framework could possibly be stretched beyond adolescent foreign language learning. It would be particularly interesting to see how it works in reciprocal (perhaps also personal?) relationships: for example, if we feel harmonious or duplicitous with somebody, will that person also feel harmonious or duplicitous with us?

A similar approach may also help elucidate what is sometimes perceived as a foreign language crisis in the UK (CILT, 2011; Coleman *et al.*, 2007; Pachler, 2002; Worton, 2009) and other English speaking countries (Martin, 2005; Pufahl & Rhodes, 2011; Shearn, 2003; Wiley, 2007). There is evidence that perceiving foreign languages as important for one's own future is related to more willingness to work hard and continue language learning after compulsory school study (Busse & Williams, 2010; Taylor, 2012), that learners who experience success with modern languages are more likely to be strategic and interested in language study (Graham, 1997, 2007; Mills *et al.*, 2007), and that explicit or implicit social pressure can have a strong influence on one's engagement with language learning (Bartram, 2010; Comănaru & Noels, 2009; Williams & Burden, 1999). However, a comprehensive model of identity like the one described in this book has yet to be applied to foreign language learning in contexts where English is an L1. Such an approach may help explain why interest in foreign languages has declined in countries like the UK, the USA and Australia in recent years, and whether relational self perceptions can elucidate the self-presentational dynamics of stereotypical beliefs such as 'nobody needs foreign languages because everybody speaks English nowadays'. Cross-sectional studies comparing foreign language learning in countries where English is an official language with learning English (and other foreign languages) in other countries may also help elucidate the role of perceived relevance, perceived difficulty and perceived competence, as well as their relationship to language learning persistence and success, while also shedding light on the role that teaching and assessment methods may have in determining foreign language uptake in contexts where language study is optional.

Implications for the classroom

The most salient red thread that has crossed this project from beginning to end is also the most important implication for the classroom: unless students are allowed to be themselves – real people, with real hopes, fears, worries, joys, disappointments, thrills and mistakes – and appreciated for what they are as real people, they are unlikely to engage genuinely in class and develop as language learners and social persons. It was sad to see that the huge potential for internalisation did not seem to be utilised in helping these Romanian teenagers integrate English language learning into their private selves by helping them see why it (should have) mattered to them personally. Even sadder still was realising that neither teachers nor parents seemed to consider that English should be more important in the students' future than in their present.

As argued in the Introduction, foreign language classes would appear to be the most suited for identity development of all academic subjects. If the students are allowed to be 'themselves' and to express 'themselves' freely about what energises them and what helps them learn better, three crucial benefits follow if this communication occurs in the foreign language itself: the teacher gains invaluable insights into the learners' own motivational processes, the students practise the real-life discourse of genuine communication in a foreign language and they have the opportunity to explore and consolidate their identity as self-determined individuals in society.

Such self-actualising communication in English would leave little room for the question-and-answer exchanges that appeared to be prevalent in my Romanian research context. If students are appreciated for what they 'really' are, then their answers in class cannot be expected to simply rise to a teacher's expectations, who decides what is and what is not a correct answer. In an environment where students can be themselves and are appreciated for that, every one of their contributions is unique and inherently valuable, as it serves the treble purpose of disclosing their 'real' identity in a safe nurturing environment, helping to consolidate the very identity thus disclosed in public and offering real-life linguistic practice.

Genuine discoursal exchanges in class would also help eliminate the 'communication wall' that my interviewees talked about, which – they felt – prevented teachers from ever knowing what their learners were really like as people and thus missing precious opportunities to make classes relevant and engaging for the learners. Both motivated and demotivated students emphasised that, if the teacher knew them as individuals and incorporated self-relevant information in the lessons, they would feel much more motivated to engage in class genuinely and really work hard (rather than pretend to). In this light, 'motivating' learners to work hard appears to be reduced to the necessity of creating a classroom environment in which they feel appreciated and nurtured for what they are as individuals.

However, when teachers themselves may not be appreciated for what they are as individuals, in a system driven mainly by assessment and administration, this may not be very easy to put into practice. Romanian (and not only) teachers may themselves be controlled and imposed upon by higher-order factors and it is quite unlikely that many of them feel 'themselves' either in the staff room or in the classroom, which may undermine their professional and personal sense of wellbeing. But in contrast to their adolescent students, teachers are mature individuals who are free to make personally relevant choices and – at least in theory – do what they like.

Conclusion

This research project started from a practice-rooted interest in the factors that may help students feel that they are personally appreciated in the classroom, and in how these factors could be used to enhance their engagement and achievement in the English class. Specifically, the aims of the project were (1) to gain new insights into the identity of Romanian adolescent learners of English as a foreign language and its relationships to classroom involvement and declared achievement; and (2) to validate the new theoretical framework, A Quadripolar Model of Identity, and its associated questionnaire.

Considering the previous chapters, it can be concluded that the two aims have been achieved to a great extent. The L2 Quadripolar Identity Questionnaire has been shown to work well in gathering quantitative data that confirmed the theoretical insights emerging from the literature reviewed, while also showing very high internal consistency coefficients for all the scales and being consolidated by the similar findings of the larger European project. The four L2 self components (private, public, ideal and imposed) have been shown to represent distinct measurable variables, clustering in different ways depending on the analysis performed (of particular interest being the difference between the L2 private self and the L2 public self displayed in response to various imposed selves).

After presenting a brief literature background in Chapters 2 and 3, I ended Chapter 3 with five reasons why I believed that more research was needed into the identity of foreign language learners, which were also the rationale for conducting my study:

- very little research had addressed the learners' actual self and the host of socio-individual factors that students bring with them into the foreign language class;
- hardly any attention had been given to strategic self-presentation in L2 classes, although evidence from educational psychology suggested that manipulative identity display was rife in school, especially in competitive performance-oriented environments;
- previous investigations into socially imposed selves had not found much support for the motivational power that these could have in foreign language learning, especially the potential uses of internalisation being overlooked;
- there was a need for comprehensive models aiming to describe not only the possible, but also the actual identity of foreign language learners, along with their relationships and their results in the L2 class; and
- as most identity research in foreign language learning had been conducted with data collection instruments borrowed – totally or partially – from older studies designed for totally different purposes, in totally different research contexts, new purposefully designed instruments were necessary in order to investigate the topic in a systematic manner.

My findings – based on data collected with new purposefully designed instruments – have depicted foreign language learners as skilled identity nego-tiators both in the classroom and outside, who choose to disclose what they perceive (and/or declare) to be their 'real' identity only in environments where they feel appreciated as individuals. When they feel they are not appreciated personally, they display context-induced public selves and they may internalise these into their private selves, although this potential does not appear to be exploited in the English language class. In addition, not only has my project shown that students' private selves sometimes have little in common with the public selves they display in class, but we have also seen that students who feel they cannot be themselves in class have lower language-learning scores than those who do. Although further research is certainly needed before drawing any definite conclusions, this link between classroom identity and achieve-ment is an important indication that we do need to care about our students' identity if we care about their achievement.

Teachers appeared to be the decisive factors in determining students' classroom identity, both through the perceived interest and appreciation that they showed to learners and through their perceived assessment fairness. Although overall students felt quite competent in English, few of them con-sidered that their competence originated in the classroom, some even indi-cating that a dislike for the teacher induced a dislike for their academic subject. There were signs that outside the classroom the participants were self-determined and mastery-oriented, whereas in class they tended to be helpless and disengaged. Both parents and teachers appeared to reinforce the importance of English-as-an-academic-subject to the detriment of English-as-a-communication-tool, reportedly downplaying the relevance that the foreign language could have in the students' future. Consequently, many participants who had strong affinities with the language and wanted to pursue English-related careers apparently had to rebel against their parents and to be duplicitous to their teachers in order to do so. By contrast, students who felt that their attributes and desires were appreciated were prepared to work hard and do what the teacher and parents asked them without even being aware of any existing 'expectations' that might redirect their actions. These students, who felt they could be 'themselves' in class and outside, appeared to be better language learners than those who felt they had to con-ceal their 'real' identity and display various public selves thought to bring immediate beneficial results but that seemed to be detrimental in the long run.

While the fivefold rationale for conducting this research project has been addressed and my findings have contributed to a better understanding of the self and identity in adolescent foreign language learning, there is no doubt that more questions were raised than were answered and I very much hope that future research will test and expand these preliminary insights in other contexts, continuing the dialogue about what it is that makes us who we are and how we can use this understanding to be more successful and more fulfilled language learners and teachers.

There were strong indications in my findings that my participants love languages and they would love to become more proficient L2 users. There were also indications that they tried to be 'themselves' in class and were not often appreciated for that. It would appear, then, that a huge learning potential is left unexplored in these classes, increasing students' demotivation and frustration, which is bound to enter a vicious circle with the teachers' demotivation and frustration. It is quite unlikely that educational systems like the one depicted in this book will change dramatically in the near future and it is equally improbable that students will be able to change anything on their own soon. The onus, then, is on teachers. They have the wonderful opportunity to work with students who seem to have a genuine desire to learn, who appear to be interested and self-determined, and who would love to learn more at school – if only they were allowed to be themselves. The 1045 voices in my study appeared to all be saying the same thing: just let us be ourselves in class and we will learn better. With this, half the motivational battle would be won. Perhaps the other half would be won if teachers, too, tried to be themselves in the classroom.

Appendix A: The L2 Quadripolar Identity Questionnaire

(Available to download from http://www.iris-database.org)

... [DESCRIPTIVE INTRO]

I. *Please read the following paragraphs very carefully and choose the one that best suits your English teacher, your classmates, your best friends and your family. Please encircle one corresponding letter in every box, as in the example. Thank you!*

A) They know very well what sort of person I am. What they would like me to do in life is different from what I would like to do, so that's why I prefer to give up my intentions and do what they think it's better for me. What they want me to do in life is more important than what I'd have liked, so I'll do what they say.

B) They don't really know what sort of person I really am, and it's not important for me that they do. They would like me to do something else in life than I would, and that's why I'll pursue my own dreams without letting them know. At the same time, I'll give them the impression that I do what they ask me to, even though I'm actually seeing about my own business. I know better.

C) What they would like me to do in life is different from what I would like to do, so that's why I'll pursue my own dreams even if I have to rebel against them. They know me well, I haven't got anything to hide, and if they want to force me into doing something, I am likely to refuse it openly. What they want me to do is less important than what I want.

D) They know me very well and appreciate me for what I am. My dreams for the future are very similar to what they'd like me to do in life. They don't want to impose anything on me, but give me the total liberty to choose, and they always appreciate my decisions about my future. They help me feel really fulfilled.

Example	my English teacher	my classmates	my best friends	my family
A B © D	A B C D	A B C D	A B C D	A B C D

II. *Please read the following statements carefully and for each of them encircle one answer that represents you best of all (e.g. if you love hazelnut chocolate but you love plain chocolate even more, choose ⑤; if you hate hazelnut chocolate, choose ①). Please remember: **one** answer for **every line**!*

HOW TRUE FOR YOU?	
1 = very untrue 2 = untrue 3 = relatively untrue 4 = relatively true 5 = true 6 = very true	
EXAMPLE: I love hazelnut chocolate.	*1 2 3 4 ⑤ 6*
I find it very easy to learn English.	very untrue very true 1 2 3 4 5 6
I am better at English than most of my classmates.	1 2 3 4 5 6
English will be a very important part of my future.	1 2 3 4 5 6
English is the hardest class of all.	1 2 3 4 5 6
What I learn during the English classes will be very useful to me in the future.	1 2 3 4 5 6
I feel great when I'm working on my English.	1 2 3 4 5 6
I am among the best students in my English class.	1 2 3 4 5 6
I can pick up English stuff faster than my classmates can.	very untrue very true 1 2 3 4 5 6
My English classes will help me become the person I want to be in the future.	1 2 3 4 5 6
I enjoy the challenges of the English class even when I don't get good marks.	1 2 3 4 5 6
The English class really helps me develop as a person.	1 2 3 4 5 6
I really love learning English.	1 2 3 4 5 6
I intend to get a degree in English.	1 2 3 4 5 6
If I know an activity is too hard for me, I still try to do it.	1 2 3 4 5 6

I am really good at English.	very untrue	very true
	1 2 3 4 5 6	
I have been more successful with English than with other subjects.	1 2 3 4 5 6	
I would love to be an English expert in the future.	1 2 3 4 5 6	
I have generally been successful in learning English so far.	1 2 3 4 5 6	
My future job will have an English language component.	1 2 3 4 5 6	
Learning English is an important part of my life.	1 2 3 4 5 6	
Learning English is easier for me than learning other subjects.	1 2 3 4 5 6	
I work hard to improve my English irrespective of the marks I get.	very untrue	very true
	1 2 3 4 5 6	
The English class is always very interesting.	1 2 3 4 5 6	
I feel I am appreciated for what I really am in the English class.	1 2 3 4 5 6	
I have a lot of fun when I work on my English.	1 2 3 4 5 6	
I have more problems with my English than some of my classmates.	1 2 3 4 5 6	
I try an activity for as many times as necessary to do it right.	1 2 3 4 5 6	
I can't wait to learn more things about English.	1 2 3 4 5 6	
The person I would like to be communicates in English very well.	1 2 3 4 5 6	
When an English task is very difficult, I feel motivated to work harder on it.	very untrue	very true
	1 2 3 4 5 6	
The English class is boring, always following the same lines.	1 2 3 4 5 6	
Compared to other subjects, English poses very few problems for me.	1 2 3 4 5 6	
My English teacher knows what my hobbies are.	1 2 3 4 5 6	
I can easily find mistakes in my classmates' English.	1 2 3 4 5 6	
I am really happy with my performance in English.	1 2 3 4 5 6	
I feel encouraged to grow and develop in the English class.	1 2 3 4 5 6	
English is one of my favourite subjects.	very untrue	very true
	1 2 3 4 5 6	

(Continued)

The English class is just right for me – not too easy, not too difficult.	1 2 3 4 5 6
My personal qualities are very much appreciated in the English class.	1 2 3 4 5 6
I feel I am really talented at English.	1 2 3 4 5 6
I have more problems with my English than with other subjects.	1 2 3 4 5 6
My English teacher is interested in my hobbies and passions.	1 2 3 4 5 6
The mistakes I make in English motivate me to work harder.	1 2 3 4 5 6
The other students in class struggle with English more than I do.	very untrue very true 1 2 3 4 5 6
What I really am as a person doesn't matter in the English class.	1 2 3 4 5 6
My English learning experience has been satisfactory to date.	1 2 3 4 5 6
I am better at English than at any other subject.	1 2 3 4 5 6

III. *We are all surrounded by people who would like us to do particular things. For the following statements, please think about your English teacher, your classmates, your best friends and your family. How much would they all like you to do these things? Please choose one answer for each of them, so that you have four encircled answers on every line, like in the example. Please remember:* **four** answers for **every line**! Thank you!

HOW MUCH WOULD THESE PEOPLE LIKE ME TO...?			
1 = very little 2 = little 3 = relatively little 4 = relatively much 5 = much 6 = very much			
These people would like me to...	*my English teacher*	*my classmates*	*my best friends*	*my family*
EXAMPLE: ...use paper tissues.	1 ② 3 4 5 6	① 2 3 4 5 6	1 2 ③ 4 5 6	1 2 3 4 5 ⑥
...work hard to improve my English.	1 2 3 4 5 6	1 2 3 4 5 6	1 2 3 4 5 6	1 2 3 4 5 6
...consider English very important for me.	1 2 3 4 5 6	1 2 3 4 5 6	1 2 3 4 5 6	1 2 3 4 5 6
...really love English.	1 2 3 4 5 6	1 2 3 4 5 6	1 2 3 4 5 6	1 2 3 4 5 6

...be really talented at English.	1 2 3 4 5 6	1 2 3 4 5 6	1 2 3 4 5 6	1 2 3 4 5 6
...always do my English homework.	1 2 3 4 5 6	1 2 3 4 5 6	1 2 3 4 5 6	1 2 3 4 5 6
...always do what the English teacher asks me.	1 2 3 4 5 6	1 2 3 4 5 6	1 2 3 4 5 6	1 2 3 4 5 6
...get a degree in English.	1 2 3 4 5 6	1 2 3 4 5 6	1 2 3 4 5 6	1 2 3 4 5 6
...have a future job with an English language component.	1 2 3 4 5 6	1 2 3 4 5 6	1 2 3 4 5 6	1 2 3 4 5 6
...be a teacher of English, or something similar.	1 2 3 4 5 6	1 2 3 4 5 6	1 2 3 4 5 6	1 2 3 4 5 6
...see English as a very important part of my future.	1 2 3 4 5 6	1 2 3 4 5 6	1 2 3 4 5 6	1 2 3 4 5 6
...be an English expert in the future.	1 2 3 4 5 6	1 2 3 4 5 6	1 2 3 4 5 6	1 2 3 4 5 6
...communicate in English very well in the future.	1 2 3 4 5 6	1 2 3 4 5 6	1 2 3 4 5 6	1 2 3 4 5 6

IV. *Sometimes, we all want to show other people particular things about ourselves. How important is it that you show the following to your English teacher, your classmates, your best friends and your family? Please choose one answer for each of them, so that you have four encircled answers on every line, like in the example. Please remember:* **four** *answers for* **every line**! Thank you!

HOW IMPORTANT TO SHOW TO THESE PEOPLE...?

1 = very unimportant   2 = unimportant   3 = relatively unimportant
4 = relatively important   5 = important   6 = very important

It's very important for me to show to these people...	to my English teacher	to my classmates	to my best friends	to my family
EXAMPLE: ...that I love sports cars.	① 2 3 4 5 6	1 2 3 4 ⑤ 6	1 2 3 4 5 ⑥	1 2 3 ④ 5 6
...that I work hard to improve my English.	1 2 3 4 5 6	1 2 3 4 5 6	1 2 3 4 5 6	1 2 3 4 5 6

...that English is very important for me.	1 2 3 4 5 6	1 2 3 4 5 6	1 2 3 4 5 6	1 2 3 4 5 6
...that I really love English.	1 2 3 4 5 6	1 2 3 4 5 6	1 2 3 4 5 6	1 2 3 4 5 6
...that I am really talented at English.	1 2 3 4 5 6	1 2 3 4 5 6	1 2 3 4 5 6	1 2 3 4 5 6
...that I always do my English homework.	1 2 3 4 5 6	1 2 3 4 5 6	1 2 3 4 5 6	1 2 3 4 5 6
...that I always do what the English teacher asks me.	1 2 3 4 5 6	1 2 3 4 5 6	1 2 3 4 5 6	1 2 3 4 5 6

V.   *How would you explain your successes and failures in the English class? Please read the following statements carefully and tick ☑ all that apply in your case. You may tick as many answers as you feel are right for you, but please remember to mark your answers in* **both columns**! Thank you!

Think about the situations when you did well in English. What do you think helped you do well? Please tick all that apply. ☑	Now think about the situations when you didn't do very well in English. What do you think were the causes? Please tick all that apply. ☑
I had worked really hard on my English.	I spent too little time preparing.
I was really-really lucky.	I'm not all that good at it.
I really love English.	My classmates didn't bother to help me at all.
I always do extra work for English.	The teacher gave me a lower mark than I deserved.
I have a true gift for English.	I haven't really got a gift for languages.
My classmates helped me do well.	I was very unlucky.
The teacher gave me a higher mark than I deserved.	The teacher doesn't always explain things well.
The lesson was very easy.	I can't understand some rules of English.
The teacher helped me along.	I couldn't concentrate very well during that lesson.
I spend a lot of time on my English.	I was having a bad day.
I was having a really good day.	The tasks were too hard for my level of English.
I am very interested in English.	I didn't try hard enough.

VI. *Finally, please fill in the following information about yourself:*

I have studied English for _____ years at school and _____ years with a private tutor.
My usual mark in English is _____. The mark I think I deserve is _____. *(Please write one number in each space.)*

I am a boy/a girl. *(Please circle.)*

IF YOU WOULD LIKE TO PARTICIPATE IN A SHORT INTERVIEW ON THE THEME OF THIS QUESTIONNAIRE, PLEASE WRITE A PASSWORD IN THIS BOX FOR IDENTIFICATION:

Appendix B: The L2 Quadripolar Identity Questionnaire with Item Numbers

... [DESCRIPTIVE INTRO]

I. *Please read the following paragraphs very carefully and choose the one that best suits your English teacher, your classmates, your best friends and your family. Please encircle one corresponding letter in every box, as in the example. Thank you!*

A) They know very well what sort of person I am. What they would like me to do in life is different from what I would like to do, so that's why I prefer to give up my intentions and do what they think it's better for me. What they want me to do in life is more important than what I'd have liked, so I'll do what they say.

B) They don't really know what sort of person I really am, and it's not important for me that they do. They would like me to do something else in life than I would, and that's why I'll pursue my own dreams without letting them know. At the same time, I'll give them the impression that I do what they ask me to, even though I'm actually seeing about my own business. I know better.

C) What they would like me to do in life is different from what I would like to do, so that's why I'll pursue my own dreams even if I have to rebel against them. They know me well, I haven't got anything to hide, and if they want to force me into doing something, I am likely to refuse it openly. What they want me to do is less important than what I want.

D) They know me very well and appreciate me for what I am. My dreams for the future are very similar to what they'd like me to do in life. They don't want to impose anything on me, but give me the total liberty to choose, and they always appreciate my decisions about my future. They help me feel really fulfilled.

example	my English teacher	my classmates	my best friends	my family
A B © D	A B C D	A B C D	A B C D	A B C D
	1	**2**	**3**	**4**

II. *Please read the following statements carefully and for each of them encircle one answer that represents you best of all (e.g. if you love hazelnut chocolate but you love plain chocolate even more, choose ⑤; if you hate hazelnut chocolate, choose ①). Please remember:* **one** answer for **every line**!

HOW TRUE FOR YOU?	
1 = very untrue 2 = untrue 3 = relatively untrue 4 = relatively true 5 = true 6 = very true	
EXAMPLE: I love hazelnut chocolate.	*1 2 3 4 ⑤ 6*
5. I find it very easy to learn English.	very untrue very true 1 2 3 4 5 6
6. I am better at English than most of my classmates.	1 2 3 4 5 6
7. English will be a very important part of my future.	1 2 3 4 5 6
8. English is the hardest class of all. **R**	1 2 3 4 5 6
9. What I learn during the English classes will be very useful to me in the future.	1 2 3 4 5 6
10. I feel great when I'm working on my English.	1 2 3 4 5 6
11. I am among the best students in my English class.	1 2 3 4 5 6
12. I can pick up English stuff faster than my classmates can.	very untrue very true 1 2 3 4 5 6

13. My English classes will help me become the person I want to be in the future.	1 2 3 4 5 6
14. I enjoy the challenges of the English class even when I don't get good marks.	1 2 3 4 5 6
15. The English class really helps me develop as a person.	1 2 3 4 5 6
16. I really love learning English.	1 2 3 4 5 6
17. I intend to get a degree in English.	1 2 3 4 5 6
18. If I know an activity is too hard for me, I still try to do it.	1 2 3 4 5 6
19. I am really good at English.	very untrue very true 1 2 3 4 5 6
20. I have been more successful with English than with other subjects.	1 2 3 4 5 6
21. I would love to be an English expert in the future.	1 2 3 4 5 6
22. I have generally been successful in learning English so far.	1 2 3 4 5 6
23. My future job will have an English language component.	1 2 3 4 5 6
24. Learning English is an important part of my life.	1 2 3 4 5 6
25. Learning English is easier for me than learning other subjects.	1 2 3 4 5 6
26. I work hard to improve my English irrespective of the marks I get.	very untrue very true 1 2 3 4 5 6
27. The English class is always very interesting.	1 2 3 4 5 6
28. I feel I am appreciated for what I really am in the English class.	1 2 3 4 5 6
29. I have a lot of fun when I work on my English.	1 2 3 4 5 6
30. I have more problems with my English than some of my classmates. **R**	1 2 3 4 · 5 6
31. I try an activity for as many times as necessary to do it right.	1 2 3 4 5 6
32. I can't wait to learn more things about English.	1 2 3 4 5 6
33. The person I would like to be communicates in English very well.	1 2 3 4 5 6

34. When an English task is very difficult, I feel motivated to work harder on it.	very untrue very true 1 2 3 4 5 6
35. The English class is boring, always following the same lines. **R**	1 2 3 4 5 6
36. Compared to other subjects, English poses very few problems for me.	1 2 3 4 5 6
37. My English teacher knows what my hobbies are.	1 2 3 4 5 6
38. I can easily find mistakes in my classmates' English.	1 2 3 4 5 6
39. I am really happy with my performance in English.	1 2 3 4 5 6
40. I feel encouraged to grow and develop in the English class.	1 2 3 4 5 6
41. English is one of my favourite subjects.	very untrue very true 1 2 3 4 5 6
42. The English class is just right for me – not too easy, not too difficult.	1 2 3 4 5 6
43. My personal qualities are very much appreciated in the English class.	1 2 3 4 5 6
44. I feel I am really talented at English.	1 2 3 4 5 6
45. I have more problems with my English than with other subjects. **R**	1 2 3 4 5 6
46. My English teacher is interested in my hobbies and passions.	1 2 3 4 5 6
47. The mistakes I make in English motivate me to work harder.	1 2 3 4 5 6
48. The other students in class struggle with English more than I do.	very untrue very true 1 2 3 4 5 6
49. What I really am as a person doesn't matter in the English class. **R**	1 2 3 4 5 6
50. My English learning experience has been satisfactory to date.	1 2 3 4 5 6
51. I am better at English than at any other subject.	1 2 3 4 5 6

R = reverse-coded item

III. *We are all surrounded by people who would like us to do particular things. For the following statements, please think about your English teacher, your classmates, your best friends and your family. How much would they all like you to do these things? Please choose one answer for each of them, so that you have four encircled answers on every line, like in the example. Please remember:* **four** answers for **every line**! Thank you!

HOW MUCH WOULD THESE PEOPLE LIKE ME TO...? 1 = very little 2 = little 3 = relatively little 4 = relatively much 5 = much 6 = very much				
These people would like me to...	*my English teacher*	*my classmates*	*my best friends*	*my family*
EXAMPLE: ...use paper tissues.	*1 ② 3 4 5 6*	*① 2 3 4 5 6*	*1 2 ③ 4 5 6*	*1 2 3 4 5 ⑥*
...work hard to improve my English.	52	53	54	55
...consider English very important for me.	56	57	58	59
...really love English.	60	61	62	63
...be really talented at English.	64	65	66	67
...always do my English homework.	68	69	70	71
...always do what the English teacher asks me.	72	73	74	75
...get a degree in English.	76	77	78	79
...have a future job with an English language component.	80	81	82	83
...be a teacher of English, or something similar.	84	85	86	87
...see English as a very important part of my future.	88	89	90	91
...be an English expert in the future.	92	93	94	95
...communicate in English very well in the future.	96	97	98	99

IV. *Sometimes, we all want to show other people particular things about ourselves. How important is it that you show the following to your English teacher, your classmates, your best friends and your family? Please choose one answer for each of them, so that you have four encircled answers on every line, like in the example. Please remember:* **four** answers for **every line**! Thank you!

HOW IMPORTANT TO SHOW TO THESE PEOPLE...?			
1 = very unimportant 2 = unimportant 3 = relatively unimportant 4 = relatively important 5 = important 6 = very important			
It's very important for me to show to these people...	*to my English teacher*	*to my classmates*	*to my best friends*	*to my family*
EXAMPLE: ...that I love sports cars.	① 2 3 4 5 6	1 2 3 4 ⑤ 6	1 2 3 4 5 ⑥	1 2 3 ④ 5 6
...that I work hard to improve my English.	100	101	102	103
...that English is very important for me.	104	105	106	107
...that I really love English.	108	109	110	111
...that I am really talented at English.	112	113	114	115
...that I always do my English homework.	116	117	118	119
...that I always do what the English teacher asks me.	120	121	122	123

V. *How would you explain your successes and failures in the English class? Please read the following statements carefully and tick ☑ all that apply in your case. You may tick as many answers as you feel are right for you, but please remember to mark your answers in* **both columns**! Thank you!

Think about the situations when you did well in English. What do you think helped you do well? Please tick all that apply. ☑		*Now think about the situations when you didn't do very well in English. What do you think were the causes? Please tick all that apply.* ☑	
I had worked really hard on my English.	124	I spent too little time preparing.	136
I was really-really lucky.	125	I'm not all that good at it.	137

I really love English.	**126**	My classmates didn't bother to help me at all.	**138**
I always do extra work for English.	**127**	The teacher gave me a lower mark than I deserved.	**139**
I have a true gift for English.	**128**	I haven't really got a gift for languages.	**140**
My classmates helped me do well.	**129**	I was very unlucky.	**141**
The teacher gave me a higher mark than I deserved.	**130**	The teacher doesn't always explain things well.	**142**
The lesson was very easy.	**131**	I can't understand some rules of English.	**143**
The teacher helped me along.	**132**	I couldn't concentrate very well during that lesson.	**144**
I spend a lot of time on my English.	**133**	I was having a bad day.	**145**
I was having a really good day.	**134**	The tasks were too hard for my level of English.	**146**
I am very interested in English.	**135**	I didn't try hard enough.	**147**

VI. *Finally, please fill in the following information about yourself:*
I have studied English for _**148**_ years at school and _**149**_ years with a private tutor.
My usual mark in English is _**150**_. The mark I think I deserve is _**151**_.
(Please write one number in each space.)

I am a boy/a girl **152***(Please circle.)* and I am _**153**_ years old.

IF YOU WOULD LIKE TO PARTICIPATE IN A SHORT INTERVIEW
ON THE THEME OF THIS QUESTIONNAIRE, PLEASE WRITE A
PASSWORD IN THIS BOX FOR IDENTIFICATION:

154

Appendix C: Questionnaire Scales with Item Numbers

No.	Scale		Subscales	Items
1.	System subtypes (not an actual scale)		English teacher	1
			Classmates	2
			Best friends	3
			Family	4
2.	**Private self**		Cognitive appraisals	5, 19, 22, 39, 44, 50
			Affective appraisals	10, 16, 24, 29, 32, 41
			Frame of reference – internal	8(R), 20, 25, 36, 45(R), 51
			Frame of reference – external	6, 11, 12, 30(R), 38, 48
3.	**Public selves**		English teacher	100, 104, 108, 112, 116, 120
			Classmates	101, 105, 109, 113, 117, 121
			Best friends	102, 106, 110, 114, 118, 122
			Family	103, 107, 111, 115, 119, 123
4.	**Ideal self**		–	7, 17, 21, 23, 33
5.	**Imposed selves**	Present	English teacher	52, 56, 60, 64, 68, 72
			Classmates	53, 57, 61, 65, 69, 73
			Best friends	54, 58, 62, 66, 70, 74
			Family	55, 59, 63, 67, 71, 75
		Future	English teacher	76, 80, 84, 88, 92, 96
			Classmates	77, 81, 85, 89, 93, 97
			Best friends	78, 82, 86, 90, 94, 98
			Family	79, 83, 87, 91, 95, 99

6.	**Learning orientation**		–	14, 18, 26, 31, 34, 47
7.	**Perceptions of the English class**		Interest; personal relevance	9, 13, 15, 27, 35(R), 42
			Freedom to be oneself; appreciation as an individual	28, 37, 40, 43, 46, 49(R)
8.	**Attributions**	Success	Internal	124, 126, 127, 128, 133, 135
			External	125, 129, 130, 131, 132, 134
		Failure	Internal	136, 137, 140, 143, 144, 147
			External	138, 139, 141, 142, 145, 146
9.	Biodata	Years of studying English	At school	148
			Privately	149
		English mark	Real	150
			Deserved	151
		Gender	–	152
		Age	–	153
		Volunteer for interview	–	154
10.	Background information (not in the questionnaire)	No. of English classes/ week	–	155
		Questionnaire administrator	–	156
		Admin. problems?	–	157
		School	–	158

Appendix D: Interview Guide – Themes Covered, with Examples of Questions and Prompts

Introduction

(Thanks and informal beginning.) How did you find the questionnaire (yesterday)? Any problems? Anything that wasn't right?

Missing Answers in the Questionnaire

There are a few blanks in your questionnaire – could you please fill these in too? I think you've skipped a few items – was that intentional or did you just overlook them?

Section 1 of the Questionnaire (Vignettes)

Vignettes right?

Have a look at your answers to the first section, please. Would you still choose the same descriptions?

Were they right for your situation? Did you feel the need for more options? Which one(s) suited you really well/didn't really suit you? How would you improve it/them?

Examples and explanations

Could you please give me some examples/details to support your choices? Why did you choose this description for those people? Could you go through this description sentence by sentence and give me some examples, please?

System Subtype Differences/Conflicts

I can see you've chosen different paragraphs for your family and your friends. What happens when you're in the same place both with your family and your friends? How do you feel? Has it ever happened that you were in the same place with your family and your friends and didn't really know how to behave? Can you give me an example? What did you do? Who did you try to 'please' first? Why?

– variants for teacher/classmates, classmates/friends

Playing Social Roles

Do you ever feel you're playing some sort of social role? That you're different from one situation to another, perhaps depending on the person you're talking to? Can you give me an example? How would you explain this? Why do you think this happens?

Conforming to Expectations

I can see from your questionnaire that your English teacher/your family/friends/classmates have certain expectations about you and you tend (not) to respond to these expectations. Can you explain a bit, please?

It seems to be quite different with your classmates/friends/family/teacher. How would you explain this? It doesn't seem to matter too much what they expect of you – why is that? It seems to matter a lot – could you expand a bit please?

English class/Teacher

Your passions and interests

You've said in your questionnaire that your English teacher doesn't really know what passions and interests you've got and doesn't seem to be too interested either. Can you give me an example, please? How would you explain that? Does this have any influence on your/the students' classroom involvement?

You've said the English teacher knows your passions and is very interested too. Can you give me an example, please? How would you explain that? Does this have any influence on your classroom involvement?

Your personal qualities

According to your questionnaire answers, you think you've got some personal qualities that aren't really appreciated (or known) in the English class. Can you give me an example, please? Does this have any influence on your classroom involvement?

You've said your personal qualities are very appreciated in the English class. An example? How does that make you feel in class? Why is that?

Mark

You've said you deserve a higher/lower mark than you normally get in English. How would you explain that? Why do you think you're usually marked in this way?

Motivation

What makes you feel really great in the English class? What makes you feel you're really yourself? That you're having a lot of fun and you're learning a lot too?

How would you describe your ideal English class? Has that happened?

Think about the English class of your life (whether it's happened or not) – how would you describe it to me? What's going on in there?

How would you motivate your students if you were a teacher (of English)?

Is there anything you'd change in your English class as it is now? Why?

How much effort would you say you put into the English class? A percentage? Why is that? What would make you work harder/not so hard?

Future job

What would you like to do in the future? How would English come into it?

Anything to Add?

Thanks and Concluding Remarks

Appendix E: Self System Graphical Representations and Vignettes

Table A. Self systems summary

Self system	Graphical representation	Vignette
Submissive	Ideal ≠ Imposed / Private = Public	They know very well what sort of person I am. What they would like me to do in life is different from what I would like to do, so that's why I prefer to give up my intentions and do what they think is better for me. What they want me to do in life is more important than what I'd have liked, so I'll do what they say.
Duplicitous	Ideal ≠ Imposed / Private ≠ Public	They don't really know what sort of person I really am, and it's not important for me that they do. They would like me to do something else in life than I would, and that's why I'll pursue my own dreams without letting them know. At the same time, I'll give them the impression that I do what they ask me to, even though I'm actually seeing about my own business. I know better.
Rebellious	Ideal ≠ Imposed / Private = Public	What they would like me to do in life is different from what I would like to do, so that's why I'll pursue my own dreams even if I have to rebel against them. They know me well, I haven't got anything to hide, and if they want to force me into doing something, I am likely to refuse it openly. What they want me to do is less important than what I want.
Harmonious	Ideal = Imposed / Private = Public	They know me very well and appreciate me for what I am. My dreams for the future are very similar to what they'd like me to do in life. They don't want to impose anything on me, but give me the total liberty to choose, and they always appreciate my decisions about my future. They help me feel really fulfilled.

Appendix F: Interviewee Profiles

Table B offers important background information about my 32 interview participants, which will be very useful in understanding their contributions in Chapter 5 and elsewhere. The table contains their chosen pseudonym, their gender, age and school, the self system type that they chose for all four relational contexts and a brief summary of their interviews. These summaries were written by myself after the data analysis stage and consist of either direct citation or very close paraphrasing, concentrating on the salience of the students' reference to identity processes.

Table B. Self system types and interview summaries for all 32 interviewees

No.	Participant (pseudonym, gender, age, school)	Self system type				Interview summary
		Teacher	Classmates	Friends	Family	
1.	Aprilie F 15 A	duplicitous	Rebellious	harmonious	submissive	Teachers help me learn and become what they want, but what they want is best for me. That's also true for my family. My previous teacher didn't know much about me because she never let me talk and she gave me low marks. Classmates and friends aren't really interested in how well I do in English, but sometimes I'm afraid to answer in class, lest I make mistakes and people laugh at me.
2.	Englezu M 16 A	rebellious	Duplicitous	submissive	submissive	I don't think my English teacher cares about what I want to do in the future; she just teaches her subject. The English class is for relaxation, not taken seriously. I'd be more involved if the teacher were more demanding. I don't talk to my classmates, only my best friends and my family know what I want to do in life. When my parents tell me something, I've got to do it, no grumbling.

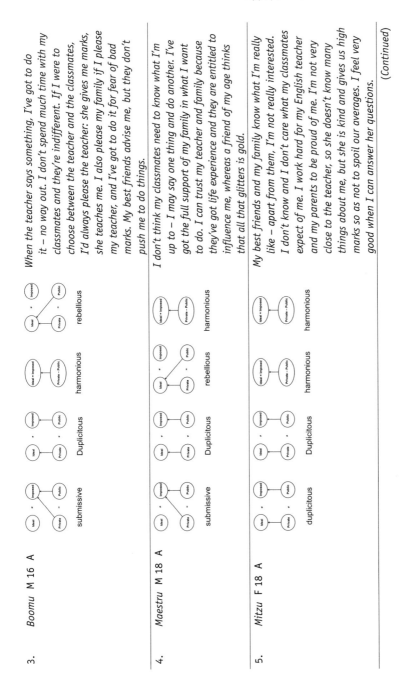

3. *Boomu M 16 A*

submissive   Duplicitous   harmonious   rebellious

When the teacher says something, I've got to do it – no way out. I don't spend much time with my classmates and they're indifferent. If I were to choose between the teacher and the classmates, I'd always please the teacher: she gives me marks, she teaches me. I also please my family if I please my teacher, and I've got to do it for fear of bad marks. My best friends advise me, but they don't push me to do things.

4. *Maestru M 18 A*

submissive   Duplicitous   rebellious   harmonious

I don't think my classmates need to know what I'm up to – I may say one thing and do another. I've got the full support of my family in what I want to do. I can trust my teacher and family because they've got life experience and they are entitled to influence me, whereas a friend of my age thinks that all that glitters is gold.

5. *Mitzu F 18 A*

duplicitous   Duplicitous   harmonious   harmonious

My best friends and my family know what I'm really like – apart from them, I'm not really interested. I don't know and I don't care what my classmates expect of me. I work hard for my English teacher and my parents to be proud of me. I'm not very close to the teacher, so she doesn't know many things about me, but she is kind and gives us high marks so as not to spoil our averages. I feel very good when I can answer her questions.

(Continued)

Table B. (Continued)

No.	Participant (pseudonym, gender, age, school)	Self system type					Interview summary
		Teacher	Classmates	Friends	Family	
6.	Kiddo M 14 B	duplicitous	Duplicitous	harmonious	rebellious	I always give a teacher the impression I do what they want. I think all students do this. That's the Romanian system – if you're not on good terms with the teacher, you're in trouble. As for my classmates, I've always said 'yes, of course' and gone on to do what I wanted. They want you to make mistakes, so they can laugh. My best friends are much older than me; they understand me and we get on very well. I've always done the opposite of what my parents say: they've got a Communist mentality.
7.	Woolf M 15 B	duplicitous	Duplicitous	rebellious	harmonious	Nobody should be influenced by anybody else. You can't let your friends decide for you – maybe your family, but not even them. You've got to be the same all the time, otherwise you won't know which person to be when you meet someone – and I'm talking from experience. I want to be perceived as a hard-working student, because I know that first impressions count. I want my teachers to think I'm hardworking, although I'm not. Well, I am, but not as much as they think. I want to create a particular image. As for this interview, I've actually been striving to look more interesting than I am.

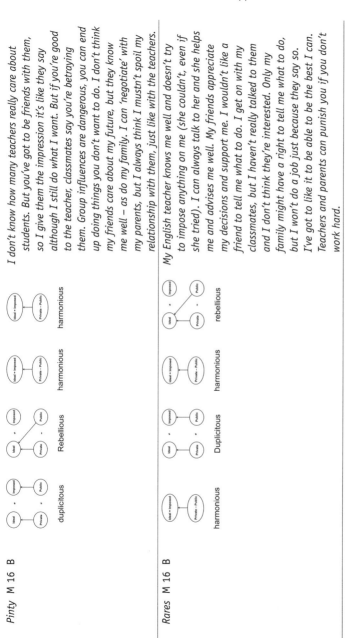

8.   *Pinty* M 16 B

duplicitous | Rebellious | harmonious | harmonious

I don't know how many teachers really care about students. But you've got to be friends with them, so I give them the impression it's like they say although I still do what I want. But if you're good to the teacher, classmates say you're betraying them. Group influences are dangerous, you can end up doing things you don't want to do. I don't think my friends care about my future, but they know me well – as do my family. I can 'negotiate' with my parents, but I always think I mustn't spoil my relationship with them, just like with the teachers.

9.   *Rares* M 16 B

harmonious | Duplicitous | harmonious | rebellious

My English teacher knows me well and doesn't try to impose anything on me (she couldn't, even if she tried). I can always talk to her and she helps me and advises me well. My friends appreciate my decisions and support me. I wouldn't like a friend to tell me what to do. I get on with my classmates, but I haven't really talked to them and I don't think they're interested. Only my family might have a right to tell me what to do, but I won't do a job just because they say so. I've got to like it to be able to be the best I can. Teachers and parents can punish you if you don't work hard.

(Continued)

Table B. (Continued)

No.	Participant (pseudonym, gender, age, school)	Self system type				Interview summary
		Teacher	Classmates	Friends	Family	
10.	Soare F 17 B	harmonious	Duplicitous	harmonious	harmonious	I only talk about class matters to my English teacher. She was really shocked when I told her what I'd like to do in the future, that's why I think she doesn't really know me, but she wouldn't push me to do things I don't want to do. My parents and my friends – few as I have – appreciate me and have always been there for me. However, I don't want to show my real face to my classmates, because they are mean and envious, and they can hurt me. I avoid showing them that I am sensitive and let them think that I'm a tough person, and never tell them what I do. Let them be shocked when they realise how wrong they've been!
11.	Prestige F 16 B	harmonious	Duplicitous	rebellious	harmonious	I always do what I want and nobody will ever influence me. My parents leave me total liberty to do what I want, and teachers are there to help us. My classmates can't possibly know what kind of person I really am, as we don't spend much time together, and I don't care what they'd like me to do. I work hard because I want my teacher and family to be proud of me, that's what motivates me. And I'm really pleased when I can show I'm better than others in class.

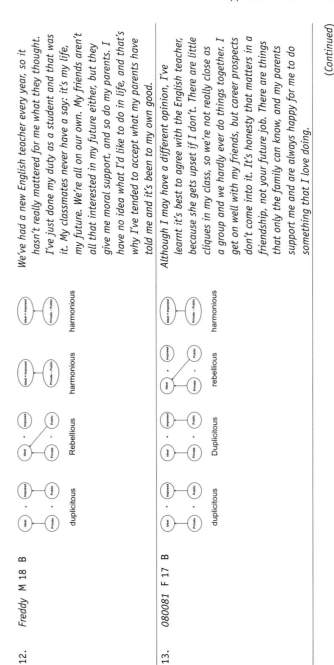

12.   Freddy M 18 B

We've had a new English teacher every year, so it hasn't really mattered for me what they thought. I've just done my duty as a student and that was it. My classmates never have a say: it's my life, my future. We're all on our own. My friends aren't all that interested in my future either, but they give me moral support, and so do my parents. I have no idea what I'd like to do in life, and that's why I've tended to accept what my parents have told me and it's been to my own good.

duplicitous   Rebellious   harmonious   harmonious

13.   080081 F 17 B

Although I may have a different opinion, I've learnt it's best to agree with the English teacher, because she gets upset if I don't. There are little cliques in my class, so we're not really close as a group and we hardly ever do things together. I get on well with my friends, but career prospects don't come into it. It's honesty that matters in a friendship, not your future job. There are things that only the family can know, and my parents support me and are always happy for me to do something that I love doing.

duplicitous   Duplicitous   rebellious   harmonious

(Continued)

Table B. (Continued)

No.	Participant (pseudonym, gender, age, school)	Self system type				Interview summary
		Teacher	Classmates	Friends	Family	
14.	Anda F 15 B	rebellious	Rebellious	harmonious	harmonious	I am what I am and people must get used to me, including my classmates and teachers. I demand more and more of myself because I want to achieve something in life and my parents push me to do the things they know I can do and help me succeed. When the teacher sees you do well, it means they've been good and you feel good in class too. From the very beginning our English teacher asked us about ourselves, what we like, what we don't, what we'd like the class to be like... When you see they're interested, of course you're interested too. I love it.
15.	Huggy M 15 B	harmonious	Rebellious	harmonious	harmonious	My friends and family have always let me choose what I wanted to do. My parents are very kind and they've created opportunities for me to learn English because they saw I was learning on my own from TV when I was really young. My English teacher has always been my friend and I've always felt great in class. I've got a real passion for English. As for my classmates, they know me as the boy who smiles all the time, but I won't do things they push me to if I don't think they're right.

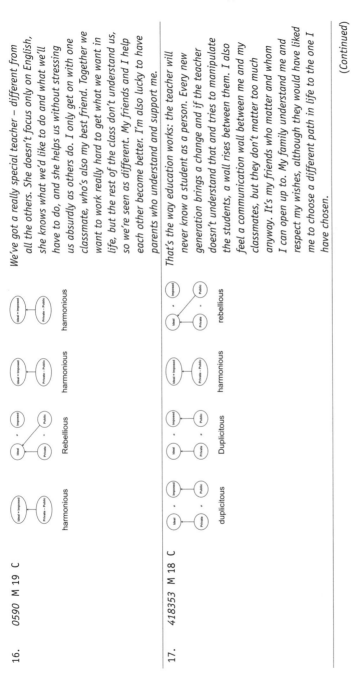

16. 0590 M 19 C

harmonious / Rebellious / harmonious / harmonious

We've got a really special teacher – different from all the others. She doesn't focus only on English, she knows what we'd like to do and what we'll have to do, and she helps us without stressing us absurdly as others do. I only get on with one classmate, who's also my best friend. Together we want to work really hard to get what we want in life, but the rest of the class don't understand us, so we're seen as different. My friends and I help each other become better. I'm also lucky to have parents who understand and support me.

17. 418353 M 18 C

duplicitous / Duplicitous / harmonious / rebellious

That's the way education works: the teacher will never know a student as a person. Every new generation brings a change and if the teacher doesn't understand that and tries to manipulate the students, a wall rises between them. I also feel a communication wall between me and my classmates, but they don't matter too much anyway. It's my friends who matter and whom I can open up to. My family understand me and respect my wishes, although they would have liked me to choose a different path in life to the one I have chosen.

(Continued)

Table B. (Continued)

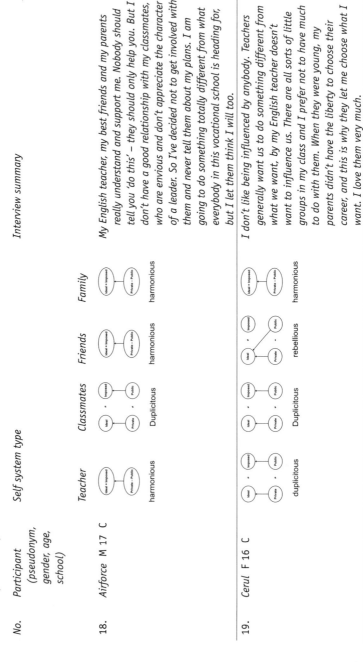

No.	Participant (pseudonym, gender, age, school)	Self system type				
		Teacher	Classmates	Friends	Family	Interview summary
18.	Airforce M 17 C	harmonious	Duplicitous	harmonious	harmonious	My English teacher, my best friends and my parents really understand and support me. Nobody should tell you 'do this' – they should only help you. But I don't have a good relationship with my classmates, who are envious and don't appreciate the character of a leader. So I've decided not to get involved with them and never tell them about my plans. I am going to do something totally different from what everybody in this vocational school is heading for, but I let them think I will too.
19.	Cerul F 16 C	duplicitous	Duplicitous	rebellious	harmonious	I don't like being influenced by anybody. Teachers generally want us to do something different from what we want, by my English teacher doesn't want to influence us. There are all sorts of little groups in my class and I prefer not to have much to do with them. When they were young, my parents didn't have the liberty to choose their career, and this is why they let me choose what I want. I love them very much.

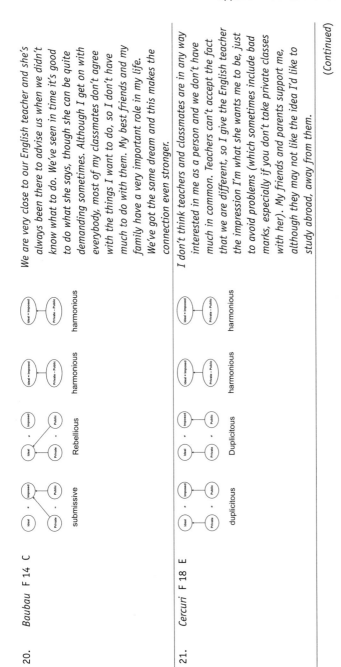

20.	*Baubau* F 14 C	submissive	Rebellious	harmonious	harmonious	We are very close to our English teacher and she's always been there to advise us when we didn't know what to do. We've seen in time it's good to do what she says, though she can be quite demanding sometimes. Although I get on with everybody, most of my classmates don't agree with the things I want to do, so I don't have much to do with them. My best friends and my family have a very important role in my life. We've got the same dream and this makes the connection even stronger.
21.	*Cercuri* F 18 E	duplicitous	Duplicitous	harmonious	harmonious	I don't think teachers and classmates are in any way interested in me as a person and we don't have much in common. Teachers can't accept the fact that we are different, so I give the English teacher the impression I'm what she wants me to be, just to avoid problems (which sometimes include bad marks, especially if you don't take private classes with her). My friends and parents support me, although they may not like the idea I'd like to study abroad, away from them.

(Continued)

Table B. (Continued)

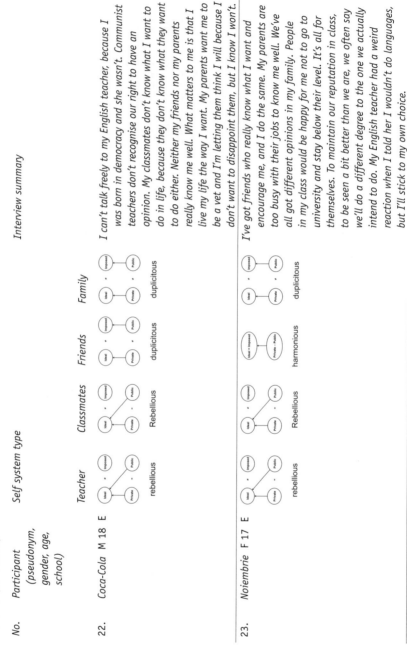

No.	Participant (pseudonym, gender, age, school)	Self system type				Interview summary
		Teacher	Classmates	Friends	Family	
22.	Coca-Cola M 18 E	rebellious	Rebellious	duplicitous	duplicitous	I can't talk freely to my English teacher, because I was born in democracy and she wasn't. Communist teachers don't recognise our right to have an opinion. My classmates don't know what I want to do in life, because they don't know what they want to do either. Neither my friends nor my parents really know me well. What matters to me is that I live my life the way I want. My parents want me to be a vet and I'm letting them think I will because I don't want to disappoint them, but I know I won't.
23.	Noiembrie F 17 E	rebellious	Rebellious	harmonious	duplicitous	I've got friends who really know what I want and encourage me, and I do the same. My parents are too busy with their jobs to know me well. We've all got different opinions in my family. People in my class would be happy for me not to go to university and stay below their level. It's all for themselves. To maintain our reputation in class, to be seen a bit better than we are, we often say we'll do a different degree to the one we actually intend to do. My English teacher had a weird reaction when I told her I wouldn't do languages, but I'll stick to my own choice.

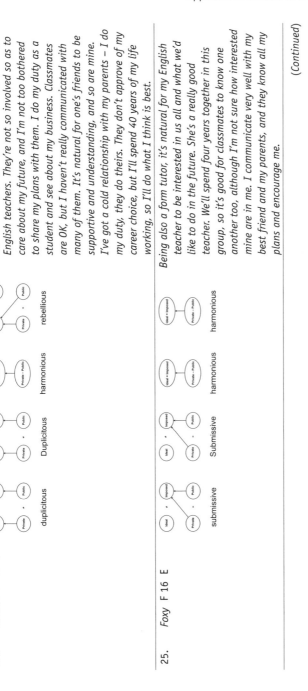

24.   Visator   M 18   E

duplicitous   Duplicitous   harmonious   rebellious

I've got a strictly professional relationship with my English teachers. They're not so involved so as to care about my future, and I'm not too bothered to share my plans with them. I do my duty as a student and see about my business. Classmates are OK, but I haven't really communicated with many of them. It's natural for one's friends to be supportive and understanding, and so are mine. I've got a cold relationship with my parents – I do my duty, they do theirs. They don't approve of my career choice, but I'll spend 40 years of my life working, so I'll do what I think is best.

25.   Foxy   F 16   E

submissive   Submissive   harmonious   harmonious

Being also a form tutor, it's natural for my English teacher to be interested in us all and what we'd like to do in the future. She's a really good teacher. We'll spend four years together in this group, so it's good for classmates to know one another too, although I'm not sure how interested mine are in me. I communicate very well with my best friend and my parents, and they know all my plans and encourage me.

(Continued)

Table B. (Continued)

No.	Participant (pseudonym, gender, age, school)	Self system type				Interview summary
		Teacher	Classmates	Friends	Family	
26.	2244 F 15 E	rebellious	Duplicitous	harmonious	harmonious	The English teacher is not really interested in every one of us, probably because she's too busy. If a teacher tells me to do a certain degree, I just don't care. I'll do what I want. My classmates don't really know me and they're not interested in me just like I'm not interested in them. Each for himself or herself in my class. My friends and my parents have always supported my decisions, even the wrong ones. You learn from your mistakes and if I want to do something I do it.
27.	Titulescu M 17 E	rebellious	Harmonious	harmonious	harmonious	I think my teacher would like me to do English at the university, but I won't. All students try to please their teacher, because a satisfied teacher is a teacher who's on your side (higher marks, better atmosphere). I do all that, but I won't change my plans for the future. My classmates, friends and family have come to know me well. They know what I intend to do and they're never tried to stop me from anything. I've always done what I wanted and it's been OK so far.

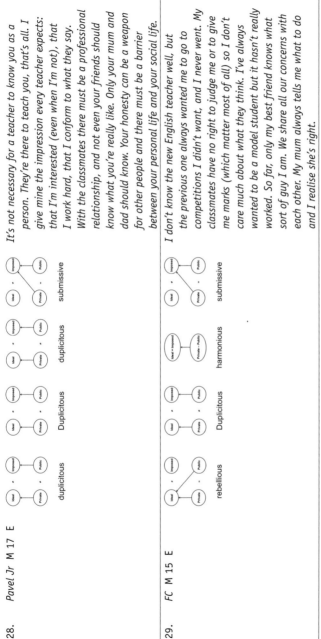

28. *Pavel Jr M 17 E*

It's not necessary for a teacher to know you as a person. They're there to teach you, that's all. I give mine the impression every teacher expects: that I'm interested (even when I'm not), that I work hard, that I conform to what they say. With the classmates there must be a professional relationship, and not even your friends should know what you're really like. Only your mum and dad should know. Your honesty can be a weapon for other people and there must be a barrier between your personal life and your social life.

29. *FC M 15 E*

I don't know the new English teacher well, but the previous one always wanted me to go to competitions I didn't want, and I never went. My classmates have no right to judge me or to give me marks (which matter most of all) so I don't care much about what they think. I've always wanted to be a model student but it hasn't really worked. So far, only my best friend knows what sort of guy I am. We share all our concerns with each other. My mum always tells me what to do and I realise she's right.

(Continued)

Table B. (Continued)

No.	Participant (pseudonym, gender, age, school)	Self system type				Interview summary
		Teacher	Classmates	Friends	Family	
30.	Sophie F 15 E	duplicitous	Duplicitous	harmonious	submissive	Teachers don't really care about us. They don't care that maybe you're ill, or you'd like to do some extra practice – they just come, teach the lesson and they're gone. They're bored, if they ever were interested. But you've got to leave them a good impression. You mustn't look too interested or too clever though, just enough so you're left alone. My classmates will never really know me, but I let them think I'm interested in them. What I am as a person only matters to my family and to myself. You've got to always be careful with the family. Sometimes you've got to do as they tell you or they say you've betrayed them and you haven't observed the family tradition. I love having a lot of trustworthy friends, but we don't talk about school.
31.	Piaf F 18 E	harmonious	Duplicitous	harmonious	rebellious	My English teacher is also my form tutor and she knows me well, she knows my hobbies, she appreciates and encourages me. I don't interact much with my classmates, so we're not close. And with all this competitiveness... My family aren't really involved in my life. They'd like me to study something lucrative, like Medicine, but I want to do Arts. It's strange, but I don't feel I can open

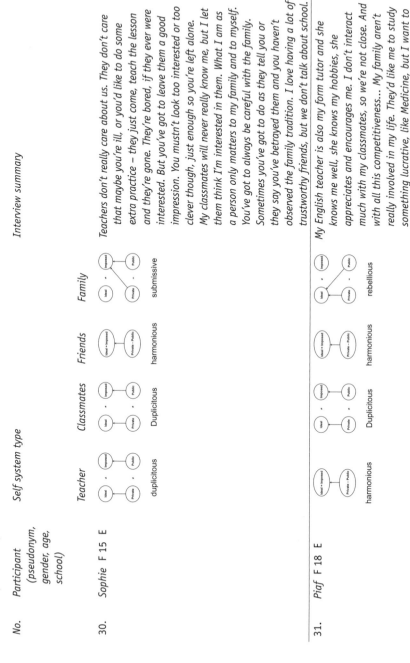

32.   *Slot F 17   E*

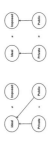

rebellious

Duplicitous

harmonious

harmonious

The English teacher knows me quite well. There have been situations when I didn't agree with her, but I told her and she understood, everything was fine. My classmates think I'm very different from what I am actually, but I'm not too bothered. I live only with my mum and we're very good friends. She encourages and appreciates me for what I am. And so do my friends. Otherwise they wouldn't be my friends, I guess.

Glossary

Duplicitous self system – A configuration of an individual's identity characterised by a strong imposed self and a strong ideal self, which results in the individual pretending to have the identity imposed on them in a particular relational context, while privately pursuing their own desired identity.

Harmonious self system – A configuration of an individual's identity characterised by an ideal self that is similar to the imposed self in a particular relational context, which results in the individual developing harmoniously along a trajectory that is both personally desired and socially encouraged.

Ideal self – A personal representation of what an individual would like to be in the future, irrespective of other people's desires and expectations about the individual.

Identity – An aggregate of internal and external selves associated with one individual. See *Quadripolar Model of Identity*.

Imposed selves – Representations of other people's hopes, desires and expectations of what an individual should achieve, the number of such representations depending on the number of relational contexts in which the individual functions.

Private self – A person's intimate representation of his/her present attributes, which may or may not be disclosed in social interaction.

Public selves – Various social presentations that a person may display depending on the relational context and audience.

Quadripolar Model of Identity – A theoretical framework that regards identity as an aggregate of four self components distributed across two axes (possible/actual and internal/external): the ideal (internal, possible), the private (internal, actual), the imposed (external, possible) and the public (external, actual) selves. These self components are regarded to cluster into four main self systems: submissive, duplicitous, rebellious and harmonious.

Rebellious self system – A configuration of an individual's identity characterised by an ideal self that is stronger than the imposed self, which results in the individual pursuing their own identity goals and openly opposing the identity imposed on them in that particular relational context.

Relational context – A given social situation where the individual interacts with other persons in a particular social capacity, responding to particular social expectations. Examples of such relational contexts are teacher-pupil, peer-group or family interactions, where social roles and expectations are usually clearly defined.

Submissive self system – A configuration of an individual's identity characterised by an imposed self that is stronger than the ideal self, which results in the individual relinquishing their ideal self and pursuing the imposed self in a particular relational context.

References

Ames, C. (1992) Classrooms: Goals, structures, and student motivation. *Journal of Educational Psychology* 84 (3), 261–271. doi:10.1037/0022-0663.84.3.261

Ames, C. and Archer, J. (1988) Achievement goals in the classroom: Students' learning strategies and motivational processes. *Journal of Educational Psychology* 80 (3), 260–267. doi:10.1037/0022-0663.80.3.260

Anderman, E.M., Anderman, L.H. and Griesinger, T. (1999) The relation of present and possible academic selves during early adolescence to grade point average and achievement goals. *Elementary School Journal* 100 (1), 3–17. doi:10.1086/461940

Andersen, S.M., Glassman, N.S. and Gold, D.A. (1998) Mental representations of the self, significant others, and nonsignificant others: Structure and processing of private and public aspects. *Journal of Personality and Social Psychology* 75 (4), 845–861. doi:10.1037/0022-3514.75.4.845

Andrei, L. (2006) Teaching English in post-modern Romanian education. *Journal of Organizational Change Management* 19 (6), 772–774. doi:10.1108/09534810610708431

Arkin, R.M. and Baumgardner, A.H. (1986) Self-presentation and self-evaluation: Processes of self-control and social control. In R.F. Baumeister (ed.) *Public Self and Private Self* (pp. 75–97). New York: Springer-Verlag.

Assor, A., Kaplan, H., Kanat-Maymon, Y. and Roth, G. (2005) Directly controlling teacher behaviors as predictors of poor motivation and engagement in girls and boys: The role of anger and anxiety. *Learning and Instruction* 15 (5), 397–413. doi:10.1016/j.learninstruc.2005.07.008

Assor, A., Kaplan, H. and Roth, G. (2002) Choice is good, but relevance is excellent: Autonomy enhancing and suppressing teacher behaviours predicting students' engagement in schoolwork. *British Journal of Educational Psychology* 72 (2), 261–278. doi:10.1348/000709902158883

Bakhtin, M. (1981) *The Dialogic Imagination: Four Essays.* Austin, TX: University of Texas Press.

Bandura, A. (1997) *Self-efficacy: The Exercise of Control.* New York: Freeman.

Barton, A. (1997) Boys' under-achievement in GCSE modern languages: Reviewing the reasons. *Language Learning Journal* 16 (1), 11–16. doi:10.1080/09571739785200211

Bartram, B. (2006a) Attitudes to language learning: A comparative study of peer group influences. *Language Learning Journal* 33 (1), 47–52. doi:10.1080/09571730685200101

Bartram, B. (2006b) An examination of perceptions of parental influence on attitudes to language learning. *Educational Research* 48 (2), 211–221. doi:10.1080/00131880600732298

Bartram, B. (2010) *Attitudes to Modern Foreign Language Learning: Insights from Comparative Education.* London: Continuum.

Baumeister, R.F. (1982) A self-presentational view of social phenomena. *Psychological Bulletin* 91 (1), 3–26. doi:10.1037/0033-2909.91.1.3

Baumeister, R.F. (ed.) (1986) *Public Self and Private Self.* New York: Springer-Verlag.

Baumeister, R.F. (1997) Identity, self-concept, and self-esteem: The self lost and found. In R. Hogan and J.A. Johnson (eds) *Handbook of Personality Psychology* (pp. 681–710). San Diego, CA: Academic Press.

Baumeister, R.F. (1999a) The nature and structure of the self: An overview. In R.F. Baumeister (ed.) *The Self in Social Psychology* (pp. 1–20). Philadelphia, PA: Psychology Press.

Baumeister, R.F. (ed.) (1999b) *The Self in Social Psychology.* Philadelphia, PA: Psychology Press.

Baumeister, R.F., Campbell, J.D., Krueger, J.I. and Vohs, K.D. (2003) Does high self-esteem cause better performance, interpersonal success, happiness, or healthier life-styles? *Psychological Science in the Public Interest 4*, 1–44.

Bell, K.L., Allen, J.P., Hauser, S.T. and O'Connor, T.G. (1996) Family factors and young adult transitions: Educational attainment and occupational prestige. In J.A. Graber, J. Brooks-Gunn and A.C. Petersen (eds) *Transitions Through Adolescence: Interpersonal Domains and Context* (pp. 345–366). Mahwah, NJ: Lawrence Erlbaum.

Berndt, T.J. and Keefe, K. (1996) Friends' influence on school adjustment: A motivational analysis. In J. Juvonen and K.R. Wentzel (eds) *Social Motivation: Understanding Children's School Adjustment* (pp. 248–278). Cambridge: Cambridge University Press.

Birch, S.H. and Ladd, G.W. (1996) Interpersonal relations in the school environment and the children's early school adjustment: The role of teachers and peers. In J. Juvonen and K.R. Wentzel (eds) *Social Motivation: Understanding Children's School Adjustment* (pp. 199–225). Cambridge: Cambridge University Press.

Blau, D.M. (1999) The effect of income on child development. *Review of Economics and Statistics* 81 (2), 261–276. doi:10.1162/003465399558067

Block, D. (1995) *Exploring Learners' Worlds: Two Studies* (Unpublished PhD thesis). University of Lancaster.

Block, D. (2000) Learners and their meta-pedagogical awareness. *International Journal of Applied Linguistics* 10 (1), 97–124. doi:10.1111/j.1473-4192.2000.tb00142.x

Block, D. (2007) *Second Language Identities.* London: Continuum.

Blumenfeld, P.C., Pintrich, P.R. and Hamilton, L.V. (1986) Children's concepts of ability, effort, and conduct. *American Educational Research Journal* 23 (1), 95–104. doi:10.3102/00028312023001095

Boggiano, A.K. and Katz, P. (1991) Maladaptive achievement patterns in students: The role of teachers' controlling strategies. *Journal of Social Issues* 47 (4), 35–51.

Bong, M. (2001) Between- and within-domain relations of academic motivation among middle and high school students: Self-efficacy, task value, and achievement goals. *Journal of Educational Psychology* 93 (1), 23–34. doi:10.1037/0022-0663.93.1.23

Bong, M. (2005) Within-grade changes in Korean girls' motivation and perceptions of the learning environment across domains and achievement levels. *Journal of Educational Psychology* 97 (4), 656–672. doi:10.1037/0022-0663.97.4.656

Bong, M. and Skaalvik, E.M. (2003) Academic self-concept and self-efficacy: How different are they really? *Educational Psychology Review* 15 (1), 1–40. doi:10.1023/A:1021302408382

Bor, D. (2012) *The Ravenous Brain: How the New Science of Consciousness Explains our Insatiable Search for Meaning.* New York: Perseus.

Bourdieu, P. (1991) *Language and Symbolic Power.* Cambridge: Polity.

Bower, G.H. and Gilligan, S.G. (1979) Remembering information related to one's self. *Journal of Research in Personality* 13 (4), 420–432. doi:10.1016/0092-6566%2879%2990005-9

Boyle, J.P. (1987) Sex differences in listening vocabulary. *Language Learning* 37 (2), 273–284. doi:10.1111/j.1467-1770.1987.tb00568.x

Brewer, J. and Hunter, A. (1993) *Multimethod Research: A Synthesis of Styles.* Newbury Park, CA: Sage.

Brinthaupt, T.M. and Lipka, R.P. (eds) (2002) *Understanding Early Adolescent Self and Identity: Applications and Interventions.* Albany, NY: State University of New York Press.

Brown, B.B. (1990) Peer groups and peer cultures. In S.S. Feldman and G.R. Elliot (eds) *At the Threshold: The Developing Adolescent* (pp. 171–196). Cambridge, MA: Harvard University Press.

Bügel, K. and Buunk, B.P. (1996) Sex differences in foreign language text comprehension: The role of interests and prior knowledge. *Modern Language Journal* 80 (1), 15–31.

Burhans, K.K. and Dweck, C.S. (1995) Helplessness in early childhood: The role of contingent worth. *Child Development*, 66 (6), 1719–1738. doi:10.2307/1131906

Burke, R.J., Greenglass, E.R. and Schwarzer, R. (1996) Predicting teacher burnout over time: Effects of work stress, social support, and self-doubts on burnout and its consequences. *Anxiety, Stress and Coping* 9 (3), 261. doi:10.1080/10615809608249406

Busch, T. (1995) Gender differences in self-efficacy and attitudes toward computers. *Journal of Educational Computing Research* 12 (2), 1–1. doi:10.2190/H7E1-XMM7-GU9B-3HWR

Busse, V. and Williams, M. (2010) Why German? Motivation of students studying German at English universities. *Language Learning Journal* 38 (1), 67–85.

Bussmann, H., Trauth, G. and Kazzazi, K. (1998) *Routledge Dictionary of Language and Linguistics.* London: Taylor & Francis.

Butler, R. (1988) Enhancing and undermining intrinsic motivation: The effects of task-involving and ego-involving evaluation of interest and performance. *British Journal of Educational Psychology* 58 (1), 1–14.

Butler, R. (1989) Interest in the task and interest in peers' work in competitive and noncompetitive conditions: A developmental study. *Child Development* 60 (3), 562–570.

Butler, R. (1992) What young people want to know when: Effects of mastery and ability goals on interest in different kinds of social comparison. *Journal of Personality and Social Psychology* 62 (6), 934–943. doi:10.1037/0022-3514.62.6.934

Byrne, B.M. (1996) *Measuring Self-Concept Across the Life Span: Issues and Instrumentation.* Washington, D.C.: American Psychological Association.

Callaghan, M. (1998) An investigation into the causes of boys' underachievement in French. *Language Learning Journal* 17 (1), 2–7. doi:10.1080/09571739885200021

Carr, J. and Pauwels, A. (2009) *Boys and foreign language learning: Real boys don't do languages* (2nd edn). Basingstoke: Palgrave Macmillan.

Ciani, K.D., Middleton, M.J., Summers, J.J. and Sheldon, K.M. (2010) Buffering against performance classroom goal structures: The importance of autonomy support and classroom community. *Contemporary Educational Psychology* 35 (1), 88–99. doi:10.1016/j.cedpsych.2009.11.001

CILT (2011) *Language Trends.* London: The National Centre for Languages. Retrieved from http://www.cilt.org.uk/home/research_and_statistics/language_trends_surveys/secondary/2010.aspx

Clark, A. (1995) Boys into modern languages: An investigation of the discrepancy in attitudes and performance between boys and girls in modern languages. *Gender and Education* 7 (3), 315–326.

Clarke, D.F. (1991) The negotiated syllabus: What is it and how does it work? *Applied Linguistics* 12 (1), 13–28.

Clemens, P. and Seidman, E. (2002) The ecology of middle grades school and possible selves: Theory, research and action. In T.M. Brinthaupt and R.P. Lipka (eds) *Understanding Early Adolescent Self and Identity: Applications and Interventions* (pp. 133–164). Albany, NY: State University of New York Press.

Cole, D.A., Martin, J.M., Peeke, L.A., Seroczynski, A.D. and Fier, J. (1999) Children's over- and underestimation of academic competence: A longitudinal study of gender differences, depression, and anxiety. *Child Development* 70 (2), 459–473. doi:10.1111/1467-8624.00033

Coleman, J.A., Galaczi, A. and Astruc, L. (2007) Motivation of UK school pupils towards foreign languages: a large-scale survey at Key Stage 3. *Language Learning Journal* 35 (2), 245. doi:10.1080/09571730701599252

Collins, W.A. (1990) Parent–child relationship in the transition to adolescence: Continuity and change in interaction, affect, and cognition. In R. Montemayor, G.R. Adams and T.P. Gullotta (eds) *From Childhood to Adolescence: A Transitional Period?* (Vol. 2, pp. 85–106). Newbury Park, CA: Sage.

Comănaru, R. and Noels, K.A. (2009) Self-determination, motivation, and the learning of Chinese as a heritage language. *The Canadian Modern Language Review* 66 (1), 131–158. doi:10.3138/cmlr.66.1.131

Connor, M.J. (1994) Peer relations and peer pressure. *Educational Psychology in Practice* 9 (4), 207–215. doi:10.1080/0266736940090403

Constantinescu, I., Popovici, V. and Ştefanescu, A. (2002) Romanian. In M. Görlach (ed.) *English in Europe* (pp. 168–194). Oxford: Oxford University Press.

Coopersmith, S. (1967) *The Antecedents of Self-esteem*. San Francisco: W. H. Freeman.

Côté, J.E. (2009) Identity formation and self-development in adolescence. In R.M. Lerner and L. Steinberg (eds) *Handbook of Adolescent Psychology: Individual Bases of Adolescent Development* (3rd edn, Vol. 1, pp. 266–304). Hoboken, NJ: Wiley.

Cotterall, S. and Murray, G. (2009) Enhancing metacognitive knowledge: Structure, affordances and self. *System* 37 (1), 34–45. doi:10.1016/j.system.2008.08.003

Covington, M.V. (1992) *Making the Grade: A Self-worth Perspective on Motivation and School Reform*. Cambridge: Cambridge University Press.

Creswell, J.W. (2008) *Research design: Qualitative, quantitative and mixed methods approaches* (3rd edn). Thousand Oaks, CA: Sage.

Crookes, G. (1997) What influences what and how second and foreign language teachers teach? *Modern Language Journal* 81 (1), 67–79.

Csikszentmihalyi, M. (1990) *Flow: The Psychology of Optimal Experience*. New York: Harper Collins.

Csikszentmihalyi, M. (1997) *Finding Flow: The Psychology of Engagement with Everyday Life*. New York: Perseus.

Csikszentmihalyi, M. and Larson, R. (1984) *Being Adolescent: Conflict and Growth in the Teenage Years*. New York: Basic Books.

Dart, B. and Clarke, J. (1988) Sexism in schools: A new look. *Educational Review* 40 (1), 41–49. doi:10.1080/0013191880400104

Day, J.D., Borkowski, J.G., Punzo, D. and Howsepian, B. (1994) Enhancing possible selves in Mexican American students. *Motivation and Emotion* 18 (1), 79–103. doi:10.1007/BF02252475

De Andrés, V. (2007) Self-esteem and language learning: Breaking the ice. In F. Rubio (ed.) *Self-esteem and Foreign Language Learning* (pp. 30–67). Newcastle, UK: Cambridge Scholars.

Deci, E.L., Koestner, R. and Ryan, R.M. (1999) A meta-analytic review of experiments examining the effects of extrinsic rewards on intrinsic motivation. *Psychological Bulletin* 125 (6), 627–668. doi:10.1037/0033-2909.125.6.627

Deci, E.L. and Moller, A.C. (2005) The concept of competence: A starting place for understanding intrinsic motivation and self-determined extrinsic motivation. In A.J. Elliot and C.S. Dweck (eds) *Handbook of Competence and Motivation* (pp. 579–597). New York: Guildford Press.

Deci, E.L. and Ryan, R.M. (1985) *Intrinsic Motivation and Self-determination in Human Behavior.* New York: Plenum.

Deci, E.L. and Ryan, R.M. (1992) The initiation and regulation of intrinsically motivated learning and achievement. In A.K. Boggiano and T.S. Pittman (eds) *Achievement and Motivation: A Social-developmental Perspective* (pp. 9–36). Cambridge: Cambridge University Press.

Deci, E.L. and Ryan, R.M. (2002) *Handbook of Self-determination Research.* Rochester, NY: University of Rochester Press.

Delamont, S. (1990) *Sex Roles and the School* (2nd edn). London: Routledge.

Doherty, K., Van Wagenen, T.J. and Schlenker, B.R. (1991) Imagined audiences influence self-identifications. Presented at the Annual meeting of the American Psychological Association, San Francisco.

Dörnyei, Z. (2005) *The Psychology of the Language Learner: Individual Differences in Second Language Acquisition.* Mahwah, NJ: Lawrence Erlbaum.

Dörnyei, Z. (2009) The L2 motivational self system. In Z. Dörnyei and E. Ushioda (eds) *Motivation, Language Identity and the L2 Self* (pp. 9–42). Bristol: Multilingual Matters.

Dörnyei, Z., Csizér, K. and Németh, N. (2006) *Motivational Dynamics, Language Attitudes and Language Globalisation: A Hungarian Perspective.* Clevedon: Multilingual Matters.

Dunkel, C.S. (2000) Possible selves as a mechanism for identity exploration. *Journal of Adolescence* 23 (5), 519–529. doi:10.1006/jado.2000.0340

Dunkel, C.S., Kelts, D. and Coon, B. (2006) Possible selves as mechanisms of change in therapy. In C.S. Dunkel and J.L. Kerpelman (eds) *Possible Selves: Theory, Research and Applications* (pp. 187–204). New York: Nova Science.

Durkin, K. (2004) Towards a developmental social psychology of the social self. In M. Bennett and F. Sani (eds) *The Development of the Social Self* (pp. 313–326). New York: Psychology Press.

Dweck, C.S. (1999) *Self-theories: Their Role in Motivation, Personality and Development.* Hove, UK: Psychology Press.

Dweck, C.S. (2007a) *Mindset: The New Psychology of Success.* New York: Random House.

Dweck, C.S. (2007b) Is math a gift? Beliefs that put females at risk. In S.J. Ceci and W.M. Williams (eds) *Why Aren't More Women in Science? Top Researchers Debate the Evidence* (pp. 47–55). Washington, DC: American Psychological Association.

Dweck, C.S. (2007c) The perils and promises of praise. *Educational Leadership* Oct.(2), 34–39.

Ehrman, M. (1996) An exploration of adult language learner motivation, self-efficacy, and anxiety. In R. Oxford (ed.) *Language Learning Motivation: Pathways to the New Century* (pp. 81–103). Honolulu, HI: University of Hawai'i Press.

Elkind, D. (1998) *All Grown Up and No Place to go: Teenagers in Crisis* (2nd edn). Cambridge, MA: Perseus.

Elliott, A. (2001) *Concepts of the Self.* Cambridge: Polity.

Elliott, E.S. and Dweck, C.S. (1988) Goals: An approach to motivation and achievement. *Journal of Personality and Social Psychology* 54 (1), 5–12. doi:10.1037/0022-3514.54.1.5

Erikson, M.G. (2007) The meaning of the future: Toward a more specific definition of possible selves. *Review of General Psychology* 11 (4), 348–358. doi:10.1037/1089-2680.11.4.348

European Commission. (2008a) *Organisation of the education system in Romania.* Brussels: EACEA, Eurydice Network. Retrieved from http://eacea.ec.europa.eu/education/eurydice/documents/eurybase/eurybase_full_reports/RO_EN.pdf

European Commission. (2008b) *Key data on teaching languages at school in Europe.* Brussels: EACEA, Eurydice Network. Retrieved from http://eacea.ec.europa.eu/education/eurydice/documents/key_data_series/095EN.pdf

Fabrigar, L.R., Wegener, D.T., MacCallum, R.C. and Strahan, E.J. (1999) Evaluating the use of exploratory factor analysis in psychological research. *Psychological Methods* 4 (3), 272–299. doi:10.1037/1082-989X.4.3.272

Feiring, C. and Taska, L.S. (1996) Family self-concept: Ideas on its meaning. In B.A. Bracken (ed.) *Handbook of Self-concept* (pp. 317–373). New York: Wiley.

Flink, C., Boggiano, A.K. and Barrett, M. (1990) Controlling teaching strategies: Undermining children's self-determination and performance. *Journal of Personality and Social Psychology* 59 (5), 916–924. doi:10.1037/0022-3514.59.5.916

Fredricks, J.A., Blumenfeld, P.C. and Paris, A.H. (2004) School engagement: Potential of the concept, state of the evidence. *Review of Educational Research* 74 (1), 59–109. doi:10.3102/00346543074001059

Friedman, T.L. (2000) *The Lexus and the Olive Tree.* New York: Anchor Books.

Furrer, C. and Skinner, E. (2003) Sense of relatedness as a factor in children's academic engagement and performance. *Journal of Educational Psychology* 95 (1), 148–162. doi:10.1037/0022-0663.95.1.148

Gardner, R.C. (1985) *Social Psychology and Second Language Learning: The Role of Attitudes and Motivation.* London: Edward Arnold.

Gardner, R.C., Tremblay, P.F. and Masgoret, A.M. (1997) Towards a full model of second language learning: An empirical investigation. *Modern Language Journal* 81 (3), 344–362. doi:10.2307/329310

Gebhard, J.G. (2006) *Teaching English as a Foreign or Second Language: A Teacher Self-development and Methodology Guide* (2nd edn). Ann Arbor, MI: University of Michigan Press.

Gilbert, F. (2005) *I'm a Teacher, Get Me Out of Here!* (2nd edn). London: Short Books.

Goldberg, E. and Noels, K.A. (2006) Motivation, ethnic identity, and post-secondary education language choices of graduates of intensive French language programs. *Canadian Modern Language Review* 62 (3), 423–447. doi:10.3138/cmlr.62.3.423

Goldstein, T. (1995) Nobody is talking bad. In K. Hall and M. Bucholtz (eds) *Gender Articulated: Language and the Socially Constructed Self* (pp. 375–400). New York: Routledge.

Goldstein, T. (1997) *Two Languages at Work: Bilingual Life on the Factory Floor.* New York: Mouton de Gruyter.

Gollwitzer, P.M. and Kirchhof, O. (1998) The wilful pursuit of identity. In J. Heckhausen and C.S. Dweck (eds) *Motivation and Self-regulation Across the Life Span* (pp. 389–423). Cambridge: Cambridge University Press.

Graham, S. (1997) *Effective Language Learning: Positive Strategies for Advanced Level Language Learning*. Clevedon: Multilingual Matters.

Graham, S. (2004) Giving up on modern foreign languages? Students' perceptions of learning French. *The Modern Language Journal* 88 (2), 171–191. doi:10.1111/j.0026-7902.2004.00224.x

Graham, S. (2007) Learner strategies and self-efficacy: Making the connection. *Language Learning Journal* 35 (1), 81–93. doi:10.1080/09571730701315832

Greene, B. and Miller, R. (1996) Influences on achievement: Goals, perceived ability and cognitive engagement. *Contemporary Educational Psychology* 21 (2), 181–192. doi:10.1006/ceps.1996.0015

Hair, F.H., Black, W.C., Babin, B.J., Anderson, R.E. and Tatham, R.L. (2006) *Multivariate data analysis* (6th edn). Upper Saddle River, NJ: Pearson Education.

Hansen, R.D. and O'Leary, V.E. (1985) Sex-determined attributions. In V.E. O'Leary, R.K. Unger and B.S. Wallston (eds) *Women, Gender, and Social Psychology* (pp. 67–99). Hillsdale, NJ: Lawrence Erlbaum.

Hardman, F. (2008) Teachers' use of feedback in whole-class and group-based talk. In N. Mercer and S. Hodgkinson (eds) *Exploring Talk in School* (pp. 131–150). London: Sage.

Hargittai, E. and Shafer, S. (2006) Differences in actual and perceived online skills: The role of gender. *Social Science Quarterly* 87 (2), 432–448. doi:10.1111/j.1540-6237.2006.00389.x

Harter, S. (1992) The relationship between perceived competence, affect, and motivational orientation within the classroom: Processes and patterns of change. In A.K. Boggiano and T.S. Pittman (eds) *Achievement and Motivation: A Social-developmental Perspective* (pp. 77–114). Cambridge: Cambridge University Press.

Harter, S. (1996) Teacher and classmate influences on scholastic motivation, self-esteem, and level of voice in adolescents. In J. Juvonen and K.R. Wentzel (eds) *Social Motivation: Understanding Children's School Adjustment* (pp. 11–42). Cambridge: Cambridge University Press.

Harter, S. (1999) *The Construction of the Self: A Developmental Perspective*. New York: Guildford Press.

Harter, S. (2012) *Construction of the Self: Developmental and Sociocultural Foundations* (2nd edn). New York: Guilford.

Harter, S., Bresnick, S., Bouchey, H.A. and Whitesell, N.R. (1997) The development of multiple role-related selves during adolescence. *Development and Psychopathology* 9 (4), 835–853. doi:10.1017/S0954579497001466

Harter, S. and Monsour, A. (1992) Developmental analysis of conflict caused by opposing attributes in the adolescent self-portrait. *Developmental Psychology* 28 (2), 251–260. doi:10.1037/0012-1649.28.2.251

Harter, S., Waters, P. and Whitesell, N.R. (1997) Lack of voice as a manifestation of false self-behavior among adolescents: The school setting as a stage upon which the drama of authenticity is enacted. *Educational Psychologist* 32 (3), 153–173. doi:10.1207/s15326985ep3203_2

Harter, S., Waters, P. and Whitesell, N.R. (1998) Relational self-worth: Differences in perceived worth as a person across interpersonal contexts among adolescents. *Child Development* 69 (3), 756–766. doi:10.1111/j.1467-8624.1998.tb06241.x

Hattie, J. (1992) *Self-Concept*. Hillsdale, NJ: Lawrence Erlbaum.

Heller, M. (1987) The role of language in the formation of ethnic identity. In J. Phinney and M. Rotheram (eds) *Children's Ethnic Socialization* (pp. 180–200). Newbury Park, CA: Sage.

Henry, A. (2009) Gender differences in compulsory pupils' L2 self-concepts: A longitudinal study. *System* 37 (2), 177–193. doi:10.1016/j.system.2008.11.003

Hidi, S. (2000) An interest researcher's perspective: The effects of extrinsic and intrinsic factors on motivation. In C. Sansone and J.M. Harackiewicz (eds) *Intrinsic and Extrinsic Motivation: The Search for Optimal Motivation and Performance* (pp. 309–339). San Diego, CA: Academic Press.

Higgins, T.E. (1987) Self-discrepancy: A theory relating self and affect. *Psychological Review* 94 (3), 319–340. doi:10.1037/0033-295X.94.3.319

Higgins, T.E. (1996) The 'self digest': Self-knowledge serving self-regulatory functions. *Journal of Personality and Social Psychology* 71 (6), 1062–1083. doi:10.1037/0022-3514.71.6.1062

Higgins, T.E. (2006) Value from hedonic experience and engagement. *Psychological Review* 113 (3), 439–460. doi:10.1037/0033-295X.113.3.439

Higgins, T.E., Roney, C.J.R., Crowe, E. and Hymes, C. (1994) Ideal versus ought predilections for approach and avoidance: Distinct self-regulatory systems. *Journal of Personality and Social Psychology* 66 (2), 276–286. doi:10.1037/0022-3514.66.2.276

Hock, M.F., Deshler, D.D. and Schumaker, J.B. (2006) Enhancing student motivation through the pursuit of possible selves. In C.S. Dunkel and J.L. Kerpelman (eds) *Possible Selves: Theory, Research and Applications* (pp. 205–221) New York: Nova Science.

Hogan, R. and Briggs, S.R. (1986) A socioanalytic interpretation of the public and the private selves. In R.F. Baumeister (ed.) *Public Self and Private Self* (pp. 179–188). New York: Springer-Verlag.

Holmberg, G.N. (1996) A model of family relational transformations during the transition to adolescence: Parent–adolescent conflict and adaptation. In J.A. Graber, J. Brooks-Gunn and A.C. Petersen (eds) *Transitions Through Adolescence: Interpersonal Domains and Context* (pp. 167–200). Mahwah, NJ: Lawrence Erlbaum.

Horberg, E.J. and Chen, S. (2010) Significant others and contingencies of self-worth: Activation and consequences of relationship-specific contingencies of self-worth. *Journal of Personality and Social Psychology* 98 (1), 77–91. doi:10.1037/a0016428

Imhof, M., Vollmeyer, R. and Beierlein, C. (2007) Computer use and the gender gap: The issue of access, use, motivation, and performance. *Computers in Human Behavior* 23 (6), 2823–2837. doi:10.1016/j.chb.2006.05.007

Istrate, O. and Velea, L.S. (2006) *Student Voice Romania*. Bucharest: Centre for Development and Innovation in Education. Retrieved from http://www.tehne.ro/resurse/TEHNE_SVR_Report_2006.pdf

James, W.J. (1890) *Principles of Psychology*. New York: Holt.

Jarvis, S. and Seifert, T. (2002) Work avoidance as a manifestation of hostility, helplessness or boredom. *Alberta Journal of Educational Research* 48, 174–187.

Johnson, B. and Turner, L.A. (2003) Data collection strategies in mixed methods research. In A. Tashakkori and C. Teddlie (eds) *Handbook of Mixed Methods in Social and Behavioral Research* (pp. 297–320). Thousand Oaks, CA: Sage.

Jones, E.E. and Pittman, T.S. (1982) Toward a general theory of strategic self-presentation. In J. Suls (ed.) *Psychological Perspectives on the Self* (Vol. 1, pp. 231–262). Hillsdale, NJ: Erlbaum.

Jones, S.M. and Dindia, K. (2004) A meta-analytic perspective on sex equity in the classroom. *Review of Educational Research* 74 (4), 443–471. doi:10.3102/00346543074004443

Juvonen, J. (1996) Self-presentation tactics promoting teacher and peer approval: The function of excuses and other clever explanations. In J. Juvonen and K.R. Wentzel (eds) *Social Motivation: Understanding Children's School Adjustment* (pp. 43–65). Cambridge: Cambridge University Press.

Juvonen, J. (2000) The social functions of attributional face-saving tactics among early adolescents. *Educational Psychology Review* 12 (1), 15–32. doi:10.1023/A%3A1009080816191

Juvonen, J. and Murdock, T.B. (1993) How to promote social approval: Effect of audience and outcome on publicly communicated attributions. *Journal of Educational Psychology* 85 (2), 365–376. doi:10.1037/0022-0663.85.2.365

Juvonen, J. and Murdock, T.B. (1995) Grade-level differences in the social value of effort: Implications for self-presentation tactics of early adolescents. *Child Development* 66 (6), 1694–1705. doi:10.2307/1131904

Juvonen, J. and Wentzel, K.R. (eds) (1996) *Social Motivation: Understanding Children's School Adjustment*. Cambridge: Cambridge University Press.

Kaplan, A. and Flum, H. (2010) Achievement goal orientations and identity formation styles. *Educational Research Review* 5 (1), 50–67. doi:10.1016/j.edurev.2009.06.004

Kay, R.H. (2009) Examining gender differences in attitudes toward interactive classroom communications systems (ICCS). *Computers and Education* 52 (4), 730–740. doi:10.1016/j.compedu.2008.11.015

Kellman, S.G. (ed.) (2003) *Switching Languages: Translingual Writers Reflect on their Craft*. Lincoln, NE: University of Nebraska Press.

Kelly, A. (1988) Gender differences in teacher-pupil interactions: A meta-analytic review. *Research in Education* 39, 1–23.

Kindermann, T.A., McCollam, T.L. and Gibson, E. (1996) Peer networks and students' classroom engagement during childhood and adolescence. In J. Juvonen and K.R. Wentzel (eds) *Social Motivation: Understanding Children's School Adjustment* (pp. 279–312). Cambridge: Cambridge University Press.

Klos, M.L. (2006) Using cultural identity to improve learning. *The Educational Forum* 70 (4), 363–370. doi:10.1080/00131720608984915

Kobayashi, Y. (2002) The role of gender in foreign language learning attitudes: Japanese female students' attitudes towards English learning. *Gender and Education* 14 (2), 181–197. doi:10.1080/09540250220133021

Kohn, A. (1993) *Punished by Rewards: The Trouble with Gold Stars, Incentive Plans, A's, Praise and other Bribes*. Boston, MA: Houghton Mifflin.

Kohn, A. (1994) The truth about self-esteem. *Phi Delta Kappan* 76 (4), 272–283.

Kohn, A. (1999) *The Schools our Children Deserve: Moving Beyond Traditional Classrooms and 'Tougher Standards'*. Boston, MA: Houghton Mifflin.

Kormos, J. and Csizér, K. (2008) Age-related differences in the motivation of learning English as a foreign language: Attitudes, selves, and motivated learning behavior. *Language Learning* 58 (2), 327–355. doi:10.1111/j.1467-9922.2008.00443.x

Kyriacou, C. and Zhu, D. (2008) Shanghai pupils' motivation towards learning English and the perceived influence of important others. *Educational Studies* 34 (2), 97–104. doi:10.1080/03055690701811099

La Guardia, J.G. (2009) Developing who I am: A self-determination theory approach to the establishment of healthy identities. *Educational Psychologist* 44 (2), 90–104. doi:10.1080/00461520902832350

Lamb, M. (2011) A 'Matthew effect' in English language education in a developing country context. In H. Coleman (ed.) *Dreams and Realities: Developing Countries and the English Language* (pp. 186–206). London: The British Council. Retrieved from http://www.teachingenglish.org.uk/publications/dreams-realities-developing-countries-english-language

Landry, R., Allard, R. and Deveau, K. (2009) Self-determination and bilingualism. *Theory and Research in Education* 7 (2), 203–213. doi:10.1177/1477878509104325

Lantolf, J. and Genung, P. (2003) 'I'd rather switch than fight': An activity theoretic study of power, success and failure in a foreign language classroom. In C. Kramsch (ed.) *Language Acquisition and Language Socialization* (pp. 175–196). London: Continuum.

Lau, I., Yeung, A.S., Jin, P. and Low, R. (1999) Toward a hierarchical, multidimensional English self-concept. *Journal of Educational Psychology* 91 (4), 747–758. doi:10.1037/0022-0663.91.4.747

Leary, M.R. (1995) *Self-Presentation: Impression Management and Interpersonal Behavior.* Madison, WI: Brown and Benchmark.

Leary, M.R. and Kowalski, R.M. (1990) Impression management: A literature review and two-component model. *Psychological Bulletin* 107 (1), 34–47. doi:10.1037/0033-2909.107.1.34

LeCompte, M.D. and Dworkin, A.G. (1991) *Giving up on School: Student Dropouts and Teacher Burnouts.* Newbury Park, CA: Sage.

Lempers, J.D. and Clark-Lempers, D.S. (1992) Young, middle, and late adolescents' comparisons of the functional importance of five significant relationships. *Journal of Youth and Adolescence* 21 (1), 53–96. doi:10.1007/BF01536983

Leondari, A., Syngollitou, E. and Kiosseoglou, G. (1998) Brief report: Academic achievement, motivation and possible selves. *Journal of Adolescence* 21 (2), 219–222. doi:10.1006/jado.1997.0143

Lepper, M.R. (1983) Extrinsic reward and intrinsic motivation: Implications for the classroom. In J.M. Levine and M.C. Wang (eds) *Teacher and Student Perceptions: Implications for Learning* (pp. 281–317). Hillsdale, NJ: Erlbaum.

Lepper, M.R. and Greene, D. (eds) (1978) *The Hidden Costs of Reward: New Perspectives on the Psychology of Human Motivation.* Hillsdale, NJ: Erlbaum.

Lepper, M.R. and Henderlong, J. (2000) Turning 'play' into 'work' and 'work' into 'play': 25 years of research on intrinsic versus extrinsic motivation. In C. Sansone and J.M. Harackiewicz (eds) *Intrinsic and Extrinsic Motivation: The Search for Optimal Motivation and Performance* (pp. 257–307). San Diego, CA: Academic Press.

Lewis, M. (1990) Self-knowledge and social development in early life. In L. Pervin (ed.) *Handbook of Personality: Theory and Research* (pp. 277–300). New York: Guildford Press.

Lexmond, J. and Reeves, R. (2009) *Building Character* (Demos Report) London: Demos.

Lightbown, P. and Spada, N. (1999) *How Languages are Learnt.* Oxford: Oxford University Press.

Little, D., Ridley, J. and Ushioda, E. (2002) *Towards Greater Learner Autonomy in the Foreign Language Classroom.* Dublin: Authentik.

Markus, H.R. (1977) Self-schemata and processing information about the self. *Journal of Personality and Social Psychology* 35 (2), 63–78. doi:10.1037/0022-3514.35.2.63

Markus, H.R. and Nurius, P. (1986) Possible selves. *American Psychologist* 41 (9), 954–969. doi:10.1037/0003-066X.41.9.954

Marsh, H.W. (1990a) The structure of academic self-concept. The Marsh/Shavelson model. *Journal of Educational Psychology* 82 (4), 623–636. doi:10.1037/0022-0663.82.4.623

Marsh, H.W. (1990b) Influences of internal and external frames of reference on the formation of math and English self-concepts. *Journal of Educational Psychology* 82 (1), 107–116. doi:10.1037/0022-0663.82.1.107

Marsh, H.W. (1992) Content specificity of relations between academic achievement and academic self-concept. *Journal of Educational Psychology* 84 (1), 35–42. doi:10.1037/0022-0663.84.1.35

Marsh, H.W. (1993) Academic self-concept: Theory, measurement, and research. In J. Suls (ed.) *Psychological Perspectives on the Self* (Vol. 4, pp. 59–98). Hillsdale, NJ: Erlbaum.

Marsh, H.W., Byrne, B.M. and Shavelson, R.J. (1988) A multifaceted academic self-concept: Its hierarchical structure and its relation to academic achievement. *Journal of Educational Psychology* 80 (3), 366–380. doi:10.1037/0022-0663.80.3.366

Marsh, H.W., Craven, R. and McInerney, D. (eds) (2005) *International Advances in Self research* (Vol. 2 New frontiers for self research). Greenwich, CT: Information Age Publishing.

Marsh, H.W., Hau, K.T. and Craven, R. (2004) The big-fish-little-pond effect stands up to scrutiny. *American Psychologist* 59 (4), 269–271. doi:10.1037/0003-066X.59.4.269

Marsh, H.W. and O'Mara, A. (2008) Reciprocal effects between academic self-concept, self-esteem, achievement, and attainment over seven adolescent years: Unidimensional and multidimensional perspectives of self-concept. *Personality and Social Psychology Bulletin* 34 (4), 542–552. doi:10.1177/0146167207312313

Marsh, H.W. and Yeung, A.S. (1998) Top-down, bottom-up, and horizontal models: The direction of causality in multidimensional, hierarchical self-concept models. *Journal of Personality and Social Psychology* 75 (2), 509–527. doi:10.1037/0022-3514.75.2.509

Marshall, S.K., Young, R.A. and Domene, J.F. (2006) Possible selves as joint projects. In C.S. Dunkel and J.L. Kerpelman (eds) *Possible Selves: Theory, Research and Applications* (pp. 141–161). New York: Nova Science.

Martin, M.D. (2005) Permanent crisis, tenuous persistence: Foreign languages in Australian universities. *Arts and Humanities in Higher Education* 4 (1), 53–75. doi:10.1177/1474022205048758

McClun, L.A. and Merrell, K.W. (1998) Relationship of perceived parenting styles, locus of control orientation, and self-concept among junior high age students. *Psychology in the Schools* 35 (4), 381–390. doi:10.1002/(SICI)1520-6807 (199810)35:4<381::AID-PITS9>3.0.CO;2-S

McKay, S. and Wong, S.C. (1996) Multiple discourses, multiple identities: Investment and agency in second language learning among Chinese adolescent immigrant students. *Harvard Educational Review* 66 (3), 577–608.

McNamara, T.F. (1987) Language and social identity: Some Australian studies. *Australian Review of Applied Linguistics* 10, 33–58.

Mead, G.H. (1934) *Mind, Self and Society* (C.W. Morris, ed.). New York: University of Chicago Press.

Medgyes, P. (1997) Innovative second language education in Central and Eastern Europe. In G.R Tucker and D. Corson (eds) *Encyclopedia of Language Education* (Vol. 4: Second language education, pp. 187–196). Dordrecht, The Netherlands: Kluwer Academic.

Meece, J., Anderman, E.M. and Anderman, L.H. (2006) Classroom goal structure, student motivation, and academic achievement. *Annual Review of Psychology* 57, 487–503. doi:10.1146/annurev.psych.56.091103.070258

Melucci, A. (1996) *The Playing Self: Person and Meaning in the Planetary Society.* Cambridge: Cambridge University Press.

Mercer, S. (2011) *Towards an Understanding of Language Learner Self-concept.* Dordrecht: Springer.

Mercer, S. (2012) Self-concept: Situating the self. In S. Mercer, S. Ryan and M. Williams (eds) *Psychology for Language Learning: Insights from Research, Theory and Practice* (pp. 10–25). Basingstoke: Palgrave Macmillan.

Merrett, F. and Wheldall, K. (1992) Teachers' use of praise and reprimands to boys and girls. *Educational Review* 44 (1), 73. doi:10.1080/0013191920440106

Mihai, F.M. (2003) *Reforming English as a Foreign Language (EFL) curriculum in Romania: The global and the local contexts* (Unpublished PhD thesis). Florida State University, Tallahassee, FL.

Miller, J. (2003) *Audible Differences: ESL and Social Identity in Schools.* Clevedon: Multilingual Matters.

Miller, R.B., Greene, B.A., Montalvo, G.P., Ravindran, B. and Nichols, J.D. (1996) Engagement in academic work: The role of learning goals, future consequences, pleasing others, and perceived ability. *Contemporary Educational Psychology* 21 (4), 388–422. doi:10.1006/ceps.1996.0028

Mills, N., Pajares, F. and Herron, C. (2007) Self-efficacy of college intermediate French students: Relation to achievement and motivation. *Language Learning* 57 (3), 417–442. doi:10.1111/j.1467-9922.2007.00421.x

Mitchell, R. (2009) Foreign language teaching and educational policy. In K. Knapp and B. Seidlhofer (eds) *Handbook of Foreign Language Communication and Learning* (pp. 79–108). Berlin: Walter de Gruyter.

Mueller, C.M. and Dweck, C.S. (1998) Praise for intelligence can undermine children's motivation and performance. *Journal of Personality and Social Psychology* 75 (1), 33–52. doi:10.1037/0022-3514.75.1.33

Murdock, T.B. and Miller, A. (2003) Teachers as sources of middle school students' motivational identity: Variable-centered and person-centered analytic approaches. *Elementary School Journal* 103(4, Special issue: New directions in motivation research: Implications for practice), 383–399. doi:10.1086/499732

National Curriculum Council (2007a) *Programe scolare pentru clasa a IX-a: Limba engleza [Syllabi for grade IX: English language].* Bucharest: Romanian Ministry of Education and Research.

National Curriculum Council (2007b) *Programe scolare pentru clasele X-XII Limba engleza [Syllabi for grades X-XII: English language].* Bucharest: Romanian Ministry of Education and Research.

Noels, K.A. (2005) Orientations to learning German: Heritage language learning and motivational substrates. *Canadian Modern Language Review* 62 (2), 285–312. doi:10.1353/cml.2006.0007

Noels, K.A. (2009) The internalisation of language learning into the self and social identity. In Z. Dörnyei and E. Ushioda (eds) *Motivation, Language Identity and the L2 Self* (pp. 295–313). Bristol: Multilingual Matters.

Noels, K.A., Clément, R. and Pelletier, L.G. (2006) Intrinsic, extrinsic, and integrative orientations of French Canadian learners of English. *Canadian Modern Language Review* 57 (3), 424–442. doi:10.3138/cmlr.57.3.424

Noels, K.A., Pelletier, L.G., Clément, R. and Vallerand, R.J. (2000) Why are you learning a second language? Motivational orientations and self-determination theory. *Language Learning* 50 (1), 57–85. doi:10.1111/0023-8333.00111

Norman, C.C. and Aron, A. (2003) Aspects of possible self that predict motivation to achieve or avoid it. *Journal of Experimental Social Psychology* 39 (5), 500–507. doi:10.1016/S0022-1031%2803%2900029-5

Norton, B. (1997) Language, identity and the ownership of English. *TESOL Quarterly* 31 (3), 409–429. doi:10.2307/3587831

Norton, B. (2000) *Identity and Language Learning: Gender, Ethnicity and Educational Change.* Harlow: Pearson.

Nyikos, M. (2008) Gender and good language learners. In C. Griffiths (ed.) *Lessons from Good Language Learners* (pp. 73–82). Cambridge: Cambridge University Press.

Oettingen, G. and Mayer, D. (2002) The motivating function of thinking about the future: Expectations versus fantasies. *Journal of Personality and Social Psychology* 83 (5), 1198–1212. doi:10.1037/0022-3514.83.5.1198

Oyserman, D., Bybee, D., Terry, K. and Hart-Johnson, T. (2004) Possible selves as road-maps. *Journal of Research in Personality* 38 (2), 130–149. doi:10.1016/S0092-6566(03)00057-6

Oyserman, D. and Fryberg, S. (2006) The possible selves of diverse adolescents: Content and function across gender, race and national origin. In C.S. Dunkel and J.L. Kerpelman (eds) *Possible Selves: Theory, Research and Applications* (pp. 17–39). New York: Nova Science.

Oyserman, D., Terry, K. and Bybee, D. (2002) A possible selves intervention to enhance school involvement. *Journal of Adolescence* 25 (3), 313–326. doi:10.1006/jado.2002.0474

Pachler, N. (2002) Foreign language learning in England in the 21st century. *Language Learning Journal* 25, 4–7.

Pajares, F. (1997) Current directions in self-efficacy research. In M. Maehr and P.R. Pintrich (eds) *Advances in Motivation and Achievement* (Vol. 10, pp. 1–49). Greenwich, CT: JAI Press.

Pajares, F. and Schunk, D.H. (2001) Self-beliefs and school success: Self-efficacy, self-concept and school achievement. In R. Riding and S. Rayner (eds) *Perception* (pp. 239–266). London: Ablex Publishing.

Pajares, F. and Schunk, D.H. (2002) Self and self-belief in psychology and education: A historical perspective. In J.M. Aronson (ed.) *Improving Academic Achievement: Impact of Psychological Factors on Education* (pp. 5–21). London: Academic Press.

Pallant, J. (2007) *SPSS Survival Manual: A Step by Step Guide to Data Analysis Using SPSS for Windows* (3rd edn). Maidenhead, UK: Open University Press.

Pavlenko, A. and Blackledge, A. (eds) (2004) *Negotiation of Identities in Multilingual Contexts.* Clevedon: Multilingual Matters.

Pavlenko, A. and Lantolf, J.P. (2000) Second language learning as participation and the (re)construction of selves. In J.P. Lantolf (ed.) *Sociocultural Theory and Second Language Learning* (pp. 155–177). Oxford: Oxford University Press.

Pedersen, S. and Macafee, C. (2007) Gender differences in British blogging. *Journal of Computer-Mediated Communication* 12 (4), 1472–1492. doi:10.1111/j.1083-6101.2007.00382.x

Pelletier, L.G., Séguin-Lévesque, C. and Legault, L. (2002) Pressure from above and pressure from below as determinants of teachers' motivation and teaching behaviors. *Journal of Educational Psychology* 94 (1), 186–196. doi:10.1037/0022-0663.94.1.186

Peterson, C., Maier, S. and Seligman, M.E. (1993) *Learned Helplessness: A Theory for the Age of Personal Control.* New York: Oxford University Press.

Phelan, P., Davidson, A.L. and Cao, H.T. (1991) Students' multiple worlds: Negotiating the boundaries of family, peer, and school cultures. *Anthropology and Education Quarterly* 22 (3), 224–250. doi:10.1525/aeq.1991.22.3.05x1051 k

Phelan, P., Davidson, A.L. and Yu, H.C. (1993) Students' multiple worlds: Navigating the borders of family, peer and school culture. In P. Phelan and A.L. Davidson (eds) *Renegotiating Cultural Diversity in American Schools* (pp. 52–88). New York: Teachers' College Press.

Phelan, P., Yu, H.C. and Davidson, A.L. (1994) Navigating the psychosocial pressures of adolescence: The voices and experiences of high school youth. *American Educational Research Journal* 31 (2), 415–447. doi:10.3102/00028312031002415

Pin, E.J. and Turndorf, J. (1990) Staging one's ideal self. In D. Brissett and C. Edgley (eds) *Life as Theatre* (pp. 163–181). Hawthorne, NY: Aldine de Gruyter.

Place, J.D. (1997) 'Boys will be boys': Boys and under-achievement in MFL. *Language Learning Journal* 16 (1), 3–10. doi:10.1080/09571739785200201

Popa, S. and Acedo, C. (2006) Redefining professionalism: Romanian secondary education teachers and the private tutoring system. *International Journal of Educational Development* 26 (1), 98–110. doi:10.1016/j.ijedudev.2005.07.019

Popovici, R. and Bolitho, R. (2003) Personal and professional development through writing: The Romanian textbook project. In B. Tomlinson (ed.) *Developing Materials for Language Teaching* (pp. 505–517). London: Continuum.

Pufahl, I. and Rhodes, N.C. (2011) Foreign language instruction in U.S. schools: Results of a national survey of elementary and secondary schools. *Foreign Language Annals* 44 (2), 258–288. doi:10.1111/j.1944-9720.2011.01130.x

Reasoner, R.W. (1992) You can bring hope to failing students. What's behind self-esteem programs: Truth or trickery? *School Administrator* 49 (4), 23–30.

Reeve, J., Bolt, E. and Cai, Y. (1999) Autonomy-supportive teachers: How they teach and motivate students. *Journal of Educational Psychology* 91 (3), 537–548. doi:10.1037/0022-0663.91.3.537

Reeve, J. and Jang, H. (2006) What teachers say and do to support students' autonomy during a learning activity. *Journal of Educational Psychology* 98 (1), 209–218. doi:10.1037/0022-0663.98.1.209

Reeve, J., Jang, H., Carrell, D., Jeon, S. and Barch, J. (2004) Enhancing students' engagement by increasing teachers' autonomy support. *Motivation and Emotion* 28 (2), 147–169. doi:10.1023/B%3AMOEM.0000032312.95499.6f

Rhodes, N.C. and Pufahl, I. (2010) *Foreign Language Teaching in U.S. schools: Results of a National Survey*. Washington, DC: Center for Applied Linguistics.

Rhodewalt, F. (1998) Self-presentation and the phenomenal self: The 'carryover effect' revisited. In J.M. Darley and J. Cooper (eds) *Attribution and Social Interaction: The Legacy of Edward E. Jones* (pp. 373–421). Washington, DC: American Psychological Association.

Rhodewalt, F. and Hill, S.K. (1995) Self-handicapping in the classroom: The effects of claimed self-handicaps in responses to academic failure. *Basic and Applied Social Psychology* 16 (4), 397–416. doi:10.1207/s15324834basp1604_1

Ricento, T. (2005) Considerations of identity in L2 learning. In E. Hinkel (ed.) *Handbook of Research in Second Language Teaching and Learning* (pp. 895–910). London: Lawrence Erlbaum.

Rigby, C.S., Deci, E.L., Patrick, B.C. and Ryan, R.M. (1992) Beyond the intrinsic-extrinsic dichotomy: Self-determination in motivation and learning. *Motivation and Emotion* 16 (3), 165–185. doi:10.1007/BF00991650

Riley, P. (2006) Self-expression and the negotiation of identity in a foreign language. *International Journal of Applied Linguistics* 16 (3), 295–318. doi:10.1111/j.1473-4192.2006.00120.x

Roeser, R.W., Peck, S.C. and Nasir, N.S. (2006) Self and identity processes in school motivation, learning, and achievement. In P.A. Alexander and P.H. Winne (eds) *Handbook of Educational Psychology* (2nd edn, pp. 391–424). Mahwah, NJ: Erlbaum.

Rogers, C.R. and Freiberg, H.J. (1994) *Freedom to Learn* (3rd edn). New York: Merrill.

Rollett, B.A. (1985) Achievement motivation versus effort avoidance motivation. In J.T. Spence and C.E. Izard (eds) *Motivation, Emotion and Personality: Proceedings of the XXIII International Congress of Psychological Science, Acapulco, Mexico, September 2-7, 1984* (Vol. 5, pp. 77–85). Amsterdam: Elsevier Science.

Rollett, B.A. (1987) Effort avoidance and learning. In E. De Corte, H. Lodewijks, R. Parmentier and P. Span (eds) *Learning and Instruction: European Research in an International Context* (Vol. 1, pp. 147–157). Leuven, Belgium: Pergamon.

Rubenfeld, S., Clément, R., Lussier, D., Lebrun, M. and Auger, R. (2006) Second language learning and cultural representations: Beyond competence and identity. *Language Learning* 56 (4), 609–631. doi:10.1111/j.1467-9922.2006.00390.x

Rubio, F. (ed.) (2007) *Self-esteem and Foreign Language Learning*. Newcastle, UK: Cambridge Scholars.

Ryan, R.M., Connell, J.P. and Grolnick, W.S. (1992) When achievement is not intrinsically motivated: A theory of internalization and self-regulation in school. In A.K. Boggiano and T.S. Pittman (eds) *Achievement and Motivation: A Social-developmental Perspective* (pp. 167–188). Cambridge: Cambridge University Press.

Ryan, R.M. and Deci, E.L. (2000) When rewards compete with nature: The undermining of intrinsic motivation and self-regulation. In C. Sansone and J.M. Harackiewicz (eds) *Intrinsic and Extrinsic Motivation: The Search for Optimal Motivation and Performance* (pp. 13–54). San Diego, CA: Academic Press.

Ryan, R.M. and Deci, E.L. (2003) On assimilating identities to the self: A self-determination theory perspective on internalization and integrity within cultures. In M.R. Leary and J.P. Tangney (eds) *Handbook of Self and Identity* (pp. 253–272). New York: Guildford Press.

Ryan, S. (2008) The ideal L2 selves of Japanese learners of English (Unpublished PhD thesis). University of Nottingham.

Ryan, S. (2009) Self and identity in L2 motivation in Japan: The Ideal L2 Self and Japanese learners of English. In Z. Dörnyei and E. Ushioda (eds) *Motivation, Language Identity and the L2 Self* (pp. 120–143). Bristol: Multilingual Matters.

Sansone, C. and Morgan, C. (1992) Intrinsic motivation and education: Competence in context. *Motivation and Emotion* 16 (3), 249–270. doi:10.1007/BF00991654

Sansone, C. and Smith, J.L. (2000) Interest and self-regulation: The relation between having to and wanting to. In C. Sansone and J.M. Harackiewicz (eds) *Intrinsic and Extrinsic Motivation: The Search for Optimal Motivation and Performance* (pp. 341–372). San Diego, CA: Academic Press.

Schlenker, B.R. (1986) Self-identification: Toward an integration of the private and public self. In R.F. Baumeister (ed.) *Public Self and Private Self* (pp. 21–62). New York: Springer.

Schlenker, B.R. (2003) Self-presentation. In M.R. Leary and J.P. Tangney (eds) *Handbook of Self and Identity* (pp. 492–518). New York: Guildford Press.

Schlenker, B.R. and Weigold, M.F. (1992) Interpersonal processes involving impression regulation and management. *Annual Review of Psychology* 43 (1), 133–168. doi:10.1146/annurev.ps.43.020192.001025

Seifert, T.L. (1995) Characteristics of ego- and task-oriented students: A comparison of two methodologies. *British Journal of Educational Psychology* 65, 125–138.

Seifert, T.L. (2004) Understanding student motivation. *Educational Research* 46 (2), 137–149. doi:10.1080/0013188042000222421

Seifert, T.L. and O'Keefe, B.A. (2001) The relationship of work avoidance and learning goals to perceived competence, externality and meaning. *British Journal of Educational Psychology* 71 (1), 81–92. doi:10.1348/000709901158406

Seligman, M.E. (1992) *Helplessness: On Depression, Development, and Death*. New York: Freeman.

Selman, R.L. and Schultz, L.H. (1990) *Making a Friend in Youth*. Chicago: University of Chicago Press.

Shah, J.Y. and Kruglanski, A.W. (2000) The structure and substance of intrinsic motivation. In C. Sansone and J.M. Harackiewicz (eds) *Intrinsic and Extrinsic Motivation: The Search for Optimal Motivation and Performance* (pp. 105–127). San Diego, CA: Academic Press.

Shashaani, L. (1997) Gender differences in computer attitudes and use among college students. *Journal of Educational Computing Research* 16 (1), 1–1. doi:10.2190/Y8U7-AMMA-WQUT-R512

Shearn, S. (2003) *Attitudes to foreign language learning in New Zealand schools* (Unpublished PhD thesis). University of Wellington, New Zealand.

Siann, G., Macleod, H., Glissov, P. and Durndell, A. (1990) The effect of computer use on gender differences in attitudes to computers. *Computers and Education* 14 (2), 183–191. doi:10.1016/0360-1315(90)90058-F

Skinner, E., Furrer, C., Marchand, G. and Kindermann, T. (2008) Engagement and disaffection in the classroom: Part of a larger motivational dynamic? *Journal of Educational Psychology* 100 (4), 765–781. doi:10.1037/a0012840

Smith, F. (1986) *Insult to intelligence: The Bureaucratic Invasion of our Classrooms*. Portsmouth, NH: Heinemann.

Soenens, B. and Vansteenkiste, M. (2005) Antecedents and outcomes of self-determination in three life domains: The role of parents' and teachers' autonomy support. *Journal of Youth and Adolescence* 34 (6), 589–604. doi:10.1007/s10964-005-8948-y

Spergel, I.A. (1995) *The Youth Gang Problem*. New York: Oxford University Press.

Spratt, M. (1999) How good are we at knowing what learners like? *System* 27 (2), 141–155. doi:10.1016/S0346-251X(99)00013-5

Stanovich, K.E. (1986) Matthew effects in reading: Some consequences of individual differences in the acquisition of literacy. *Reading Research Quarterly* 21 (4), 360–407. doi:10.1598/RRQ.21.4.1

Steinberg, L. (1990) Interdependency in the family: Autonomy, conflict, and harmony in the parent–adolescent relationship. In S.S. Feldman and G. Elliot (eds) *At the Threshold: The Developing Adolescent* (pp. 255–276). Cambridge, MA: Harvard University Press.

Steinberg, L. and Monahan, K.C. (2007) Age differences in resistance to peer influence. *Developmental Psychology* 43 (6), 1531–1543. doi:10.1037/0012-1649.43.6.1531

Stipek, D.J. and Weisz, J.R. (1981) Perceived personal control and academic achievement. *Review of Educational Research* 51 (1), 101–137. doi:10.3102/00346543051001101

Strahan, E.J. and Wilson, A.E. (2006) Temporal comparisons, identity, and motivation: The relation between past, present, and possible future selves. In C.S. Dunkel and J.L. Kerpelman (eds) *Possible Selves: Theory, Research and Applications* (pp. 1–15). New York: Nova Science.

Sunderland, J. (2004) *Gendered Discourses*. Basingstoke, UK: Palgrave.

Swann, J. (1992) *Girls, Boys, and Language*. Oxford: Blackwell.

Swann, J. and Graddol, D. (1994) Gender inequalities in classroom talk. In D. Graddol, J. Maybin and B. Stierer (eds) *Researching Language and Literacy in Social Context* (pp. 151–167). Clevedon: Multilingual Matters.

Syed, Z. (2001) Notions of self in foreign language learning: A qualitative analysis. In Z. Dörnyei and R. Schmidt (eds) *Motivation and Second Language Acquisition* (pp. 127–147). Honolulu, HI: University of Hawai'i Press.

Tabachnick, B.G. and Fidell, L.S. (2007) *Using Multivariate Statistics* (5th edn). Boston, MA: Pearson Education.

Taguchi, T., Magid, M. and Papi, M. (2009) The L2 motivational self system among Japanese, Chinese and Iranian learners of English: A comparative study. In Z. Dörnyei and E. Ushioda (eds) *Motivation, Language Identity and the L2 Self* (pp. 66–97). Bristol: Multilingual Matters.

Taylor, F. (2008) Involvement Avoidance in the English class: Romanian Insights (Unpublished MEd dissertation). University of Exeter.

Taylor, F. (2009) Some grim effects of a nationally imposed English curriculum in Romania. *Romanian Journal of English Studies 6*, 417–427.

Taylor, F. (2010) Surreptitious teacher development: Promoting change from within. *Romanian Journal of English Studies 7*, 401–409.

Taylor, F. (2012) *Influencing the perceived relevance of Modern Foreign Languages in Year 9: An experimental intervention (Research report)* (No. 30). York: Centre for Language Learning Research, University of York. Retrieved from http://www.york.ac.uk/depts/educ/research/ResearchPaperSeries/index.htm

Taylor, F. (2013a) Listening to Romanian teenagers: Lessons in motivation and ELT methodology. In E. Ushioda (ed.) *International Perspectives on Motivation: Language Learning and Professional Challenges* (pp. 35–59). Basingstoke: Palgrave Macmillan.

Taylor, F. (2013b, forthcoming) Relational views of the self in SLA. In S. Mercer and M. Williams (eds) *Multiple Perspectives on the Self in SLA*. Bristol: Multilingual Matters.

Taylor, F., Busse, V., Gagova, L., Marsden, E. and Roosken, B. (2013) Identity in foreign language learning and teaching: Why listening to our students' and teachers' voices really matters. *British Council ELT Research Papers*. Retrieved from http://www.teachingenglish.org.uk/publications

Teddlie, C. and Tashakkori, A. (2009) *Foundations of mixed methods research: Integrating quantitative and qualitative approaches in the social and behavioral sciences*. Thousand Oaks, CA: Sage.

Tesser, A., Crepaz, N., Beach, S.R.H., Cornell, D. and Collins, J.C. (2000) Confluence of self-esteem regulation mechanisms: On integrating the self-zoo. *Personality and Social Psychology Bulletin 26* (12), 1476–1489. doi:10.1177/01461672002612003

Toohey, K. (2000) *Learning English at School: Identity, Social Relations and Classroom Practice*. Clevedon: Multilingual Matters.

Ushioda, E. (1996a) *Language learners' motivational thinking: A qualitative study* (Unpublished PhD thesis). Trinity College, University of Dublin.

Ushioda, E. (1996b) Developing a dynamic concept of motivation. In T. Hickey and J. Williams (eds) *Language, Education and Society in a Changing World* (pp. 215–228). Clevedon: Multilingual Matters.

Ushioda, E. (1996c) *Learner Autonomy: The Role of Motivation*. Dublin: Authentik.

Ushioda, E. (1998) Effective motivational thinking: A cognitive theoretical approach to the study of language learning motivation. In E.A. Soler and V.C. Espurz (eds) *Current Issues in English Language Methodology* (pp. 77–89). Castelló de la Plana, Spain: Universitat Jaume I.

Ushioda, E. (2008) Motivation and good language learners. In C. Griffiths (ed.) *Lessons from Good Language Learners* (pp. 19–34). Cambridge: Cambridge University Press.

Ushioda, E. (2009) A person-in-context relational view of emergent motivation, self and identity. In Z. Dörnyei and E. Ushioda (eds) *Motivation, Language Identity and the L2 Self* (pp. 215–228). Bristol: Multilingual Matters.

Van Hook, E. and Higgins, T.E. (1988) Self-related problems beyond the self-concept: Motivational consequences of discrepant self-guides. *Journal of Personality and Social Psychology* 55 (4), 625–633. doi:10.1037/0022-3514.55.4.625

Van Lier, L. (1996) *Interaction in the Language Curriculum: Awareness, Autonomy and Authenticity*. Harlow, UK: Longman.

Vandenberghe, R. and Huberman, A.M. (eds). (1999) *Understanding and Preventing Teacher Burnout: A Sourcebook of International Research and Practice*. Cambridge: Cambridge University Press.

Vansteenkiste, M. and Deci, E.L. (2003) Competitively contingent rewards and intrinsic motivation: Can losers remain motivated? *Motivation and Emotion* 27 (4), 273–299. doi:10.1023/A%3A1026259005264

Vignoles, V.L., Schwartz, S.J. and Luyckx, K. (2011) Introduction: Towards an integrative view of identity. In S.J. Schwartz, K. Luyckx and V.L. Vignoles (eds) *Handbook of Identity Theory and Research* (Vol. 1, pp. 1–27). New York: Springer.

Vygotsky, L.S. (1978) *Mind in society*. Cambridge, MA: Harvard University Press.

Walberg, H.J. and Tsai, S.L. (1983) Matthew effects in education. *American Educational Research Journal* 20 (3), 359–373. doi:10.3102/00028312020003359

Weiner, B. (2005) Motivation from an attribution perspective and the social psychology of perceived competence. In A.J. Elliot and C.S. Dweck (eds) *Handbook of Competence and Motivation* (pp. 73–84). New York: Guildford Press.

Whitley, B.E. (1997) Gender differences in computer-related attitudes and behavior: A meta-analysis. *Computers in Human Behavior* 13 (1), 1–22. doi:10.1016/S0747-5632 (96) 00026-X

Wicklund, R.A. and Gollwitzer, P.M. (1982) *Symbolic Self-Completion*. Hillsdale, NJ: Erlbaum.

Wigfield, A. and Eccles, J.S. (2002) Students' motivation during the middle school years. In J. Aronson (ed.) *Improving Academic Achievement: Impact of Psychological Factors on Education* (pp. 159–184). San Diego, CA: Academic Press.

Wigfield, A., Eccles, J.S., Schiefele, U., Roeser, R. and Davis-Kean, P. (2006) Development of achievement motivation. In N. Eisenberg (ed.) *Handbook of Child Psychology* (6th edn, Vol. 3. Social, emotional, and personality development, pp. 933–1002). New York: Wiley.

Wiley, T.G. (2007) The foreign language 'crisis' in the United States: Are heritage and community languages the remedy? *Critical Inquiry in Language Studies*, 4(2-3), 179–205. doi:10.1080/15427580701389631

Williams, M. and Burden, R. (1999) Students' developing conceptions of themselves as language learners. *Modern Language Journal* 83 (2), 193–201. doi:10.1111/0026-7902.00015

Williams, M., Burden, R. and Lanvers, U. (2002) 'French is the language of love and stuff': Student perceptions of issues related to motivation in learning a foreign language. *British Educational Research Journal* 28 (4), 503–528. doi:10.1080/0141192022000005805

Woodward, K. (2002) *Understanding Identity*. London: Arnold.

Wortham, S. (2006) *Learning Identity: The Joint Emergence of Social Identification and Academic Learning*. Cambridge: Cambridge University Press.

Worton, M. (2009) *Review of Modern Foreign Languages provision in higher education in England*. London: Higher Education Funding Council for England. Retrieved from http://www.hefce.ac.uk/pubs/hefce/2009/09_41/09_41.pdf

Wurf, E. and Markus, H.R. (1991) Possible selves and the psychology of personal growth. In D.J. Ozer, J.M. Healy Jr. and A.J. Stewart (eds) *Perspectives in Personality* (Vol. 3, pp. 39–62). London: Kingsley.

Wylie, R.C. (1989) *Measures of Self-concept*. Lincoln, NE: University of Nebraska Press.

Xu, H.C. (2009) English Learning Motivational Self System: A Structural Equation Modeling study on Chinese university students (Unpublished PhD thesis). Peking University.

Zeigler-Hill, V. (ed.) (2013) *Self-Esteem*. Hove, UK: Psychology Press.

Zentner, M. and Renaud, O. (2007) Origins of adolescents' ideal self: An intergenerational perspective. *Journal of Personality and Social Psychology* 92 (3), 557–574. doi:10.1037/0022-3514.92.3.557

Subject Index

ability, 6, 10, 15, 16, 17, 19, 20, 34, 36, 44, 45, 46, 47, 49, 97, 107, 110, 117
amotivation, 12, 58, 59, 115
assessment, 3, 15, 30, 38, 45, 48, 75, 88, 91, 100, 105, 109, 114, 126, 127, 129
attributions, 16, 20, 34, 36, 44, 46, 87, 88, 89, 90, 106, 107, 108, 110, 114, 120, 146
autonomy, 1, 12, 14, 15, 23, 28, 30, 101, 106, 107, 111, 113, 115, 116, 117, 120, 124

behaviourism, 109
beliefs, 10, 12, 15, 18, 29, 36, 42, 45, 48, 64, 85, 95, 97, 98, 126

carryover effect, 19, 51
classmates, 2, 6, 9, 13, 15, 16, 17, 24, 37, 38, 39, 45, 53, 62, 64, 66, 71, 72, 77, 78, 79, 82, 83, 86, 87, 88, 89, 90, 92, 93, 94, 95, 97, 98, 99, 100, 103, 105, 117, 123
choice, 1, 11, 12, 13, 23, 25, 28, 38, 47, 50, 57, 64, 70, 72, 73, 74, 77, 83, 107, 127, 148
competence, 2, 4, 10, 12, 15, 16, 19, 28, 29, 30, 47, 59, 91, 93, 106, 107, 109, 111, 114, 115, 117, 126, 129
competition/competitiveness, 15, 16, 20, 21, 45, 71, 74, 92, 97, 101, 107, 111, 117, 128
communication, 2, 4, 14, 26, 28, 33, 37, 44, 68, 70, 72, 77, 82, 91, 92, 93, 99, 109, 111, 112, 114, 119, 126, 127, 129
Communism, 68, 74, 75, 122
cooperation, 15, 16, 21, 47, 92

desired/undesired selves, 17, 18, 19, 21, 38, 43, 44, 50, 59

effort, 4, 10, 15, 16, 17, 20, 32, 43, 44, 45, 46, 47, 49, 90, 106, 107, 114, 117
expectations, 2, 7, 9, 15, 21, 22, 30, 35, 42, 45, 47, 49, 50, 52, 64, 66, 73, 75, 78, 79, 83, 87, 88, 95, 97, 98, 99, 100, 103, 114, 117, 118, 119, 122, 123, 127, 129

failure, 16, 34, 38, 44, 46, 49, 59, 68, 79, 87, 88, 89, 90, 107, 108, 110, 113, 114, 122
family, 1, 3, 13, 14, 24, 30, 35, 47, 48, 49, 51, 53, 57, 62, 64, 65, 66, 67, 72, 74, 75, 77, 78, 79, 85, 86, 88, 89, 93, 94, 95, 97, 98, 99, 102, 105, 119 (see also parents)
feedback, 15, 29, 57, 110, 113, 114
flow, 58
fluency, 48, 68, 75
friends, 3, 6, 9, 13, 14, 15, 18, 24, 38, 43, 49, 53, 60, 62, 63, 64, 66, 70, 71, 72, 74, 75, 76, 78, 80, 83, 86, 87, 88, 89, 92, 93, 94, 95, 97, 98, 99, 100, 101, 103, 105, 108, 109, 110, 116, 117, 119, 123
fully functioning persons, 6, 17, 22, 23, 25, 38, 40, 107, 120

gender, 5, 7, 9, 36, 37, 62, 63, 89, 90, 91, 92, 93, 95, 96, 97, 122
goal orientations, 15, 16, 19, 29, 30, 44, 46, 87, 88, 90, 97, 106, 110, 111, 119, 120
grades, see marks

helplessness, see learnt helplessness
heritage languages, 30, 35, 125

ideal self, 22, 32, 33, 34, 39, 42, 43, 44,
    46, 47, 50, 51, 52, 53, 54, 55, 56, 57,
    59, 86, 88, 89, 90, 94, 103, 104, 106,
    119, 124
identity display, 3, 7, 38, 39, 46, 85, 88,
    93, 97, 98, 99, 100, 105, 106, 111,
    120, 122, 123, 125, 128
imposed selves, 39, 42, 45, 46, 48, 49,
    50, 51, 52, 53, 54, 55, 56, 58, 83, 85,
    86, 87, 88, 89, 90, 93, 94, 95, 96,
    97, 99, 100, 111, 118, 119, 122, 123,
    124, 128
impression management, 55, 59, 97, 122
internalisation, 2, 8, 11, 13, 18, 19, 20, 38,
    39, 42, 43, 44, 45, 49, 51, 53, 54, 79,
    80, 105, 107, 110, 116, 117, 118, 119,
    120, 122, 123, 124, 126, 128, 129

law of generalised mediocrity, see norm
    of low achievement
learnt/learned helplessness, 12, 59, 107,
    110, 111, 114, 122, 129

marks/grades, 8, 16, 17, 36, 37, 46, 60,
    65, 66, 69, 75, 76, 78, 87, 88, 89,
    90, 91, 92, 101, 102, 106, 107, 108,
    109, 110, 111, 113, 114, 116, 117,
    119, 120
motivation, 1, 2, 4, 7, 12, 15, 20, 21, 24,
    27, 30, 31, 32, 33, 34, 35, 36, 37, 38,
    39, 41, 43, 46, 52, 58, 59, 60, 77, 80,
    82, 97, 101, 106, 107, 109, 111, 116,
    120, 122, 124, 126, 128, 130
Modern Foreign Languages, 8, 46,
    100, 115

norm of low achievement/ law of gener-
    alised mediocrity, 16, 21, 45, 47, 90,
    116, 117, 118, 122

overjustification effect, 109

parents, 3, 6, 9, 13, 14, 18, 31, 32, 36, 37,
    38, 39, 48, 49, 50, 51, 59, 60, 64, 66,

67, 68, 70, 72, 73, 74, 75, 77, 78, 79,
    87, 88, 99, 100, 101, 102, 103, 118,
    119, 120, 126 (see also family)
peers, 2, 13, 14, 16, 17, 20, 36, 37, 44, 45,
    47, 49, 53, 64, 71, 72, 77, 79, 80, 88,
    98, 103, 107, 116, 117, 123
peer pressure, 6, 16, 17, 48, 56, 76,
    90, 117
possible selves, 17, 19, 20, 21, 32, 33, 42,
    43, 46, 58, 119, 122
praise, 15, 92, 109, 110, 113
private self, 17, 18, 19, 39, 42, 43, 46, 47,
    49, 50, 51, 52, 54, 55, 86, 88, 89, 90,
    94, 95, 96, 97, 98, 103, 104, 106, 107,
    119, 120, 123, 124, 128
public selves, 17, 19, 20, 21, 38, 39, 42, 46,
    48, 49, 50, 51, 52, 53, 54, 55, 57, 59,
    85, 88, 90, 93, 96, 97, 99, 100, 117,
    118, 119, 122, 123, 124, 129

regulation/self-regulation, 3, 12, 29, 116,
    120, 124
relatedness, 12, 30, 92, 107, 117
relational context, 1, 2, 9, 11, 12, 13, 15,
    20, 21, 29, 36, 37, 38, 42, 44, 45, 46,
    48, 50, 53, 59, 60, 62, 63, 64, 77, 85,
    88, 90, 93, 95, 96, 97, 98, 99, 100,
    101, 102, 103, 116, 117, 118, 119,
    122, 124
rewards, 108, 109, 110, 111, 113

self-concept, 9, 10, 12, 14, 18, 19, 20, 21,
    22, 28, 29, 30, 31, 34, 38, 39, 47, 50,
    51, 52, 56, 107, 108, 118
self-determination, 1, 11, 19, 30, 106,
    107, 111, 115, 116, 117, 122, 127,
    129, 130
self-efficacy, 12, 27, 29, 30, 31
self-esteem, 9, 10, 27, 28, 30, 31, 38
self-handicapping, 59, 107
self-presentation, 18, 19, 20, 21, 22, 39,
    48, 52, 93, 122, 128
self-worth, 9, 10, 16, 29, 31, 46, 47, 59, 102
success, 15, 29, 34, 36, 38, 44, 46, 87, 88,
    90, 106, 107, 108, 111, 114, 119, 120,
    126

truancy, 101, 106

Author Index

Acedo, Clementina, 115
Allard, Réal, 108
Allen, Joseph P., 14
Ames, Carole, 15, 16, 107
Andrei, Luminita, 3, 4
Archer, Jennifer, 107
Anderman, Eric, M., 16, 21, 97
Anderman, Lynley H., 16, 21, 97
Andersen, Susan M., 17
Anderson, Rolph E., 85
Arkin, Robert M., 18
Aron, Arthur, 20
Assor, Avi, 15, 119
Astruc, Lluïsa, 125
Auger, Réjean, 26

Babin, Barry J., 85
Bakhtin, Mikhail, 26
Bandura, Albert, 12, 29
Barch, Jon, 115
Barrett, Marty, 115
Barton, Amanda, 90
Bartram, Brendan, 36, 37, 90, 98, 126
Baumeister, Roy F., 10, 11, 18, 19, 28, 31
Baumgardner, Ann H., 18
Beach, Steven R. H., 9
Beierlein, Constanze, 91
Bell, Kathy L., 14
Berndt, Thomas J., 14
Birch, Sondra, H., 104
Blau, David M., 14
Black, William C., 85
Blackledge, Adrian, 26
Block, David, 37
Blumenfeld, Phyllis C., 15, 111

Boggiano, Ann K., 15, 115
Bolitho, Rod, 3
Bolt, Elizabether, 119
Bong, Mimi, 12, 29
Bor, Daniel, 50
Borkowski, John G., 21
Bouchey, Heather A., 13, 14
Bourdieu, Pierre, 26
Boyle, Joseph P., 90
Bower, Gordon H., 10
Bresnick, Shelley, 13, 14
Brewer, John, 5
Briggs, Stephen, 17, 18
Brinthaupt, Thomas M., 13
Brown, Bradford B., 14
Bügel, Karin, 90
Burden, Robert, 34, 36, 38, 90, 98, 110, 126
Burhans, Karen K., 107
Burke, Ronald J., 115
Busch, Tor, 91
Busse, Vera, 32, 33, 34, 98, 104, 111, 124, 125, 126
Bussmann, Hadumod, 27
Butler, Ruth, 16, 111
Buunk, Bram P., 90
Bybee, Deborah, 20, 21
Byrne, Barbara M., 10

Cai, Yi, 15, 119
Callaghan, Martine, 90
Campbell, Jennifer D., 10, 31
Cao, Hanh T., 14, 100, 101
Carr, Jo, 48, 90
Carrell, Dan, 115
Chen, Serena, 10

Ciani, Keith, 111
Clark, Ann, 90
Clarke, David F., 115
Clarke, John A., 92
Clark-Lempers, Dania S., 14, 15, 99
Clemens, Peggy, 21
Clément, Richard, 26, 30, 107, 108
Cole, David A., 91
Coleman, James, A., 125
Collins, Jon C., 14
Collins, W. Andrew, 9
Comănaru, Ruxandra, 30, 108, 126
Connell, James P., 120
Connor, Michael J., 14
Constantinescu, Ilinca, 4
Coon, Brian, 20
Coopersmith, Stanley, 28
Cornell, David, 9
Côté, James E., 10
Covington, Martin V., 10, 16, 18, 97, 107, 117
Cotterall, Sarah, 35
Craven, Rhonda, 28, 110
Crepaz, Nicole, 9
Creswell, John W., 5
Crookes, Graham, 115
Crowe, Ellen, 21, 22
Csikszentmihalyi, Mihaly, 13, 14, 58
Csizér, Kata, 32

Dart, Barry C., 92
Davidson, Ann L., 14, 97, 99, 100, 101
Davis-Kean, Pamela, 119
Day, Jeanne D., 21
de Andrés, Veronica, 31
Deci, Edward L., 107, 109, 110, 114, 117, 120
Delamont, Sara, 92
Deshler, Donald D., 21
Deveau, Kenneth, 108
Dindia, Kathryn, 92
Domene, Jos F., 119
Dörnyei, Zoltán, 31, 32, 33
Dunkel, Curtis S., 20
Durkin, Kevin, 26
Durndell, A., 91
Dweck, Carol S., 10, 15, 16, 91, 92, 97, 107, 110, 113, 117
Dworkin, Anthony G., 115

Eccles, Jacquelynne S., 15, 119
Ehrman, Madeline, 30
Elkind, David, 14
Elliott, Anthony, 26
Elliott, E. S., 97
Erikson, Martin G., 20, 21

Fabrigar, Leandre R., 85
Feiring, Candice, 14
Fidell, Linda S., 88
Fier, Jonathan, 91
Flink, Cheryl, 115
Flum, Hanoch, 16
Fredricks, Jeniffer A., 15
Freiberg, H. Jerome, 22, 106, 120
Friedman, Thomas L., 3
Fryberg, Stephanie, 20, 21, 119
Furrer, Carrie, 15, 92

Gagova, Lubina, 98, 104, 111, 124, 125
Galaczi, Árpád, 125
Gardner, Robert C., 32, 33
Gebhard, Jerry G., 27
Genung, Patricia, 37, 38
Gibson, Ellsworth, 15
Gilbert, Francis, 115
Gilligan, Stephen G., 10
Glassman, Noah S., 17
Glissov, P., 91
Gold, David A., 17
Goldberg, Erin, 30
Goldstein, Tara, 26, 27
Gollwitzer, Peter M., 11, 19
Graddol, David, 92
Graham, Suzanne, 29, 48, 126
Greene, Barbara A., 16, 91, 97, 119
Greene, David, 109
Greenglass, Esther R., 115
Griesinger, Tripp, 21
Grolnick, Wendy S., 120

Hair, Joseph F., 85
Hamilton, Lee V., 11
Hansen, Ranald D., 92
Hardman, Frank, 114
Hargittai, Eszter, 91
Harter, Susan, 10, 11, 13, 14, 15, 17, 21, 26, 29, 99, 104, 106

Hart-Johnson, Tamera, 21
Hattie, John, 10, 91
Hau, Kit T., 110
Hauser, Stuart T., 14
Henderlong, Jennifer, 109
Henry, Alastair, 32
Herron, Carol, 29, 126
Hidi, Suzanne, 120
Higgins, Tory E., 13, 19, 21, 22, 32, 100
Hill, S. Kristian, 107
Hock, Michael F., 21
Hogan, Robert, 17, 18
Holmberg, G. N., 14
Horberg, E. J., 10
Howsepian, Barbara, 21
Huberman, A. Michael, 115
Hunter, Albert, 5
Hymes, Charles, 21

Imhof, Margarete, 91
Istrate, Olimpius, 4

James, William J., 18, 31
Jang, Hyungshim, 107, 114, 115
Jarvis, Sharon, 107
Jeon, Soohyun, 115
Jin, Patai, 29
Johnson, Burke, 5
Jones, Edward E., 11, 18
Jones, Susanne M., 92
Juvonen, Jaana, 16, 20, 39, 98, 117

Kanat-Maymon, Yaniv, 15
Kaplan, Avi, 16
Kaplan, Haya, 15, 119
Kay, Robin H., 91
Kazzazi, Kerstin, 27
Katz, Phyllis, 15
Keefe, Keunho, 14
Kellman, Steven G., 27
Kelly, A., 92
Kelts, Daniel, 20
Kindermann, Thomas A., 15
Kiosseoglou, Grigoris, 21
Kirchhof, Oliver, 11, 19
Klos, Maureen L., 97
Kobayashi, Yoko, 90
Koestner, Richard, 109

Kohn, Alfie, 1, 10, 31, 109, 110, 111, 112, 115
Kormos, Judit, 32
Kowalski, Robin M., 19, 97
Krueger, Joachim I., 10, 31
Kruglanski, Arie W., 120
Kyriacou, Chris, 37, 38

Ladd, Gary W., 104
La Guardia, Jennifer G., 12, 19
Landry, Rodrigue, 108
Lanvers, Ursula, 34, 36, 38, 90, 98
Lantolf, James, 26, 27, 37
Larson, Reed, 13, 14
Lau, Ivy C., 29
Leary, Mark R., 11, 18, 19, 97
Lebrun, Monique, 26
LeCompte, Margaret D., 115
Legault, Louise, 115
Lempers, Jacques D., 14, 15, 99
Leondari, Angeliki, 21
Lepper, Mark R., 109
Lewis, M., 9
Lexmond, Jen, 14
Lightbown, Patsy, 27
Lipka, Richard P., 13
Little, David, 90, 119, 120
Low, Renae, 29
Lussier, Denise, 26
Luyckx, Koen, 11

Macafee, Caroline, 91
MacCallum, Robert C., 85
Macleod, P., 91
Magid, Michael, 32, 33
Maier, Steven F., 107
Marchand, Gwen, 15
Markus, Hazel R., 10, 13, 18, 20, 21, 36, 119
Marsden, Emma, 98, 104, 111, 124, 125
Marsh, Herbert W., 10, 28, 29, 31, 91, 110
Marshall, Sheila K., 119
Martin, Joan M., 91
Martin, Mario, D., 120, 125
Masgoret, Anne-Marie, 33
Mayer, Doris, 21
McClun, Lisa A., 14
McCollam, Tanya L., 15

McInerney, Dennis M., 28
McKay, Sandra, 26, 27
McNamara, Tim F., 26
Mead, George H., 26, 35
Meece, Judith L., 16, 97
Medgyes, Peter, 4
Melucci, Alberto, 26
Mercer, Sarah, 28, 29, 39
Merrell, Kenneth W., 14
Merrett, Frank, 92
Middleton, Michael M., 111
Mihai, Florin M., 3, 4
Miller, Angela, 15
Miller, Raymond B., 16, 91, 97, 119
Miller, Jennifer, 15, 26, 27
Mills, Nicole, 29, 126
Mitchell, Rosamond, 48
Moller, Arlen C., 107, 120
Monahan, Kathryn C., 17
Monsour, Ann, 13
Montalvo, Fregory P., 91, 97, 119
Morgan, Carolyn, 111
Mueller, Claudia M., 113
Murdock, Tamera B., 15, 16, 20, 39, 98
Murray, Garold, 35

Nasir, Nellah S., 119
Németh, Nora, 32
Nichols, Joe D., 91, 97, 119
Noels, Kimberly A., 30, 107, 108, 126
Norman, Christina C., 20
Norton, Bonny, 26, 27
Nurius, Paula, 13, 18, 36
Nyikos, Martha, 90

O'Connor, Thomas G., 14
Oettingen, Gabriele, 21
O'Keefe, B. A., 16, 117
O'Leary, Virginia E., 92
O'Mara, Alison, 28, 31
Oyserman, Daphna, 20, 21, 119

Pachler, Norbert, 125
Pajares, Frank, 10, 12, 29, 126
Pallant, Julie, 85, 88
Papi, Mostafa, 32, 33
Paris, Alison H., 15
Patrick, Brian C., 120
Pauwels, Anne, 48, 90

Pavlenko, Aneta, 26, 27
Peck, Stephen C., 119
Pedersen, Sarah, 91
Peeke, Lachlan A., 91
Pelletier, Luc G., 30, 107, 108, 115
Peterson, Christopher, 107
Phelan, Patricia, 14, 97, 99, 100, 101
Pin, Emile J., 19
Pintrich, Paul R., 111
Pittman, Thane S., 11, 18
Place, J. Dianne, 90
Popa, Simona, 115
Popovici, Ruxandra, 3
Popovici, Victoria, 4
Pufahl, Ingrid, 48, 120, 125
Punzo, Diana, 21

Ravindran, Bhuvaneswari, 91, 97, 119
Reasoner, Robert W., 10
Reeve, Johnmarshall, 15, 107, 114, 115
Reeves, Richard, 14
Renaud, Olivier, 21
Rhodes, Nancy C., 48, 120, 125
Rhodewalt, Frederick, 19, 107, 118
Ricento, Thomas, 26
Ridley, Jennifer, 90, 119, 120
Rigby, C. Scott, 120
Riley, Philip, 35
Roeser, Robert W., 119
Rollett, Brigitte A., 106
Roney, Christopher J. R., 21, 22
Rogers, Carl R., 6, 17, 22, 23, 24, 25
Roosken, Barbara, 98, 104, 111, 124, 125
Roth, Guy, 15, 119
Rubenfeld, Sara, 26
Rubio, Fernando, 31
Ryan, Richard M., 30, 107, 109, 110, 114, 117, 120
Ryan, Stephen, 32, 33, 99

Sansone, Carol, 111, 120
Schiefele, Ulrich, 119
Schultz, Lynn H., 14
Schunk, Dale H., 10, 12, 29
Schlenker, Barry R., 11, 18, 19, 97
Schumaker, Jean B., 21
Schwartz, Seth J., 11

Schwarzer, Ralf, 115
Séguin-Lévesque, Chantal, 115
Seidman, Edwards, 21
Seifert, Timothy L., 16, 17, 107, 117
Seligman, Martin E. P., 107
Selman, Robert L., 14
Seroczynski, A. D., 91
Shafer, Steven, 91
Shah, James Y., 120
Shashaani, Lily, 91
Shavelson, Richard J., 28, 29
Shearn, Sandra, 120, 125
Sheldon, Kennon, 111
Siann, G., 91
Skaalvik, Einar M., 12, 29
Skinner, Ellen, 15, 92
Smith, Frank, 110
Smith, J. L., 120
Soenens, Bart, 14
Spada, Nina, 27
Spergel, Irving A., 14
Spratt, M., 114
Stanovich, Keith E., 93
Ştefănescu, Ariadna, 4
Steinberg, Laurence, 14, 17
Stipek, Deborah J., 107
Strahan, Erin J., 21, 85
Summers, Jessica J., 111
Sunderland, Jane, 92
Swann, Joan, 92
Syed, Zafar, 35
Syngollitou, Efi, 21

Tabachnick, Barbara G., 88
Taguchi, Tatsuya, 32, 33
Tashakkori, Abbas, 5
Taska, Lynn, 14
Tatham, Ronald L., 85
Taylor, Florentina, 3, 4, 13, 30, 33, 36, 41, 46, 98, 99, 104, 108, 111, 115, 120, 124, 125, 126
Teddlie, Charles, 5
Terry, Kathy, 20, 21
Tesser, Abraham, 9
Toohey, Kelleen, 26, 27
Trauth, Gregory P., 27
Tremblay, Paul F., 33
Tsai, Shiow L., 93
Turndorf, Jamie, 19

Turner, Lisa A., 5

Ushioda, Ema, 33, 34, 90, 108, 115, 119, 120

Vallerand, Robert J., 30, 107
Vandenberghe, Roland, 115
Van Hook, Elizabeth, 22, 100
van Lier, Leo, 120
Vansteenkiste, Maarten, 14, 109
Velea, Luciana S., 4
Vignoles, Vivian L., 11
Vohs, Kathleen D., 10, 31
Vollmeyer, Regina, 91
Vygotsky, Lev S., 35

Walberg, Herbert J., 93
Waters, Patricia L., 13, 14, 15
Wegener, Duane T., 85
Weigold, Michael F., 97
Weiner, Bernard, 107
Weisz, John R., 107
Wentzel, Kathryn R., 117
Wigfield, Allan, 15, 119
Wiley, Terrence G., 125
Williams, Marion, 32, 33, 34, 36, 38, 90, 98, 108, 110, 126
Wilson, Anne E., 21
Wheldall, Kevin, 92
Whitesell, Nancy R., 13, 14
Whitley, Bernard E., 91
Wicklund, Robert A., 11
Wong, Sau-Ling, C., 26, 27
Wortham, Stanton E. F., 97
Woodward, Kath, 26
Worton, Michael, 125
Wurf, Elissa, 20, 21, 119
Wylie, Ruth C., 10

Xu, Hong C., 33

Yeung, Alexander S., 10, 29
Young, Richard A., 119
Yu, Hahn, C., 97, 99, 100, 101

Zeigler-Hill, Virgil, 10
Zentner, Marcel, 21
Zhu, Die, 37, 38

Country Index

Apart from language teaching, learning and education in general, the book discusses research evidence and implications for Romania and the following countries:

Argentina, 31
Australia, 27, 120, 126
Austria, 28

Bulgaria, 98, 124

Canada, 27, 30, 32
China, 33, 37, 38, 90, 124

'English speaking countries', 8, 46, 48,
    100, 120, 125, 126

France, 35

Germany, 27, 37, 98

Hong Kong, 29
Hungary, 32

Iran, 32, 33
Ireland, 34

Japan, 32, 33, 35, 99

Netherlands, 37, 90, 98, 124
New Zealand, 120

Spain, 98, 124
South Korea, 29

UK, 24, 34, 37, 46, 108, 115, 120, 125, 126
USA, 29, 30, 35, 37, 124, 126